phac

3-17-06

Hidden Treasures
of the
American West

Hidden Treasures
OF THE
American West

Muriel H. Wright,
Angie Debo,
AND
Alice Marriott

Patricia Loughlin

UNIVERSITY OF NEW MEXICO PRESS

ALBUQUERQUE

09 08 07 06 05   1 2 3 4 5

Library of Congress Cataloging-in-Publication Data

Loughlin, Patricia, 1971–
  Hidden treasures of the American West : Muriel H. Wright,
Angie Debo, and Alice Marriott / Patricia Loughlin.
       p. cm.
  Includes bibliographical references and index.
  ISBN 0-8263-3801-1 (cloth : alk. paper)
 1. Indians of North America—Oklahoma—Historiography.
 2. Indians of North America—Oklahoma—Social life and customs.
 3. Indians in literature—History and criticism. 4. Women historians—Oklahoma—History. 5. Women authors—Oklahoma—
History. 6. Wright, Muriel H. (Muriel Hazel), 1889–1975—Relations
with Indians. 7. Debo, Angie, 1890–1988 —Relations with Indians.
8. Marriott, Alice, 1910–1992 —Relations with Indians. I. Title.
  E78.O45L68 2005
  976.6004'97'0072022—dc22
                      2005009968

Chapter three of this book is based on an article previously
published as "The Battle of the Historians of Round Mountain:
An Examination of Muriel Wright and Angie Debo," *Heritage of
the Great Plains* 31 (Spring/Summer 1998): 5–18.

Book design and composition by Damien Shay
Body type is Utopia 10/13.
Display is Park Avenue and Columbus.

For

Gerry Schaefer

Oklahoma educator

and friend

❧ Contents ❧

List of Illustrations

MAPS

FIGURES

LIST OF ILLUSTRATIONS

❧ Acknowledgments ❧

I have accumulated many debts during this decade-long research project exploring women's intellectual pursuits in the American West. My interest in Oklahoma women's history began in California, during my studies with W. David Baird at Pepperdine University. During evening seminars on the history of the American West, I would walk into class after observing a spectacular sunset—literally watching the sun drop into the Pacific Ocean—and listen to Baird discuss with intense passion the smell of a wheat field in Oklahoma. He was living in Malibu, California, yet he longed for home. In 1995 I relocated to Oklahoma and enrolled as a graduate student at Oklahoma State University, where I had the opportunity to study with L. G. Moses. I quickly discovered that Oklahoma history and historians provided a treasure trove of untapped sources on women public intellectuals and their desire to preserve American Indian history.

Archivists and librarians provided valuable assistance as I gathered materials. Depositories such as the Oklahoma Historical Society, the Western History Collections at the University of Oklahoma, and Archives and Special Collections at Oklahoma State University contain ample manuscript collections and oral histories on western women's history. I am indebted to the kindness and expertise of Bill Welge at the Oklahoma Historical Society. Welge encouraged me to explore the life and writings of Muriel Wright for a seminar paper. Others at the historical society including Mary Jane Warde, Mary Ann Blochowiak,

ACKNOWLEDGMENTS

Rodger Harris, Chester Cowen, and Judith Mitchener provided valuable insights and introduced me to extensive manuscript and oral history collections. John Lovett and his helpful staff at the Western History Collections have always been willing to listen to new developments in this project and to track down boxes of materials with a smile. In the same vein, Todd Kosmerick of the Carl Albert Congressional Studies and Research Center at the University of Oklahoma and John Phillips of Oklahoma State University aided me in locating government documents pertinent to this project. I give special thanks to Jennifer Paustenbaugh and her staff at Archives and Special Collections at Oklahoma State University, including Steve Kite, Tom Jorsch, and the late Heather Lloyd, for their willingness to share the oral histories and manuscript collection of Angie Debo. I am grateful to Diane Bird of the Laboratory of Anthropology in Santa Fe.

I have been fortunate to have had the mentoring and valuable suggestions on earlier drafts of the manuscript from Nancy Parezo, Shirley Leckie, Theresa Harlan, Virginia Scharff, Clyde Ellis, Carol Rachlin, Jean Hurtado, Linda Reese, Amy Carreiro, Susanne Weinberger, and Catherine Lavender. I am grateful for additional suggestions from dissertation committee members Ron Petrin, Bill Bryans, Joan Jensen, Elizabeth Williams, Laura Belmonte, and the late Louis Seig at Oklahoma State University.

My colleagues in the department of history and geography at the University of Central Oklahoma (UCO), especially Kenny Brown, Dan Donaldson, Xiaobing Li, and Cathi Dunkle, continue to provide a stimulating environment in which to grow as a scholar and instructor. I owe special thanks to Erica Johnson, Kathi Nehls, Dana Jackson, and Brandy Taylor, students in the history program at UCO. Beginning with T. H. Baughman as dean until 2004 and with continuing support from Dean Pam Washington, administrators continued to nurture this project to completion. Dean S. Narasinga Rao and Associate Dean John Garic of the Joe C. Jackson College of Graduate Studies and Research have actively supported this project for several years, demonstrating their interest in cultivating research at a teaching institution through an incentive grant for new faculty and other grants. Provost Don Betz remained steadfast in his vision to encourage professors like myself to seek balance

ACKNOWLEDGMENTS

between scholarship and teaching. Other vice presidents in academic affairs, including Bill Radke and Pat LaGrow, consistently sought out the resources I needed to complete the project.

Two Scholar Research Grants from the Oklahoma Humanities Council and the National Endowment for the Humanities in 2001 and 2003 provided timely summer support for revising the manuscript and securing images. I would like to give special thanks to Anita May, director of the Humanities Council, and David Pettyjohn, program officer, for their interest in the project.

At the University of New Mexico Press, Maya Allen-Gallegos, Evelyn Schlatter, Jill Root, David Holtby, and Glenda Madden embraced this project with enthusiasm and a deep commitment to supporting intellectual histories of the American West.

My wonderful neighbors in Stillwater, Lynn and Denise Roberts, and Sidney and Margaret Ewing, continued to encourage me to finish the book. In addition, Gerry Schaefer, Marshall resident, OSU booster, and longtime friend of Angie Debo, continues to educate me on what it means to be an Oklahoman. Her insight and thoughtfulness continue to motivate me to share my findings with others, and I dedicate this book to her.

My parents, Pat and Chris Loughlin, and my sisters, Kristin and Kate Loughlin, provide immeasurable family support and ongoing interest in the project. My grandmothers, Emma Loughlin and Frieda Kuklewicz, continue to inspire me with their strength. Phyllis Beemsterboer, my godmother, guides my professional development with her sound advice. My children, Owen and Bryce Logan, have never known life without this project. Their boundless curiosity and energy have structured my life around them and I do not want to miss a minute of their development. I share all of this with my husband, Mike Logan, whose calming disposition helps balance mine. He has nurtured this book to completion so that I may share it with you. I am beginning to understand the deep sense of place that connects Oklahomans to the region, so that the distinct smell of a wheat field overshadows the penetrating colors of a sunset.

❧❦ *Preface* ❦❧

A lot of people don't like Indians," Muriel H. Wright, Choctaw and editor of the *Chronicles of Oklahoma*, the state's historical quarterly, stated in 1965. "But I think in Oklahoma, of all the states of the Union, you have the finest feeling for the Indians. The American race is developing. The nucleus, whether you like it or not, is the Indian with the frontiersman."[1] With this notion of Oklahoma's national significance in mind, Wright produced publicly funded and publicly accessible documents in an effort to promote Oklahoma history. Wright had been documenting American Indian history since the 1920s, and her contributions to the *Chronicles of Oklahoma* emphasized her consistent theme of the positive aspects of Indian history: progress, strength, and endurance. She envisaged Oklahoma's place in American history as unique owing to the historical forces of the Indian removals to the twin territories and the encroachment of white settlement.

Angie Debo, Wright's contemporary and author of *And Still the Waters Run* (1940), also devoted her life to the study of American Indian history and Oklahoma's distinct identity as a place of frontier possibilities and American Indian settlement. Like Wright, Debo participated in the larger national discourse concerning the history of the United States and the history of American Indian people. What compelled Debo to pursue the tenuous career of freelance writing, particularly on the subject of American Indians that she claimed people were not interested in reading? She answered some of these questions in a lecture in 1951 entitled "Indian History from an Author's Point of View," presented at the Ohoyohoma Club, an American Indian women's club, in Tulsa. For Debo, Indian history enticed her to such a degree that she continued to write it, even against her "practical judgment." She found something deeply satisfying in revising American Indian topics that had been misrepresented in prior accounts—in erasing what she called "falsehoods from the popular mind." Debo also discovered "universal human experiences" in her research on American Indians that she broadened into "universal lessons" for the public at large.[2] This theme of teasing out universal truths from the study of American Indian history is a common theme throughout the literature of women historians and anthropologists during the first half of the twentieth century.

The general trend among women public intellectuals such as Wright and Debo was to study American Indian history as a means of offering a general social critique of the United States rather than commenting specifically on gender discrimination based on personal experience. Many women writers of the period viewed themselves as reformers, kindly "reflecting" and rectifying social ills by mirroring these social problems back to the larger society. "In [the white man's] philosophic moods," Debo wrote in the preface to *The Road to Disappearance: A History of the Creek Indians* (1941), "he may appraise his own civilization and see a reflection of his own problems and failures in the history of their tiny republic."[3] As historian Catherine Jane Lavender has maintained, white women writers during the early twentieth century studied Native communities in order to critique their own.[4] Debo was no exception. The story becomes far more interesting and complicated, however, when we examine Debo and Wright together. Muriel Wright was interested in controlling and disseminating her vision of Oklahoma's privileged place as a blending of American Indian and pioneer history—reflecting her own life as an educated Choctaw woman editing the *Chronicles of Oklahoma* for over three decades.

By the mid-twentieth century, one-third of all American Indian people lived in the state of Oklahoma. According to Commissioner of Indian Affairs John Collier's 1933 report, Oklahoma had the

Figure 1.
Alice Marriott conducting interviews with Maria Montoya Martinez during the early 1940s for her biography *Maria: The Potter of San Ildefonso* (Courtesy of Alice Marriott Collection, Western History Collections, University of Oklahoma, Norman).

largest Indian population in the United States.[5] As the state license plate now proclaims, Oklahoma is "Native America." With the state claiming the largest American Indian population and demonstrating marked diversity among tribes—home to fifty-seven federally recognized tribes—Oklahoma has provided a fertile place for historians and anthropologists, both women and men, to study American Indians.

Alice Marriott, anthropologist and author of *The Ten Grandmothers* (1945), contributes an important addition to this story. I view her in many ways as a counterpoint to Wright and Debo in that she eschewed the traditional approaches of her discipline (the formal, often patriarchal style of anthropological texts) in favor of experimental ethnography, providing the reader with insight into her own life as the anthropologist or participant-observer. Many anthropologists during the 1930s and 1940s considered experimental ethnography to be a feminine and unscholarly approach, but anthropologist Barbara Tedlock among others has identified anthropologists such as Marriott and Gladys Reichard as the forerunners of this method.[6] Marriott spent more time in western Oklahoma than Debo and Wright, writing about the Kiowas, for example, and later in New Mexico researching the famous potter Maria Martinez and the people of San Ildefonso Pueblo. As a field representative for the Indian Arts and Crafts Board during the 1930s, Marriott often needed to justify Oklahoma Indians as "real Indians" to her superiors at the board, only to be overshadowed by the romanticization of American Indian arts and crafts of New Mexico and Arizona. She tackled the daunting task of asking largely white collectors of American Indian arts and crafts to consider Native arts and crafts from Oklahoma as "authentic," valuable acquisitions to growing American Indian art collections. Such misconceptions lingered as many Oklahomans looked to the arts and crafts of tribes in the Southwest as somehow more authentic than the arts and crafts of tribes in Oklahoma.

As Virginia Scharff has reminded us in her recent study *Twenty Thousand Roads*, these women were mobile, active agents in the American West.[7] Raised in eastern Oklahoma, Wright attended Wheaton Seminary in Massachusetts, and also took some classes at Barnard in New York, before returning to Oklahoma and creating a life for herself as a permanent fixture at the Oklahoma Historical Society. Debo, too, was a woman on the move. Born in Kansas, as a young girl she relocated to Oklahoma Territory with her family as part of a pattern of movement—people in search of a better life and land ownership. She then resided in Chicago for her M.A. in history, followed by a decade-long teaching position at West Texas while completing a Ph.D. at the University of Oklahoma, before returning to Oklahoma, where she lived in Stillwater and Marshall for the remainder of her life. Born in Illinois, Marriott also moved to Oklahoma as a young girl when her parents found better jobs in the Oklahoma City area. Marriott's position at the Indian Arts and Crafts Board required extensive travel throughout the state of Oklahoma and took her to the far reaches of the continental United

States, specifically New York, Florida, and San Francisco for extended periods of time. During World War II, Marriott worked for the Red Cross along the New Mexico–Texas border and then moved to the Santa Fe area for over a decade before returning to Oklahoma City. There is no question that these women were mobile agents in the American West. But Oklahoma called them back—as a place of personal meaning, relationships, and family. As we read their historical record and the manuscripts they produced, we gain a strong sense of regional identity and sense of place. Oklahoma was home for these writers.

Professional women writers in the American West often embarked on their literary careers through studies of Native American culture and history. The intellectual work of women writers in New Mexico and Arizona has received extensive attention by scholars of the West, but the lives and texts of Oklahoma women remain largely overlooked. The three women in this study illustrate various degrees of this literary invisibility. Of the three, Angie Debo is the most well known, but she never achieved a career in academia that would match the success of her literary production. Ethnologist Alice Marriott is partially visible to academics, although her work is often disparaged as superficial, written for a nonintellectual public audience. Public historian Muriel Wright remains little known beyond a small circle of Oklahoma historians. All three writers made significant contributions to the historiography of American Indian communities in Oklahoma and the American West while occupying professional careers on the periphery of academia. The literary work of these women anticipated later methodologies and historical interpretations. The women's lives and their texts contribute to the understanding of state and regional history, to shifting federal Indian policy, and to interpretations of Native American culture.

In the longer view, this study explores the ways in which women have interpreted and left a visible record of historical interpretation in the American West—how they have shaped and filtered Oklahoma's self-described image as a unique place of American Indian and other settlers' history. Angie Debo recognized this regional identity or Oklahoma exceptionalism.

According to Debo, Oklahomans are unique because of their "peculiar history"—American Indian history and settler history coming together with the merger of Indian Territory and Oklahoma Territory in 1907. Both Wright and Debo embraced Turnerian thought—westward expansion and settlement—and explained Oklahoma history as a microcosm of rapid western expansion. But Wright and Debo told separate stories, with striking differences in their texts and historical interpretation according to issues of race, class, religion, and memory.

These women created careers and a body of literature at a time when academia was almost exclusively the domain of men. In some cases explicitly and in others simply through their successful careers, these women embody both the limitations faced and the opportunities enjoyed by women scholars in the 1930s and 1940s. Their work was not submerged beneath or hidden within the work of men because they strived so diligently to establish their own voices through the written record. I argue that if anything, these public intellectuals sought out challenging projects and took risks because they were not bound or limited by the confines of the academy. Instead, they pursued studies in American Indian history that interested them, that they believed would make significant contributions to the literature of American Indian history and particularly American Indians in Oklahoma, and that would also appeal to the general public. They were doing this work at a time when academics often shunned the idea of writing for a popular audience. For many years I have considered it detrimental and even lamentable that these women had so much to offer—and did offer in their writings—but could not train graduate students because they were not in academic positions. The tradition of academic discourse emphasizes the importance of citing the larger literature and those who came before you. We can only estimate the additional academic weight of Wright, Debo, and Marriott had they trained graduate students who in turn continued their pacesetting work on a larger scale. Recently I have begun to explore the inverse notion—that because these writers were in fact beyond the boundaries of the academy, they were free to pursue interesting aspects of American Indian history. Their writings—quite voluminous—are their legacy to Oklahoma history, American Indian history, and western history, and serve as an important reminder as we approach the centennial of Oklahoma's statehood in 2007.

Marriott, Wright, and Debo participated in the larger tradition of western women writers during the first half of the twentieth century and made significant contributions—as precursors to later models of experimental ethnography, American Indian history, and ethnohistory—to the literature of the American West. They were western women who examined American Indians through the lens of regional history. This regional history assumes certain historiographical paths in Oklahoma, as the next chapter explains in a brief examination of state development coupled with the birth of the University of Oklahoma and the Oklahoma Historical Society. Following this initial examination of Oklahoma's regional identity, I then offer the biographical sketches of Wright, Debo, and Marriott alongside their significant texts, placing them in the larger literature of regionalism and women public intellectuals in the American West. When studied in this way, women's regional identity and literary investment in the West, especially Oklahoma, are unmistakable.

Chapter One

Regional Identity and Historiography in Oklahoma

Writing in the early 1980s, legal scholar Rennard Strickland noted that the historiography of Oklahoma was "rich" and "good." Oklahoma's historical accounts and analysis were better on the whole, he argued, than those of the neighboring states of Arkansas, Kansas, Missouri, or Colorado. Even New Mexico's story had "great gaps" because the bulk of the literature focused on the colonial period, and Texas struggled with moving beyond legend and adventure lore. "The tradition of Joseph Thoburn, Grant and Carolyn Foreman, Edward Everett Dale, Muriel Wright and Angie Debo is a proud one," Strickland observed. "Indeed, few states can point to such a distinguished group of scholars."[1] In recent decades, he maintained, the University of Oklahoma and Oklahoma State University have been more interested in European history than Oklahoma history. "The time has come," Strickland rallied, "for the state's history departments to accord to the state's history the support it deserves."[2] Strickland's words remain valid today. Oklahoma and many scholars within Oklahoma continue to wrestle with regionalist identity, as some scholars are too concerned with provincialism to recognize the value of state and local topics.

Then as now, some academics have scoffed at regional history, particularly its embrace of a broader readership. Public intellectuals like Wright, Debo, and Alice Marriott told regional stories and produced an abundance of historical texts for public consumption. They shaped Oklahoma's self-image as a blending of American Indian history and settler history—they wrote Oklahoma history textbooks for state adoption in primary and secondary education; they wrote state guides and articles in scholarly journals, popular magazines, and local newspapers. Marriott tapped the public interest in her experimental ethnographies, combining her fieldwork experiences with American Indian people and allowing much of her personal observations and daily living into her stories. She also wrote several children's books with the same idea in mind: to make American Indian history accessible to readers.

During the first decades of the twentieth century, local history lost prestige in the academic world, as it became more "feminized" and "commercialized."[3] Most women writers were not part of the academy, but they did participate in the regionalist movement as public intellectuals. Rather than viewing this absence from the academy as gender discrimination, which it was in Debo's case, we can view it as an asset, a freedom—for they were relieved from academic pressures and political concerns. At the same time, in Oklahoma and throughout the United States, amateurs and history enthusiasts were writing local histories, raising the question, can anyone be a local historian? For historian John Walton Caughey, writing in the mid-1940s, local history meant state history. Caughey listed the perils of local history as bias, being close to one's subject, provincialism, and censorship. Censorship was particularly problematic for local historians as they relied on local sources, local funds, and local presses.[4] For example, Debo's mentor, Edward Everett Dale, lectured on the graft and corruption that took place in Oklahoma's development, but he never wanted to

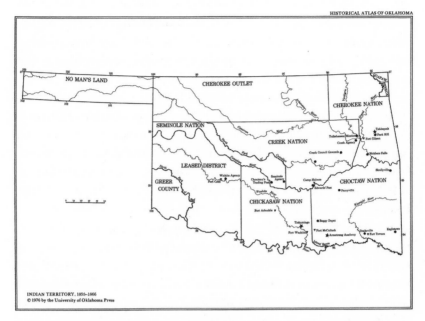

Map 1.

Indian Territory, 1855–66. From John W. Morris, Charles R. Goins, and Edwin C. McReynolds, *Historical Atlas of Oklahoma*, 3d ed. Copyright © 1965, 1976, and 1986 by the University of Oklahoma Press. Reprinted by permission.

put his lecture notes into print—it would be politically unwise for him to offend "friends" of the University of Oklahoma.[5] Debo, however, working on the margins of academia, could tackle these topics with unequaled passion and scholarly rigor because she was not tied to the university and she did not write for tenure; she wrote for a larger audience and larger purpose: that of the public intellectual. To be fair to Dale and others holding academic posts at the time, Debo also did not partake in academic networking—sharing drafts, seeking feedback—another problem or freedom, depending on one's viewpoint.

Beginning in the 1890s and into the early twentieth century, the University of Oklahoma and the Oklahoma Historical Society worked collaboratively to secure Oklahoma's regionalist identity. In this alliance, professional historians and amateurs, politicians and

3

boosters, came together in the name of Oklahoma statehood and the preservation of its history. Individuals such as Muriel Wright, Angie Debo, and Alice Marriott participated in the regionalist tradition of public intellectuals bent on producing both scholarly and readable texts in American Indian history.

Robert L. Dorman, in his study of the regionalist movement in the United States during the interwar period, accepts Debo as a key figure in the regionalist movement. He breaks the movement down further, classifying Debo along with novelists John Joseph Mathews (Osage) and D'Arcy McNickle (Salish-Kootenai) as "Indian subregionalists." Mathews and McNickle were American Indians whereas Debo was not. These writers, Dorman argues, viewed American history from the "Indians' side of the frontier" and, during the 1930s, they commenced writing a new narrative of American history from this vantage point. Rather than upholding historian Frederick Jackson Turner's frontier thesis as waves of settlement extending from east to west—and the frontier line where savagery meets civilization—these Indian subregionalists focused on conflict and oppression.[6] In order to gain an understanding of Oklahoma's place in national context, the general discussion that follows traces the disciplines of history and anthropology, the movement and settlement of Oklahoma by American Indian tribes, and the importance of institution-building and regional identity in a state formed from two territories in 1907.

With the professionalization of history and anthropology during the late nineteenth century, leading figures such as anthropologist Franz Boas at Columbia University and Turner at the University of Wisconsin established new frameworks for the study of Indian communities and the American West. Boas denied the notion of universal evolutionary stages as championed by the Bureau of American Ethnology, and advanced the theory of cultural relativism, or the idea that culture could be evaluated according to detailed studies of specific societies. As Curtis M. Hinsley Jr. points out, by World War I graduate programs in anthropology, first established by Boas at Columbia in 1895, represented the decline of government anthropology, specifically the Smithsonian Institution founded in 1846 followed by the Bureau of American

Ethnology in 1879, and the rise of anthropology as a university-trained science.[7] With the federal government's assimilation policy in full motion at the turn of the century, Boas and his students took to the field to preserve what were thought to be vanishing cultures. Boasian thought became the new paradigm in the discipline of anthropology.[8]

Similarly, Turnerian thought became the new paradigm in western history. Beginning with the frontier thesis in 1893 and followed by the frontier-section theory in the 1920s, Turner and his students advanced the notion that successive waves of frontier settlement explain the social process of "Americanization," which included freedom, democracy, and individualism as leading principles.[9] We must acknowledge both traditions in this discussion of women anthropologists and historians, for these central theories were present during the early decades of the twentieth century and represent the highly gendered world of academia.

According to the 1890 census, 250,000 American Indian people lived in the United States. More than one-fourth lived in what would become Oklahoma—51,279 in Indian Territory, 13,167 in Oklahoma Territory, for a total of 64,000. Oklahoma statehood was achieved in 1907, and by 1910 American Indians had increased to 74,825.[10] The Five Tribes—Cherokees, Choctaws, Chickasaws, Creeks, and Seminoles—represented the majority of the Indian population, the largest being the Cherokees, with 22,015 members and possessing one-fifth of Indian Territory, followed by the Choctaws with over 10,000 and one-fourth of the territory.[11]

The federal government had relocated the Five Tribes to Indian Territory during the late 1820s and early 1830s, a place where they could flourish and thrive away from U.S. development but that was still very eastern-centered. Historians such as Debo and Douglas Hale have identified internal dissension within the Five Tribes, split largely along progressive or "modernizer" versus traditionalist lines. The progressives within each tribe participated in the capitalist economy, and promoted education and private property. By the 1890s, individual Five Tribes progressives had already gained control of tribal land through long-term leases. Traditionalists, on the other hand, remained centered on family and tribal ties, communal property, and a subsistence economy. As Hale indicates, the balance of power between the two groups varied among the Five Tribes, but in general the progressives made gains in eastern Oklahoma. Modernizers, for example, welcomed the range cattle industry, mining, and railroads to the region. "In their pursuit of the modern and progressive," Hale maintains, "[progressives] ultimately doomed the tribal system, based as it was upon the common ownership of the soil." Elites controlled a significant land base within the Five Tribes. A wealthy Choctaw, in one case, possessed 17,600 acres. One-third of Creek lands was controlled by sixty-one Creek individuals.[12]

With regard to certain terms and labels to imply factions within a tribe, Erik M. Zissu, in *Blood Matters*, while recognizing the problems with and limitations of labels, prefers "conservative" and "progressive" to express the deepest division within tribes, rather than terms linked in some way to blood quantum or categories based on the social construction of race. Conservatives, according to Zissu, "tended to shy from white society and preferred lives lived among their tribal fellows where older traditions and practices might be preserved. They more likely possessed significant levels of Indian ancestry, a fact that they were well aware of and used for various purposes." "Progressives," according to Zissu, "displayed greater familiarity with, and attraction to, white values. They moved more easily within white society and embraced economic development of Indian Territory and, subsequently, the state of Oklahoma. Progressives, almost exclusively, derived from mixed white-Indian parentage and not infrequently had only the scantest biological ties to their tribes."[13]

The selection of terminology and how we elect to use it in American Indian studies is an interesting argument in and of itself. Craig S. Womack, in *Red on Red*, argues that our need to create such labels is "far too simplistic" and "reductionist," when we should be striving to complicate the narrative rather than bifurcating it or categorizing people with labels.[14] In my own work, I have often relied on the notion of "cultural broker" or "cultural mediator," terms used by Margaret Connell Szasz and Clara Sue Kidwell,[15] to describe American Indian people who seemingly "moved between two worlds," but Native scholars such as Womack and Devon Abbott Mihesuah remind me to wrestle with the individuals and their texts rather than compartmentalize them with a term such as "cultural broker." As Mihesuah maintains in her recent study *Indigenous American Women*, to write from an "Indian perspective" or to adopt an "authoritative voice" is a false claim, but historians do it all the time. Again, such claims are too simplistic. "Rather," Mihesuah agues, "there exists a spectrum of multi-heritage women in between 'traditional' and 'progressive,' possessing a multitude of opinions about what it means to be a Native female. There is no one voice among Natives because there is no such thing as the culturally and racially monolithic Native woman."[16]

Not only did freedmen become citizens of the Five Tribes following the Civil War, but the Five Tribes also lost significant portions of their land base to the federal government. During the Reconstruction treaties of 1866, the Five Tribes surrendered the western half of Indian Territory to the federal government as retribution for their support of the Confederacy. In her recent study of Cherokee freedwomen, historian Linda W. Reese points out, "The historians Annie Heloise Abel and Angie Debo believed that in dealings with the Indian Territory peoples, the federal government showed partiality toward former Indian slaves, to the deliberate disadvantage and disruption of the Indian nations."[17] Many Five Tribes people, including Muriel Wright, with Confederate ties and a slaveholding heritage maintained a disdain for African Americans. Freedmen who received tribal membership status received an allotment of 40 to 160 acres of land. By 1890 there were 18,636 African Americans in Indian Territory. When the government opened Oklahoma Territory to settlement after 1889, additional African Americans participated in settlement, and many flocked to all-black towns mostly located in Indian Territory near Muskogee. By 1910 Oklahoma had an African American population of 137,612, or 8.3 percent; 23,405 were enrolled as members of the Five Tribes.[18]

Following the Reconstruction treaties, the government relocated southern Plains tribes to the western part of Indian Territory. This coerced movement and collectivization of tribes also speaks

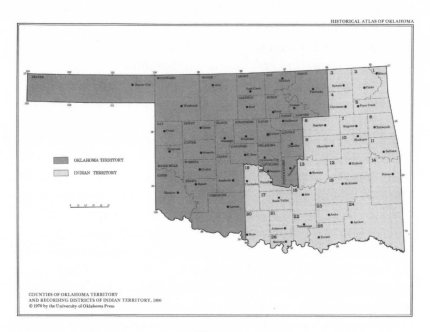

Map 2.
Counties of Oklahoma Territory and Recording Districts of Indian Territory, 1906. From John W. Morris, Charles R. Goins, and Edwin C. McReynolds, *Historical Atlas of Oklahoma*, 3d ed. Copyright © 1965, 1976, and 1986 by the University of Oklahoma Press. Reprinted by permission.

to the differences and conflicts among American Indian people in Oklahoma. Regional divisions occur between the Five Tribes in eastern Oklahoma and southern Plains tribes in western Oklahoma. From the outside, and from the federal government's perspective at the time, Oklahoma represented a place to remove American Indian people. But as David La Vere argues in *Contrary Neighbors,* an examination of Five Tribes and southern Plains Indians in Oklahoma, they were "two wholly different peoples."[19] When forced to live side by side in Indian Territory during the nineteenth century, "instead of creating a middle ground of cooperation and unity, they remained different, suspicious, and separate." In this east-west divide, Indianness became contested, as Five Tribes people viewed southern Plains Indians as "wild Indians" and southern Plains Indians viewed the Five Tribes as "effete, weak Indians" and "allies of the white man."[20]

Beginning in 1889, the federal government opened the western and central regions of Oklahoma to settlement, once again resulting in a regional split. There were two major trends of white migration. In general, midwesterners settled in northwestern Oklahoma, while southerners tended to settle in southeastern Oklahoma. This settlement pattern, as Hale points out, created a "cultural dichotomy" in Oklahoma that was particularly distinct in its inception and remains visible today in many respects. "In general terms midwestern values and attitudes were implanted north and west of a band roughly coincident with Interstates 40 and 44 from about Elk City through Oklahoma City to Miami," Hale maintains. "Southern perceptions were predominant south and east of this corridor."[21] Southerners emigrating to Indian Territory following the Civil War and into the 1880s and 1890s tended to be farmers, Christian fundamentalists, localistic, and family oriented. "[Southerners] were sometimes prone to use private violence," Hale states, "to settle disputes."[22] For these settlers, education was not a high priority. In contrast, Hale views the midwestern migrants as "more enterprising and progressive," the "'movers and shakers' of territorial Oklahoma."[23] Midwesterners were more committed to education, tended to vote Republican, and were more interested in town development than farming, although many were farmers.[24]

Such regional divisiveness is exemplified in the early development of higher education in Oklahoma. Western boosters lobbied for institutions of education in their towns, as a commitment to progressive thought and economic stimulation. In many ways, according to Hale, eastern Oklahoma was twenty years behind the west. In 1890, for example, the Oklahoma territorial legislature appropriated funds for a university, an agricultural college, and a normal school. Eastern Oklahoma, on the other hand, did not receive the benefits until after statehood, when eight schools opened in 1908–9 in the region. By 1910, Oklahoma operated seventeen colleges and universities, with a total enrollment of 2,363 students.[25] The University of Oklahoma was founded in 1890, in

Oklahoma Territory, seventeen years before statehood. As Albert L. Hurtado indicates in his study of western universities and regionalism before World War II, the University of Oklahoma had less funding and was smaller than its counterparts, the University of California and the University of Texas.[26]

When William Bizzell became president of the University of Oklahoma in 1925, he had visionary plans to carve out a distinct regional identity for OU, emphasizing American Indian history. Bizzell viewed Oklahoma as "a sort of laboratory which invites experiment; a place not bound by tradition," as Osage writer John Joseph Mathews has observed.[27] Although not a new approach—California and Texas had launched similar regionalist campaigns—the Oklahoma vision was the only one to promote Indian studies in its regional program, as Hurtado maintains, making it "distinctive" among western universities.[28] In his inaugural address, Bizzell stressed the importance of a university not only to educating its students, but to reaching a broader audience through a university press publishing scholarly texts. He initiated the University of Oklahoma Press in 1928, a bold action for a young university.

Bizzell and Joseph A. Brandt, the press director and former *Tulsa Tribune* city editor, realized that Oklahoma's American Indian population was the largest in the country and wanted OU to serve as the center for the preservation of Native heritage and identity. Brandt had ambitious plans for OU that included establishing the university as the center for Indian Studies in the United States. As part of this effort, Dale's new course in 1930, "The American Indian," was the first American Indian history course in the nation to be offered at the university level. Brandt also envisioned a special building on campus that would house an Indian museum, research center, and meeting rooms for the Indian studies program. In 1932 they launched the "Civilization of the American Indian Series" as one component of Bizzell's plan. This series remains special to Native American historians because it was conceived and sustained at a time when the historical profession showed limited interest in American Indian history.[29] Although many of Brandt's original plans were not actualized, his new series on American Indians offered a press that was interested in manuscripts on Indian topics at a time when many presses were reluctant to follow suit.[30]

Osage writer John Joseph Mathews is best known for his first book, *Wah-kon Tah: The Osage and the White Man's Road* (1932), published by the University of Oklahoma Press as the third volume in the Civilization of the American Indian Series. Within the first year, *Wah-kon-Tah*, meaning "the Great Spirit of the Osage people," sold fifty thousand copies and was a *New York Times* Book-of-the-Month Club selection. Such success bolstered the prestige of the University of Oklahoma Press. Angie Debo has maintained that her first book, *The Rise and Fall of the Choctaw Republic* (1934), the sixth volume in the Civilization of the American Indian Series, was well received following on the heels of Mathews's national acclaim.

Mathews's great-grandfather was a missionary to the Osages and married an Osage woman. With Brandt's encouragement, Mathews depicted life on the Osage reservation by using the diaries of Major Laban J. Miles, Indian agent of the Osages in the late 1870s. He pairs the diary with Osage oral histories. Mathews learned that Osage elders were concerned about preserving their oral history, "[s]o they talked eagerly, with precision and with meticulous care, preserving with the sanctity of every word that had been handed down to them from their fathers."[31]

Born near the Osage Agency at Pawhuska, Indian Territory, in 1894, Mathews received his early education at government schools and later attended the University of Oklahoma. During World War I, Mathews was in the U.S. Flying Service as a pilot. Following the war, he resumed studies at Oxford and graduated in 1923 with a degree in natural sciences from Merton College. Except for the war years and three years spent in Los Angeles, Mathews resided in the Osage hills. He was a member of the Osage Tribal Council from 1934 to 1942 and published other books with the University of Oklahoma Press including *The Life and Death of an Oilman* (1951) and *The Osages* (1961).

Although pleased with the success of his first book, Mathews was critical of the University of Oklahoma Press for its reluctance to embrace the region's folk culture and colloquialisms. In a 1942 review of the press for *Saturday Review,* Mathews remarked that most University of Oklahoma Press publications have a "scholarly smugness." He lamented that the language of the region's people— their "idioms, metaphors, dialects, and song"—has been deleted out of manuscripts. He called for the press to look for this regional identity in the people, perhaps encouraging more nonacademic writers to add to the literature of regional consciousness.[32] Mathews's critique of the University of Oklahoma Press addressed the schism between scholars and amateur historians. Although professionals and amateurs coalesced in many regional efforts, a steady tension persisted, much like the east-west tension within the state. To its credit, the press under Brandt's leadership captured national attention by defining the Southwest, including Oklahoma, as a "distinct cultural region."[33]

But Hurtado also recalls the time when the University of Oklahoma Press, at Bizzell's insistence, would not publish Debo's *And Still the Waters Run,* not wanting to offend friends of the university or lose potential donors. Debo's manuscript debacle assumes new meaning when considered in a regional context. University presses in the American West were in a precarious financial position during the first half of the twentieth century. Political interests, censorship, and friendly relations with the legislature held sway over academic freedom. And, Hurtado notes, many administrators such as Bizzell and department heads such as Dale privileged the university's vitality and funding over individual research agendas. Oklahoma was not an aberration but the norm, as other western institutions such as Texas and California did the same.[34]

By the mid to late 1930s the regional program was on the decline. Brandt's acceptance of Bizzell's regionalist plan quickly faded with the cancellation of Debo's contract for *And Still the Waters Run.* Brandt published the manuscript in 1940 when he became editor of the Princeton University Press. Three years later he returned to OU to serve as the sixth president of the university following Bizzell's retirement. But others were not so quick to accept Oklahoma's regional identity crisis. Benjamin Albert Botkin, an English professor at OU and a leading figure in the regional movement and American folklore, noted, "Oklahoma is still pioneering, a pioneering society is not a place for tradition or for literature."[35] By 1940 the University of Oklahoma Press had shifted from its specialty in regional studies to broader themes.

In ascribing Oklahoma's place within a regionalist framework, writers often fell into the trap of Oklahoma exceptionalism. Oklahoma textbooks, for example, lauded Oklahoma's uniqueness. "No state possesses a story more replete with sacrifices," Charles Evans wrote in *Lights on Oklahoma History* (1926), "with courage and spirit."[36] Such exceptionalist assertions pervade Oklahoma history textbooks and state texts in general, as authors attempt to instill state pride and patriotism in young minds. Many Oklahoma texts follow the structure of Frederick Jackson Turner's stages of civilization, contending that the process was exceptionally rapid in Oklahoma, perhaps occurring within one generation, as Debo has maintained. Optimism and progress are plentiful in these texts. Two University of Oklahoma history professors, James Shannon Buchanan and Edward Everett Dale, a Turner student, applied Turnerian thought to the development of Oklahoma in *A History of Oklahoma* (1924): "Everywhere and at every time progress is to be noted, in the steady and rapid rise of a vast region from savagery through pastoral life and pioneer agriculture, up through all the stages of human society to towns and cities and all the complex organizations of commercial and industrial life."[37] Dale and Buchanan continued to offer a romantic, regionalist interpretation of Oklahoma history in their joint editorship of the first issues of the *Chronicles of Oklahoma*, beginning in 1921.[38]

Residents of the twin territories realized they were participating in a historic moment in the decades preceding Oklahoma statehood in 1907. They recognized the importance of saving records, telling the stories, and preserving the history for future generations to learn and interpret. These primary accounts speak to the boomer mentality of many of the journalists and city planners, and to the optimistic fervor of settling the territories and of early state development. But, as Rennard Strickland has observed, these firsthand accounts and impressions are also problematic. "The state's historical literature is long on vivid remembrances," he has contended, "and short on deep analysis."[39]

The Oklahoma Historical Society (OHS) emerged during the early 1890s as the vehicle through which to secure Oklahoma's place in public memory. Newspapermen such as William P. Campbell, editor of the Kingfisher newspaper, and other members of the Oklahoma Territory Press Association recognized the importance of preserving Oklahoma history by saving territorial newspapers. Following the Kansas Historical Society model, Campbell and others collected complete sets of nine daily and forty-seven weekly newspapers, books, and documents. They would expand their mission to include maps, paintings, photographs, and manuscript collections. The University of Oklahoma housed the OHS during the 1890s. In 1901, the society moved to Oklahoma City, expanded its staff, and continued collecting materials.[40]

Another newspaperman and early proponent of the OHS was Joseph B. Thoburn. Raised on a Kansas farm and a graduate of Kansas Agricultural College, he first visited Indian Territory in 1889 and again in 1896, before settling in Oklahoma in 1899. Thoburn combined his interest in history with his printing business and journalism. His first periodical, *The Last Frontier*, was dedicated to the history of the Kiowa-Comanche country. A city booster, Thoburn helped organize the Oklahoma City Chamber of Commerce in 1903. Thoburn's varied interests put him in contact with a cross-section of Oklahomans. "[Thoburn] gained wide knowledge and had personal acquaintance with Indians, white settlers, and officials," Muriel Wright has observed, "both Territorial and State, among whom he was well known for his unfailing interest in the part they had had in the development of Oklahoma."[41]

During this time Thoburn was a central figure in the development of the historical society, serving on the board of directors and as director of research. He wrote historical articles for the *Chronicles of Oklahoma* and newspapers. He also gathered material for *A History of Oklahoma* (1908), the first textbook on Oklahoma history for state adoption. Working with the University of Oklahoma and the OHS, Thoburn performed excavation work throughout the state and showed particular interest in Spiro Mounds.

What becomes clear as we piece together state development and historic preservation is that many early Oklahoma historians were journalists and city boosters like Thoburn or federal employees like Grant Foreman. An attorney for the Dawes Commission before he retired and devoted his attention to history, Foreman played an important leadership role during the early years of the OHS and was particularly dedicated to preserving and publishing Oklahoma's historical documents. On the OHS Board of Directors since 1924, Foreman and former governor Robert L. Williams successfully agitated for the current Oklahoma Historical Society building.[42] Foreman was acutely aware of the historical value of the state's development and the documents that told Oklahoma's history. Fostering this awareness was a difficult task during the 1920s, as Stanley Clark has pointed out, for Oklahoma "was not deeply interested in its cultural heritage."[43] Foreman joined the early journalists in recognizing the importance of their historic moment, even if the majority of Oklahoma residents did not. Foreman and others worked to preserve contemporary stories for future use. They participated in a regionalist movement to document Oklahoma history and preserve it in a state historical society.

In 1927, the OHS Board of Directors voted to house all Indian files as they became available owing to the closing of Indian agencies. Foreman lobbied key members of Congress for the release of these records when Oklahoma could provide suitable storage facilities. Five Tribes governmental records had been held at Union Agency in Muskogee since 1908. In March 1934, when Congress passed a bill transferring all tribal records in Oklahoma to the OHS, Foreman created the Indian Archives Division, a federal repository. He also successfully lobbied for agency and tribal records in western Oklahoma, when agents to the Kiowa, Comanche, Cheyenne, Arapaho, Shawnee, Sac, and Fox tribes anticipated the closing of their offices.[44]

Born in western Illinois in 1869, Foreman attended public schools and enrolled in the University of Michigan's law school without undergraduate training in 1889. Health reasons dictated his move to a warmer climate, so after practicing law in the Chicago area for eight years, Foreman relocated to Muskogee, Indian Territory, where he worked for the Dawes Commission.[45]

The Dawes Commission, or the Commission of the Five Civilized Tribes, established in 1893, carved out allotments in severalty among the Five Tribes. Henry L. Dawes, former Massachusetts senator and sponsor of the 1887 General Allotment Act (also called the Dawes Act), chaired the commission. By the 1890s Congress broadened its authority to coerce reluctant or unwilling tribes to accept allotment policy. The Curtis Act, for example, passed by Congress in 1898, required the Dawes Commission to create allotments on Five Tribes land with or without their consent. Joining the Dawes team at this time, Foreman appraised and classified land, and later joined the commission's legal team.[46]

Historian Michael D. Green argues that Foreman's work with the Dawes Commission shaped his interpretation of Oklahoma history, particularly Five Tribes history. According to allotment policy, individual allotments were held in trust for twenty-five years, to protect Indians from speculators. Surplus lands, however, could be sold. By the early twentieth century, Foreman viewed firsthand the frenzy of surplus land speculation. He watched as land speculators and grafters capitalized on the purchase of Creek mixed-blood allotments and Creek freedmen's surplus lands. These activities left an indelible impression on Foreman. According to Green, Foreman's "outrage at the unprincipled, if not illegal, treatment of allotted Indians and his deep interest in history all came together to work a change in his priorities."[47] As a result, Foreman joined the Indian Rights Association and campaigned for the protection of Indian allotments. In other words, Foreman wanted more stringent regulations in place to ward off speculators.

In 1903, Foreman joined the law offices of John R. Thomas, formerly one of the first federal judges in Indian Territory appointed by President William McKinley. Two years later, Foreman married Thomas's daughter, Carolyn Thomas. Grant and Carolyn Foreman shared a passionate interest in Oklahoma history, and culled national and international depositories in search of primary source material. They were a research team, collectively producing more than two hundred books and articles. "It is difficult to separate the historical contributions made by Carolyn Foreman from Grant Foreman," Green notes.[48]

Like her husband, Carolyn Foreman was not a professionally trained historian, but her dedication and interest in regional history, almost exclusively Indian Territory and pointedly in the Cherokee and Creek nations, compelled her to write seven books and at least eighty-eight *Chronicles* articles on American Indian history. Some historians have claimed that she contributed the most articles to the *Chronicles*, although Muriel Wright wrote over one hundred articles for the journal.

Carolyn Foreman was educated in private schools in Washington, D.C., while her father, John R. Thomas, served as congressman from Illinois, and at Monticello Seminary, a girls' school, in Godfrey, Illinois, and studied French and German for a year in Europe. In 1897 at the age of twenty-five, she came to Muskogee because her father had been appointed by President William McKinley as one of the first federal judges in Indian Territory. Muskogee was in its infancy at the time, an unincorporated town with less than 3,500 residents. As J. Stanley Clark describes, Carolyn Foreman was interested in the development of Muskogee and the territory, "a city to be incorporated and developed, a state to be built, and Indians to be guided to a new and different citizen status as their tribal governments were terminated through the work of the Dawes Commission."[49]

Both Grant and Carolyn Foreman have contributed key texts in the early growth and development of Oklahoma historiography. Grant Foreman's most important work was *Indian Removal* (1932), the second volume in the Civilization of the American Indian Series at the University of Oklahoma Press. This book offers a negative assessment of President Andrew Jackson's removal policy of the Five Tribes from their homes in the southeast to Indian Territory. Foreman describes Five Tribes people of the 1820s as farmers; many were Christians, and some were educated. He discusses the misery of westward removal, sharing stories of insufficient supplies, poor medical treatment, and deaths with hasty burials. This text remains the standard reference for Indian removal.[50]

The next phase of the book focuses on the restoration of Five Tribes institutions in Indian Territory. By reestablishing their governments, churches, schools, and farms in Indian Territory, or the "raw frontier," Foreman argues, a "higher civilization of Indians" emerges. He continues, "this was an achievement unique in our history that compares favorably with the best tradition of white frontier civilization."[51] Foreman's telling of the Five Tribes story begins as a negative portrayal of forced removal westward, and then shifts to a story of redemption as the Five Tribes flourish in Indian Territory. He then equates the Five Tribes' frontier experiences with white frontier experiences. This interpretation of Oklahoma history as a positive blending of American Indian people and settler history is reminiscent of many of the writings of Muriel Wright and, to a lesser extent, of Angie Debo.

Grant Foreman's legal training aided his meticulous note-taking, but, as Green points out, Foreman was not a good historian and he shared weaknesses similar to those of many other historians of the period. First, his concern with cultural evolution, or what Green calls "ethnographic assumptions"—this notion of a cultural hierarchy with the apex being civilization and the dearth being savagery—is a point of contention. Second, in Green's assessment, Foreman did not accurately evaluate his sources; instead he quoted large passages from primary sources and provided limited or no analysis, which is a common tendency for amateur historians. Interestingly, Green does mention that Annie Heloise Abel and Angie Debo, both historians of American Indian tribes in Indian Territory and contemporaries of Foreman, offered "careful, critical historical scholarship" in their books, while Foreman did not.[52]

Carolyn Foreman's first book, *Oklahoma Imprints, 1835–1907* (1936), traces the history of printing in Oklahoma prior to statehood. As a result of her research, she encouraged her husband to lead a Works Progress Administration (WPA) project to index all newspapers at the OHS from the earliest territorial issues through 1936. An article in the *Daily Oklahoman* from 1936 echoes the importance of her research on printing: "She saw these early prints as carrying the torch of civilization, the early newspaper as the chronicle of buried pioneer struggles and progress, the surviving witness of events that were making history."[53] The Foremans also launched another WPA project, the Indian-Pioneer Papers, an oral history project recording life experiences of American Indian people and other territorial settlers before and after the Civil War.

Carolyn Foreman's second book, *Indians Abroad* (1943), published by the University of Oklahoma Press, received the most scholarly attention. This book was selected by the Office of War Information as one of the texts to be housed in overseas libraries and available to the military. In a second printing, OU Press made eighty thousand copies to meet the demand. In preparation for this book, Foreman utilized the Library of the British Museum in London and the National Libraries in Paris and Brussels. Her other books include *Indian Women Chiefs* (1954), *The Cross Timbers* (1947), *Park Hill* (1948), and *North Fork Town* (1963).

The Foremans had the financial resources to cull major libraries and archives in the United States and Europe, collecting primary source material related to Oklahoma such as correspondence, diaries, and newspapers. For example, they gathered federal reports and documents from the Indian Office and War Department before the creation of the National Archives. The Foremans bequeathed their private library to the Oklahoma Historical Society; it provides a treasure trove for researchers.

The Foremans worked as institution-builders at the historical society alongside Muriel Wright and others during the early decades of the twentieth century. Politicians, city boosters, journalists, and historians preserved and created spaces for the celebration of Oklahoma history. Throughout the United States, particularly at the state and local level, women were at the center of this mission to collect and preserve and interpret the stories, documents, and memories of state development. As the next chapter illustrates, Muriel Wright personifies the individual historian as gatekeeper. From her position on the staff at the Oklahoma Historical Society, she negotiated her role as an arbiter of public memory in Oklahoma.

PART ONE
Muriel H. Wright
(1889–1975)

Figure 2.
Muriel H. Wright (1889–1975), ca. 1922 (Courtesy of Archives and Manuscripts Division, Oklahoma Historical Society).

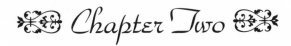

Chapter Two

Muriel H. Wright

Marking and Preserving
Five Tribes History

I n 1965, at seventy-six years of age, Muriel Hazel Wright, an Oklahoma Choctaw, reflected on her ties to the state: "I don't own Oklahoma," she said, "but I have a very deep feeling [for the state] because of being in the historical field."[1] This identification with Oklahoma, this deep sense of place, shaped Wright's presentation of Oklahoma history. She served as editor of the *Chronicles of Oklahoma*, the state's historical quarterly, from 1943 to 1973. From her position as editor, Wright successfully implanted her interpretation of Oklahoma history from within the historical society.

Educated American Indian women, Nancy Shoemaker maintains, often selected professions that were considered women's professions such as education, social welfare, and health care. Some women may have been constrained by "gendered limitations," but the majority of American Indian women in these professions assumed the role of "expert" and provided an important service to

Figure 3.
Birthplace of Muriel H. Wright near Lehigh, Choctaw Nation, Indian Territory
(Courtesy of Archives and Manuscripts Division, Oklahoma Historical Society).

their communities.[2] Muriel H. Wright's career at the Oklahoma Historical Society, for example, underscores Shoemaker's generalizations. Many women throughout the country were editors of state history journals. Under Wright's leadership, the *Chronicles of Oklahoma* consistently produced articles on American Indian history and state and local topics during a period when few national journals provided a forum for such research. During her thirty-year tenure at the historical society and her leadership role in the development of the historic sites program, Wright firmly embedded her presence in Oklahoma as an early public historian.

In an autobiographical sketch, Wright described her identity as "one-fourth Choctaw" and "also from distinguished colonial ancestry."[3] Born in 1889 at Lehigh, Choctaw Nation, Indian Territory, to a notable Choctaw family, Wright's heritage and education provided the solid foundation for her future work. Her mother, Ida Belle Richards, educated at Lindenwood College of

Muriel H. Wright

Figure 4.
Muriel H. Wright at age
two, ca. 1891 (Courtesy of
Archives and Manuscripts
Division, Oklahoma
Historical Society).

St. Charles, Missouri, came to the Indian Territory in 1887 as a Presbyterian missionary teacher. Her father, Dr. Eliphalet Nott (E. N.) Wright, a graduate of Union College and Albany Medical College in New York, returned to the Choctaw Nation to establish his private practice and serve as company physician for the Missouri-Pacific Coal Mines at Lehigh. E. N. Wright entrenched himself within the Choctaw Nation not only as a doctor but also as a businessman who was interested in improving his nation. His interests included the development of oil in the Choctaw Nation, and he became the first president of the Choctaw Oil and Refining Company in 1884. An active supporter of allotment in his negotiations with the Dawes Commission on behalf of the Choctaws, Wright was also a strong proponent for bringing together Oklahoma and Indian Territories in statehood.[4]

The pursuit and preservation of her biracial heritage remained an ever-present concern in Muriel Wright's personal

Figure 5.
Muriel H. Wright's father,
Eliphalet Nott (E. N.)
Wright (Courtesy of
Archives and Manuscripts
Division, Oklahoma
Historical Society).

life, career, and historical interpretation. On both sides of the family tree, Wright proudly traced her genealogy to descendants aboard the *Mayflower* in 1620 and the *Anne* in 1623.[5] Her paternal grandmother, Harriet Newell Mitchell Wright, for example, was a descendant of two *Mayflower* passengers, William Brewster and Edward Doty. She came from Dayton, Ohio, to Choctaw Nation as a Presbyterian missionary teacher to the Choctaws. Put another way, both Wright's grandmother and mother were white missionary teachers and married Choctaw men. According to Devon A. Mihesuah in her examination of Five Tribes census records, "many white men married full- and mixed-blood women, but few white women married Indian men—even those of mixed blood."[6] In the Wright family, however, the opposite was true, for Wright's mother and grandmother married Choctaw men. The Wright family was a Choctaw family with powerful political and economic ties in Choctaw Nation. As Mihesuah indicates in her

Figure 6.
Muriel H. Wright's mother,
Ida Belle Richards Wright
(Courtesy of Archives
and Manuscripts
Division, Oklahoma
Historical Society).

recent study of Native women, *Indigenous American Women: Decolonization, Empowerment, Activism*, "wealthy families often were educated, progressive, and Christian and did not value tribal traditions. Many saw themselves as morally superior to the uneducated, non-Christian, and less wealthy traditionalists (usually, but not always, full-bloods). Their 'white blood' also contributed to their feelings of importance. From their point of view, they were in the superior 'class.'"[7] Mihesuah's analysis of racism and class stratification among Five Tribes people is important to consider in a discussion of Muriel H. Wright. Wright was from a "progressive" family and worked to uphold the prestige and privilege of her family as she documented Choctaw Nation, Indian Territory, and Oklahoma history. A member of the Daughters of the American Revolution and the Colonial Dames, Wright maintained these commitments in addition to active participation in Choctaw Nation politics.

Figure 7.
Chief Allen Wright and Harriet Newell Mitchell Wright and family, ca. 1860s
(Courtesy of Archives and Manuscripts Division, Oklahoma Historical Society).

Wright's most distinguished relative, and her favorite to discuss, was her Choctaw grandfather, Reverend Allen Wright. A graduate of Union College and Union Theological Seminary in New York, he served as principal chief of the Choctaw Nation from 1866 to 1870. As Wright pointedly recalled, her grandfather was the "first Indian from Indian Territory to have earned the master's degree."[8] In 1866 during the Choctaw-Chickasaw Reconstruction Treaty delegation's visit to Washington, D.C., this learned man first suggested the name "Oklahoma" for the territory. Muriel H. Wright remembered the story vividly:

> My grandfather was sitting at the desk. As a linguist, he
> knew Choctaw. On one side of the sheet he was writing
> Choctaw and on the other English. One of the officials,
> probably the Commissioner of Indian Affairs, said what

would you call the territory? Grandfather was sitting absentmindedly, writing around, and he said immediately, Oklahoma. Well that Choctaw name is synonymous with Indian; there isn't any word in the Choctaw language for Indian. Oklahoma means "red people."[9]

Muriel Wright recalled that her grandfather used to laugh when he told this story, because he had spoken out of turn in the eyes of the "older, dignified Indian delegates."[10] The name "Oklahoma" quickly gained popularity among Indians and other settlers. When the twin territories merged during statehood in 1907, the popular name of choice was that offered by Wright's grandfather in 1866.[11] The Wright family roots run deep within the state's history. She took hold of this history in a personal, almost proprietary way, carefully preserving her Choctaw ties with the state's development.

Beginning in 1897 with the Atoka Agreement and continuing with the Curtis Act of 1898, the Dawes Commission systematically sectioned the Choctaw National landscape into individual allotments in severalty. Such federal government interference dramatically altered the organization of Choctaw institutions, including education. During this transition, formerly reputable tribal schools deteriorated in the hands of the federal government. As a result, Wright received most of her primary and secondary education at home from her mother, although she studied several years at the Presbyterian Mission School and the Baptist Academy in Atoka. Boarding school was not an option for Wright because her mother said she was "too small" to attend Indian boarding school.[12]

Following a family tradition of eastern education extending back to her grandfather, Wright attended Wheaton Seminary in Norton, Massachusetts. Overall, her experience at Wheaton was pleasant, although she later recounted that being "a Choctaw Indian was no asset."[13] She was a southerner and an Indian from Indian Territory, two distinctions that set her apart from her mostly northern, mostly white classmates at Wheaton and that sometimes caused friction. In her own words she maintained that her Choctaw ancestry was somehow detrimental during her time at Wheaton, but her comment may also indicate an awakening of her

Figure 8.
Muriel H. Wright, studio portrait by G. V. Buck in Washington, D.C., in 1909.
During this time, the Wright family lived in Washington, D.C., while her father
served a two-year term as resident delegate for the Choctaw Nation (Courtesy
of Archives and Manuscripts Division, Oklahoma Historical Society).

Indian identity. Being forced to confront issues of race and identity away from family and tribal ties prompted Wright's future work as an interpreter of Oklahoma's Indian history. Two years later, in 1908, she joined her parents in Washington, D.C., where her father served a two-year term as resident delegate of the Choctaw Nation.

Muriel Wright's formal introduction to Washington society provides a glimpse of her adeptness at "playing Indian" when called upon to perform, to borrow the useful term from historian Philip J. Deloria.[14] Deloria notes that in the early twentieth century, Indian people participated in such performances as never before—as he describes it, they were "imitating non-Indian imitations of Indians."[15] Muriel Wright had attended the event wearing a white dress, and was described by one Washington newspaper as "demure and dainty as any conventional sweet girl graduate." Then Wright left the party to change attire. When she returned, to quote the article, Wright had been "transformed, idealized, a creature of a different race—an Indian girl in all the picturesque trappings of her ancestral tribe."[16] But, interestingly, Wright was not wearing traditional Choctaw dress; she was wearing Cheyenne buckskin attire with her hair in braids, thereby projecting an image that the Eastern audience identified as "Indian," though largely representative of Plains Indian people. In other words, Wright was fulfilling eastern expectations of "Indianness," while simultaneously validating her family's status among Washington's elite. "Miss Muriel Wright will be a social success in Washington," the article concluded.[17]

This type of performance was typical among prominent Indian women during the early twentieth century. For example, in 1925, Ruth Muskrat Bronson, a Cherokee student at Mount Holyoke, donned similar attire in her presentation to President Calvin Coolidge.[18] Wright's and Bronson's performances appear to coincide with decades of federal assimilation policy, rather than challenging assumptions of Indian identity. The story is far more complicated in these very public performances. How did Wright's Indian performances in turn redefine her sense of Indian identity? Put another way, and borrowing from Deloria's discussion of Indian identity and authenticity, "To what extent had acting like Indian Others formed a part of their identities around the very

Figure 9.
Muriel H. Wright in
Cheyenne buckskin, 1947.
Photo by Pierre Tartoué
(Courtesy of Archives
and Manuscripts
Division, Oklahoma
Historical Society).

images they attempted to change?"[19] Coincidentally, in 1947 Wright was photographed wearing Cheyenne buckskin similar to the attire she had worn at the Washington function, and she was also photographed on another occasion wearing a traditional Choctaw dress. In this way, she adds complexity to the meaning of Indianness in her own Indian identity. When wearing so-called Indian dress, must she wear only clothes identified as part of her Choctaw identity, or is she free to wear a variety of styles? By donning such attire and being photographed, she is at once reflecting and challenging the viewer's notion of what it means to be Indian. Wright's interest in Indian performance paralleled her interest in educating the general public and dispelling stereotypes about American Indian people and their diverse histories. She helped erode stereotypes of Indians using her own life as an example, as well as dedicating her life's work to promoting her own heritage within Oklahoma history.

Muriel H. Wright

Figure 10.
Muriel H. Wright in
Choctaw dress, 1947.
Photo by Pierre Tartoué
(Courtesy of Archives
and Manuscripts
Division, Oklahoma
Historical Society).

Recently, historians have debated the question of Indian identity and the preservation of Indian culture. Historically, the Five
Tribes have embraced cultural change through accommodation
and encounter with Euro-Americans. Prior to removal to Indian
Territory, the Five Tribes had established schools, adopted
Christianity, and participated in the market economy. Some individuals were wealthy landowners with slaves, and two of the tribes
had drafted written constitutions in the southeastern part of the
United States. The Five Tribes exemplified the success of government policy and missionary work among Indians—they were
viewed as proof that Indians could be "civilized." The success of
assimilation policy prompted a question that historian W. David
Baird poses: "Are the Five Tribes of Oklahoma 'Real' Indians?" His
response is clear: yes, they are. Baird maintains that to create a hierarchy of Indian identity, by determining who is "more Indian" based
on a rejection of acculturation, is ahistorical and dangerous. By

making these kinds of distinctions, Baird continues, "we deny the vitality of Native American society and its ability to adapt dynamically to change. We assume instead that culture is static, and that once it is altered, regardless of extent, the real Indians disappear."[20] Similarly, Clara Sue Kidwell's research on the Choctaws of Mississippi has led her to conclude, "dynamic change over time does not necessarily mean the loss of culture."[21] Muriel Wright's career exemplifies Kidwell's and Baird's position regarding Indian identity and the preservation of culture. Wright created a significant space for herself as a historian of Oklahoma history, and she is no less Indian because of her embrace of "progress" or "assimilation." She made conscious decisions to represent herself as a mixed-blood Choctaw woman professional who dedicated her life to documenting the contributions made by American Indian people in the state of Oklahoma.

If anything, Wright added complexity to the notion of "Indianness." She was a confident, progressive Choctaw woman. She was proud of her Choctaw grandfather's role as principal chief and her father's leading role in the Choctaw Nation. Simultaneously, she made connections to her Anglo past, a past of Christian missionaries and educational leaders. Wright's identity was a composite of these roles. Secure in her Indian identity, she was able to "play" with it and participate in Indian performance. She was no less Indian because of this participation. Rather, through Indian performance, Wright educated her audience on Indian identity and challenged stereotypes of Indianness in her public role, first while accompanying her family and supporting their political role in Washington, D.C., and in Choctaw Nation, and later as an independent career woman working at the Oklahoma Historical Society.

Upon returning to the family allotment in Lehigh, Wright prepared for a career in teaching as she completed a teacher education course—though she never received her bachelor's degree—at the newly founded East Central Normal School in Ada, Oklahoma, in 1912.[22] One-room or two-room rural schools predominated in the Oklahoma countryside in the 1910s and 1920s. As historian James Smallwood indicates, Oklahoma had 12,390 teachers in 1915, and more than half of them were dispersed throughout the state in rural schools.[23] Wright's educational theory courses at East Central emphasized the importance of new teachers visiting the students' families at home in order to gain insight into their backgrounds and home life. Wright conducted these home visits throughout her teaching career and discovered that this method helped reduce discipline problems in the classroom.[24]

In the early twentieth century, women held the majority of teaching positions in public schools, but the men involved in elementary and secondary education received higher salaries and obtained the bulk of the administrative posts. In 1912, Wright began as an English and history instructor at Wapanucka, Oklahoma, in Johnston County. Her initial salary was $50 per month. Some women, however, ascended to administrative positions. For instance, in 1914, sixteen of seventy-seven county superintendents in Oklahoma were women. By the early 1930s, almost half of the county superintendents were women.[25] By 1914, not only had Wright risen to high school principal, but she was also earning $95 per month. Wright's position as a principal was a rarity among women teachers.[26] In 1916, women high school principals, according to Courtney Ann Vaughn-Roberson, represented 16 percent of all high school principals in Oklahoma, and by mid-century their representation dropped to 7 percent.[27] For a brief period beginning in 1916, she attended Barnard College, the women's college of Columbia University, to pursue a master's degree in history and English. World War I interfered with her education at Barnard and she returned home.[28]

From 1918 to 1924, Wright was principal of Hardwood District School, a rural school in Coal County near her family home. The local economy centered on the timber industry, with bois d'arc timber and oak railroad ties as the leading commodities. Wright described the people of the district as an all-white "renter class," renting from the Choctaws. The region and school were closed to African Americans. The nearest black settlement was approximately nine miles southeast of Boggy Creek in the upland timber region.[29]

Hardwood School stood on the section line road at the south of the Wright family allotment, comprised of some 735 acres. The school building was situated on a five-acre tract and was heated by two large wood-burning stoves. Again Muriel Wright acted as both teacher and principal, this time with a salary of $150 per month. Wright had one assistant teacher who taught the first through fourth grades, and Wright taught the fifth through eighth grades. Wright took an active interest in the welfare of her students. For example, she introduced a student-administered assistance program for students who could not afford school supplies. Most of the Hardwood students, Wright noted, earned their money for textbooks, new coats, and shoes by harvesting cotton on their parents' farms.[30]

In addition to teaching, Wright actively participated in Choctaw Nation politics. Beginning in 1922, while her father served as chair of the Choctaw Committee, she held the office of secretary. The council supported educational and welfare programs, making improvements at Wheelock Academy, Jones Academy, and Goodland Indian Orphanage, and constructing and maintaining the Indian hospital in Talihina. In addition, Muriel Wright successfully implemented a program to restore and preserve the Choctaw Council House at Tuskahoma, defeating an initiative to move the house to Southeastern State College in Durant.

Her early efforts as secretary of the Choctaw Committee provided Wright with the springboard and experience for her later political activities during the mid-twentieth century. Regarded as "one of the most accomplished women in the Choctaw nation," according to one newspaper, Wright became a candidate for principal chief of the Choctaws in 1930.[31] "Being of Choctaw descent," she wrote in a statement addressing her candidacy, "and having been closely associated with my father in his work for a number of years, some knowledge of the Choctaw people is second nature to me." Wright also noted that her "exceptional opportunities," such as serving on the Choctaw Committee, were opportunities that "no other person among the younger Choctaws has had."[32] In the mid-1930s, she helped create and served as secretary of the Choctaw Advisory Council, a governing body recognized by the U.S. Indian Office in Oklahoma and Washington, D.C., and served as the Choctaw delegate from Oklahoma City until 1944. During this period the council worked to secure final settlement of Choctaw properties still outstanding.[33] Wright viewed the council's commitment to welfare and education in the mid-1930s as an outgrowth of the Choctaw Committee's earlier work, sharing the "same vision that now seems to be materializing into real results."[34] She was part of a mixed-blood elite that had participated in the benefits of statehood, and her historical interpretation conveyed this message. Wright served her community as teacher, politician, and researcher.

Her interest in Choctaw history began as a "hobby" in 1914, the year she met Joseph B. Thoburn, a journalist, Oklahoma City booster, and early supporter of the Oklahoma Historical Society during the first years of the twentieth century. Thoburn served the OHS as a board member, historian, and archaeologist. One year after statehood, Thoburn produced the first Oklahoma history textbook for state adoption, *A History of Oklahoma* (1908). In the early 1920s, Thoburn encouraged Wright to pursue historical research on the Cherokees and Choctaws. Building on her classroom training in history and her familiarity with the land and its people, she began studying the geography of southeastern Oklahoma, mapping Choctaw Nation and conducting fieldwork almost every year from 1922 to 1929.[35]

Thoburn and Wright collaborated on a four-volume Oklahoma history set, *Oklahoma: A History of the State and Its People* (1929).[36] As a marketing device to promote the set's uniqueness, Thoburn emphasized Wright's Choctaw heritage and the authenticity of her historical approach. This work, Thoburn wrote to booksellers in California, "includes the most complete and accurate account of the old Indian Territory." He claimed—in a self-promotional exaggeration—that Wright was "possibly the first of her race in the United States to become recognized as a historical writer."[37]

Wright's writings reflected her sensitivity and interest in preserving the delicate balance of Oklahoma's American Indian and (mostly white) settler history. Drawing on her teaching experience and initial work with Thoburn, Wright wrote several history textbooks for adoption in the public schools. As a result, she understood the need for Oklahoma texts that would present balanced accounts of the contributions made by the state's Indian population as well as by Anglo participants and other ethnic groups. Along with this intensified interest in historical writing, and with Thoburn's assistance, Wright produced *The Story of Oklahoma* (1929), a text-book for public school children.[38] In addition, supplemental work-books required active student participation in piecing together Oklahoma's history.[39] Oklahoma's state textbook commission adopted *The Story of Oklahoma* for the public schools, and by 1939 it had sold over twenty thousand copies and had gone through sev-eral editions.

Wright dedicated *The Story of Oklahoma* to her grandfather, Allen Wright, pointing out the fact that he had named the state in the late nineteenth century. Wright's editor was pleased with her choice, and remarked that he was "proud of the fact that the name was suggested by a fullblood Choctaw Christian and Statesman." The editor also indicated that the book should prompt future research of "the vanishing race."[40] Although Wright and other pro-gressive Five Tribes people demonstrated through living example that some aspects of their Native heritage could be preserved while at the same time some aspects of the larger society could be embraced, popular thought in the 1920s still used terms such as "the vanishing race" to describe Native American people.

The state textbook commission also adopted two more of Wright's books, *Our Oklahoma* (1939) and *The Oklahoma History* (1955), and both volumes went through several editions.[41] In a review of *Our Oklahoma*, Thoburn commented on Wright's straightforward presentation of material: "Although both by hered-ity and environment, she might easily have manifested a measure of prejudiced feeling in some instances of text expression, her statements concerning controversial issues are noticeably fair-minded and free from any hint of personal bias."[42] He also remarked on the positive qualities that Wright's credentials and heritage brought to the textbook: "Lastly is a fact worthy of men-tion that this book is the first history of Oklahoma that has been entirely planned and written by a native of the state, one who has been a successful teacher in the public schools and one, who, in her own personality, combines much that is best and most desir-able in both the Caucasian and native American elements of its citizenship."[43] Again, Wright is promoted by her coauthor as a successful biracial Oklahoman who can speak as an authority on Oklahoma history and on the privileged place of American Indians in that story.

As more and more public schools across the state adopted her textbooks, Wright deepened her involvement with the Oklahoma Historical Society. Wright began working for the historical society in August 1929 on temporary assignment for a special research project on the history of the Choctaws and Chickasaws. Judge Robert L. Williams, former governor and OHS board member residing in Muskogee, and other OHS members launched the project to collect biographical material of the "pioneers of Oklahoma."[44] Apparently a longtime professional rivalry existed between Williams and Thoburn, and Wright's allegiance to Thoburn got caught in the middle of OHS politics. Fred Smith Standley, in his 1986 master's thesis on the Oklahoma Historical Society, recounted the situation and called Wright "an innocent pawn in a very foolish situation."[45] Williams questioned Wright's historical research credentials, perhaps referring to her lack of a bachelor's degree, and she had to make extensive reports to him on the project. She had studied Latin, Greek, and French in school, but knew little Choctaw grammar. When her own work required it, she consulted others. Under this special project, Wright assisted in the preparation of an OHS-sponsored Chickasaw dictionary. Williams told other OHS officers and board members that Wright was a temporary employee.

Through it all, Wright remained above the political fray, continued her fieldwork, and produced *Chronicles* articles related to her Five Tribes research. "As you say," she wrote in a letter to Williams, "it is a shame that all the old timers are not interviewed before they pass on, for when they go much of the history of the Indian Territory and early days in Oklahoma will be lost."[46] She requested permission from Williams to conduct more fieldwork. She was disappointed when she had to come to Oklahoma City in August 1929 and work at OHS rather than conduct fieldwork from her family home in eastern Oklahoma. "Since then," Wright lamented, "a number of old timers, some of them special friends of my father's, have died. It grieves me to think their life stories have been lost."[47] The special project ended in 1931 due to Depression-related budget cuts and the alleged conflict with Williams. She gained several other temporary assignments at the historical society before gaining her permanent position as associate editor of the *Chronicles of Oklahoma* in 1943.

From the 1940s to the 1970s, Muriel Wright worked as an institution-builder at the Oklahoma Historical Society, preserving both American Indian history and settler history through her role as associate editor and then editor of the *Chronicles of Oklahoma* and through her active historic preservation program. The *Chronicles of Oklahoma* served as Wright's vehicle through which to promote her interpretation of Oklahoma history, an interpretation emphasizing the positive aspects of state history. Others such as Grace Raymond Hebard, Mari Sandoz, and Louise Phelps Kellogg also worked as public historians—often as leaders of their state historical societies—protecting local history for future generations.

During this time Wright guided the *Chronicles of Oklahoma*, shaping the journal's content through her many scholarly contributions and as editor. In this way, she used her position and influence as editor to influence the historiography of American Indian history in Oklahoma. As editor of the *Chronicles of Oklahoma*, Wright claimed she "practically rewrote" many of the articles submitted by other historians.[48] Described as "a persistent and exacting editor" by Daniel F. Littlefield Jr., Wright controlled the interpretive product produced by the historical society during these three decades.[49]

A member of the historical society from its inception in 1922, Wright contributed her first book review to the journal's third issue. From 1943, she performed all editorial duties without the title, owing to an OHS constitutional requirement that the executive director serve as editor of the *Chronicles*. "Now, when it comes down to the facts and truth, I should be listed as the Editor," Wright wrote to her uncle in 1947. "Doctor Evans doesn't do anything except to inquire and let on as if he is working on it. I get along with him all right and he has been kind in his attitude but he really hampers instead of helps in the editorial work; and he doesn't

Figure 11.
Muriel H. Wright wrote the text for over five hundred historical markers in Oklahoma. The marker, "Old Boggy Depot," explains to visitors that this was the home of Principal Chief Allen Wright, who named Oklahoma in 1866. He was Wright's grandfather (Courtesy of Archives and Manuscripts Division, Oklahoma Historical Society).

know anything—except his own experiences, mostly political—about Oklahoma history."[50] After serving twelve years in this capacity, Wright became editor in 1955 when the board amended the constitution.

At the editorial helm, Wright produced well over one hundred issues, which included sixty-six of her own articles. Wright's contributions to the journal emphasized local topics such as military history, Indian history, biographical sketches of notable Oklahoma women, and historic preservation. Wright published a steady stream of articles in the *Chronicles,* with regular contributions beginning in 1923 and continuing until 1971. In many years, Wright contributed at least three and often four articles. Such productivity indicates a continuous record of publication, and also provides an excellent opportunity to trace her position or interpretation on different facets of Oklahoma history over a period of forty-eight years.

One of her first contributions to the *Chronicles of Oklahoma* was a 1927 article on Old Boggy Depot, once a bustling town in Choctaw Nation during the mid-1800s.[51] This town was where her grandfather, Allen Wright, had resided and where her father was raised. During the Civil War, Confederate troops were stationed at Boggy Depot, and the Confederate flag "floated bravely" in the center of town, Wright wrote in the article.[52] In the early 1870s, Allen Wright opened a flour mill and cotton gin in town. People traveled as far as seventy-five miles to have their wheat ground at the mill. Former slaves and servants of Allen Wright and other Choctaw families worked there.[53] Little remained of the town in the 1920s except her grandfather's house, built in 1860, and the remains of three other houses. In preparation for the article, Wright and her father had traveled to Old Boggy Depot, where they retraced the old town site and made a map that accompanied the article. According to Muriel Wright, her *Chronicles of Oklahoma* article resulted in the restoration and repair of her grandfather's house. For many years her grandfather's house was preserved as one of the last prominent pre–Civil War houses in southeastern Oklahoma.[54] This article is also significant because it provides a glimpse of Wright's family background. Her family was an affluent Choctaw family. They had been slaveholders at one time and had supported the Confederacy. Wright's grandfather and father had been political leaders in the Choctaw Nation, and Wright had also held political posts in the nation.

Wright's heritage was interlinked with the development of the state. Her Choctaw grandfather was a participant in the Indian removals of the 1830s and, as mentioned, later served as principal chief of the Choctaw Nation. Her father and mother met in the Choctaw Nation where her father was a doctor and her mother was a Presbyterian missionary teacher. In many ways, Wright symbolizes a cadre of multiheritage Oklahomans whose identity was connected with the state's history. What makes Wright and her work distinct, however, was her willingness to share her interest in history, storytelling, and family history with the state at large. She invested her energies in the Oklahoma Historical Society, particularly in the *Chronicles of Oklahoma*, and in the preservation of

Oklahoma's historic sites. In these ways Wright influenced the historiography of Oklahoma from her post at the historical society. She told the story of the state's development from her perspective, which generally concentrated on the positive aspects of Oklahoma's American Indian history.

In her articles on Indian history, Wright often described the participation and the significant contributions made by Native Americans to the development of the nation and, in particular, Oklahoma. In 1937, in an article entitled "Contributions of the Indian People to Oklahoma," Wright stated, "the story of Oklahoma centers around the story of the Red Man—the Indian or Amerind."[55] When Indian Territory and Oklahoma Territory joined to form the state of Oklahoma in 1907, the Five Tribes contributed "educated and experienced citizens who took an active part in the founding of our state institutions and have continued in the upbuilding of Oklahoma."[56] She listed the men and women of Indian descent who had made significant political and cultural contributions to the state. Wright revealed her personal beliefs concerning the future of Oklahoma's Indian population. Education, Christianity, and the preservation of Native traditions and customs were three paths that Wright emphasized in her article, and she encouraged other Indians to follow suit.[57] Although she acknowledged that some Five Tribes people faced economic hardship, particularly during the 1930s, she remained firm in her convictions regarding the importance of Christianity, education, and Native cultural contributions to the development of Oklahoma.[58] She upheld the importance of these three leading principles throughout her life.

Sometimes her articles served as correctives, educating the *Chronicles*' readership on popular misconceptions regarding Indian people. For example, in 1957 Wright wrote an article on the "marriage" of Oklahoma Territory and Indian Territory during the statehood celebrations. Writers often portrayed the bride, "Miss Indian Territory," as a Plains Indian woman who wore her hair in braids, with a feather headdress and a beaded buckskin dress and moccasins. The groom, "Mr. Oklahoma," was popularly identified as a cowboy. These images were incorrect, as Wright indicates.

Figure 12.
Muriel H. Wright on field trip at Fort Arbuckle, 1930 (Courtesy of Archives and Manuscripts Division, Oklahoma Historical Society).

During the 1907 statehood ceremony in Guthrie, the bride was a Choctaw woman who wore a floor-length satin dress in lavender, with long sleeves and a high collar, which was fashionable at the time. Mr. Oklahoma wore a black coat and striped pants. According to Wright, the Five Tribes people of Indian Territory did not wear buckskin and were sensitive to this misrepresentation of their people as "uncultured." The exquisite satin gown worn by the bride represented the "civilized ways" of the Five Tribes. They were not to be mistaken for the less acculturated Plains tribes of western Oklahoma.[59]

In addition to her work as editor and regular contributor of her own articles to the *Chronicles of Oklahoma*, Wright expended a great deal of energy and interest in historic preservation, and viewed it as an important facet of her role as a public historian. She was raised with a conscious appreciation of her surroundings and her Indian heritage, taking trips as a child with her father to her grandparents' home at Boggy Depot and touring the state with her uncle, James B. Wright, a U.S. Indian Service employee, and his family.[60] She was also encouraged by Thoburn to take an active role in identifying and interpreting historic sites. The initial interest in launching a historic preservation movement in Oklahoma began in the 1920s under the auspices of the Oklahoma Historical Society. Muriel Wright's research interests paralleled these early efforts to identify and study historic sites in Oklahoma. Her article on Old Boggy Depot was Wright's first historic sites article. Other early articles promoted her interest in and familiarity with Choctaw history in Oklahoma, including the Choctaw Council House and the Choctaw Chief's House. These articles centered on her family relations and regional identification that formed the backbone of her sense of Oklahoma history.

Many of Wright's articles for the *Chronicles* and newspapers such as the *Daily Oklahoman* and the *Tuskahoman*, a Choctaw newspaper, promoted her active interest in identifying and preserving a sense of Oklahoma's Indian heritage through the historic preservation program. This interest is illustrated, for example, in Wright's use of photographs to identify historic sites. She made special field trips on behalf of the historical society beginning in 1922, in which she located historic sites, took photographs, and compiled brief histories.

During the summer of 1930, Wright and two other members of the Oklahoma Historical Society took a six-week tour of southeastern Oklahoma in order to identify, photograph, map, and temporarily mark the region's historic sites.[61] "Some very fine pictures of historic sites were secured while we were out," she reported to Judge Williams, "with my own camera and Mrs. Bryce's small kodak. I am mounting these pictures with special notes as to their historical significance, in an album for the Library." The resulting album, prepared in 1931 and housed in the Oklahoma Historical Society, contains brief sketches of 75 historic sites and 125 photographs identifying these locations. Recognizing the value of these photographs for future historical work, she said, "Fifty to one hundred years from now, the collection will be all the more valuable because the pictures will show the historical sites as they appeared in 1930."[62] Her cognizance of the importance of documenting and preserving historic sites, and her attention to collecting, photographing, and mapping Oklahoma's historic sites speak to her

Figure 13.
In her album documenting her field experience in southeastern Oklahoma,
Wright recorded: "Creek Graves. Located in Okfuskee County. The custom of
covering a grave with a small house as shelter was common among all the
Five Civilized Tribes. Many examples can be found throughout the eastern
part of Oklahoma." Photo taken by Wright, July 22, 1930 (Courtesy of Archives
and Manuscripts Division, Oklahoma Historical Society).

awareness that she was part of a national commitment—comprising quite often women working in state historical societies as public historians—to valuing and preserving state and local history.

The following example from the album demonstrates Wright's meticulous recording, collection, and interpretation of her fieldwork. The image (fig. 13) depicts Creek graves, another indication of Wright's interest in educating the public on Five Tribes traditions. She has provided a narrative next to her photograph: "The custom of covering a grave with a small house as shelter was common among all the Five Civilized Tribes. Many examples can be found throughout the eastern part of Oklahoma."[63] She took these photographs in 1930 as part of her larger effort to identify and mark historic sites, with a heavy emphasis on the preservation of Five Tribes history. Her photography of American Indian sites was essential in preserving a native-based identity for Oklahoma.

Wright's travels throughout Oklahoma were not limited to American Indian sites. As a member of the historic sites committee, beginning in 1929, Wright conducted research on the Butterfield Overland Mail Route, which transported passengers and mail between Tipton, Missouri, and San Francisco, California, during the late 1850s and early 1860s. She identified all twelve stations in southeastern Oklahoma. Wright took several field trips, wrote the inscriptions, and photographed old buildings in preparation for the onsite marker program.[64] She published an article on the mail route along with a map in the *Chronicles of Oklahoma* in 1933.[65] So while her primary interest in historic preservation revolved around the Five Tribes, particularly the Choctaws, her secondary interest in preserving and interpreting the larger vision of Oklahoma history was also evident in her long career at the Oklahoma Historical Society.[66]

These early efforts at historic preservation in Oklahoma grew into the larger program of the 1950s with the support of legislative funding. Wright and her colleagues launched this program in an effort to promote a new sense of historical awareness across the state. George H. Shirk chaired the Oklahoma Historic Sites Committee and Wright conducted most of the research for the inscriptions on the historical markers. Wright also helped identify or mark hundreds of sites in Oklahoma. She drafted a list of 512 historic sites for additions and modifications by the committee. By 1958 the completed list contained 557 historic sites arranged by counties. The *Chronicles of Oklahoma* published the list in the Autumn 1958 issue and then republished it as a pamphlet. As LeRoy H. Fischer indicates, "the completion of the basic sites survey produced among many historically minded people an appreciation for the first time of the magnitude and significance of Oklahoma's historic sites."[67]

The initial survey fostered numerous other works on historic preservation published by the Oklahoma Historical Society. In 1958, Wright and Shirk compiled and edited *Mark of Heritage: Oklahoma Historical Markers*. This publication focused on 131 historic sites, provided the location and inscription of each marker, and included accompanying photographs taken by Thoburn and Wright.

Wright engaged in another collaborative historic sites effort in 1966 with Fischer, "Civil War Sites in Oklahoma," first published in the *Chronicles* and later as a pamphlet. Again, the publication identified the site location along with a description of its historical significance. "Without her long interest and dedication to the historic site identification, preservation, restoration and marker program in Oklahoma," Fischer writes of Muriel Wright, "the state could not today be a leader in the nation in its historic site program."[68] Rounding out this effort to educate the state's citizens on local history, Wright conducted OHS-sponsored public tours of these historic sites.

Because of Wright's Republican allegiance and her reverence for the political stances of her grandfather and father, one could infer that Wright would not have supported the Indian Reorganization Act of 1934, which was intended to reverse the federal government's policy of 150 years of assimilationist policies. As David Baird maintains, most Oklahoma Indians ignored the legislation.[69] However, she was an active participant in Choctaw policy-making, serving as secretary of the Choctaw Committee during the 1920s and later elected secretary and member of the Choctaw Advisory Council in 1934. She also served as a Choctaw delegate to the Intertribal Indian Council from the late 1930s to the early 1940s in Oklahoma City and Tulsa. In a letter written in 1932, Wright expressed disdain for the Bureau of Indian Affairs and its meddling in Indian communities: "one can point to the results of the Bureau control of the Indians as an example of what bureaucracy will do for the whole American people if allowed to widen its scope. I believe that assistance is only going to come through Christian education, for real Christian education among the Indians involves his spiritual, social, and economic welfare."[70] Her solution to rely on Christian education in many ways follows the missionary work of her grandmother, mother, and uncle, and her eastern boarding school education—again, a long-standing family tradition. Her position reaffirms her Choctaw family ties to Christian education, the Republican Party, and the positive aspects of assimilation. She continues that although she is a Republican, she is first of all an American Indian citizen. Once again, she returned to the ideas of

Figure 14.
Muriel H. Wright at the
dedication of the
Pocahontas tribute at
Anadarko in 1965
(Courtesy of Archives
and Manuscripts
Division, Oklahoma
Historical Society).

her father: "For a definite period of years, a board of Indians should be chosen to act in an advisory capacity at Washington with regard to Indian affairs in general, correlating its work with that of the representative council of Indians in each tribe."[71]

It is clearly evident that Wright's concern for American Indian issues reached beyond historical research. She was acutely aware of American Indian boarding schools and viewed them as a necessity. In May 1947, Wright wrote to Senator Elmer Thomas expressing concern that some Indian schools in Oklahoma would close because of declining appropriations. These schools included Wheelock Academy, Jones Academy, and Goodland Indian Orphanage near Hugo, the same Choctaw schools she helped maintain as a member of the Choctaw Committee in the 1920s. She protested the closing of these schools for, she charged, "[the schools] are doing the work that no State school is prepared to give." Many of the Indian children who attend these schools, she continued, are isolated from good public schools. "These children in many instances," she contended, "are personally handicapped in adjusting themselves to the public school program as set up to-day. There are many orphan children attending the Indian schools. What provision is made *right now* for their living? Where are they being placed?"[72] "I am opposed to closing Wheelock Academy, Jones Academy, the provisions made at Goodland, or any Indian school in Oklahoma until definite assurance is given whereby the children will be provided the foundations of an education."[73] Thomas responded that the Republicans controlled Congress and pledged to cut taxes and reduce appropriations.[74] In September 1947, as Wright later indicated in *A Guide to the Indian Tribes of Oklahoma* (1951), the Office of Indian Education was established in the Oklahoma Department of Public Instruction. "Orphans and children from broken homes," she argued, "especially older boys and girls (of one-fourth Indian blood or more) who have no high school opportunities, attend the Indian boarding schools operated by the federal government in the state, preference being given to fullblood applicants. These schools offer home training and other advantages that cannot be given in public schools."[75] She was a Native activist and historian who championed education, and access to education for all American Indian children. So even if she did not choose to spend much time talking about the detrimental aspects of American Indian issues in her published texts, she did discuss them in her correspondence to policymakers. In a real sense, she was continuing her longtime emphasis on funding for education, the preservation of Choctaw institutions, and the incorporation of Five Tribes history into the larger Oklahoma narrative.

Muriel H. Wright's legacy of historical writing remains preserved within Oklahoma and regional history. Her strong connection with Oklahoma's past, her steadfastness as an editor of a state historical journal, and her enthusiasm for educating the public are qualities she injected into the historical society, and they remain evident today. In April 1993, the Oklahoma Historical Society launched the Oklahoma Historians Hall of Fame. Muriel Wright was among the four inductees named during the inaugural year—a testament to her work and dedication to the Oklahoma Historical Society. Although she did not "own" Oklahoma history, as she insisted, she came close, leaving an indelible mark on the early work produced by the historical society and ensuring a welcome presence for Five Tribes people. The historical marker program alone leaves a tangible reminder of Muriel Wright's presence throughout the state.

Chapter Three

Contested Places
The Battle of the Historians
of Round Mountain

O n January 30, 1995, Oklahoma State University hosted a 105th birthday celebration for Angie Debo. Historian Kenny Brown from the University of Central Oklahoma delivered the keynote address. He noted with enthusiasm that the Angie Debo Elementary School had recently opened in Edmond. Interestingly, when the Edmond School District solicited names for the new school, Brown recommended Angie Debo, only to learn that someone else had already made the suggestion. Edmond resident Allen Wright III, Muriel Wright's nephew, had proposed naming the school after Muriel Wright or Angie Debo. Brown lobbied the school board to consider and approve Debo as their selection. "So if you know anything about the relationship between the two historians," Brown cautioned, "then you know that there is a great deal of irony there."[1]

In Oklahoma history lore, the relationship between Debo and Wright is legendary. The Oklahoma Historical Society remained uninterested in sponsoring a conference panel on the Battle of Round Mountain, or Twin Mounds, the first Civil War battle in Oklahoma, because of its reluctance to stir up local hot button issues. In the 1940s Wright had proposed a site near Tulsa and erected a historical marker to denote the battlefield location, while Debo remained convinced that the Round Mountain site was outside Yale, near Stillwater. But this is just the most public issue that surfaced between these two historians. In studying their relationship through the years, one discovers both mutual respect and bristling disagreement, but overall a shared concern for historical research and accuracy in telling Oklahoma's story, particularly histories of Oklahoma's American Indian people.

The interpretation of Oklahoma history is the crux of the problem. Wright argued that Debo's work suffered from sweeping generalizations, lumping all American Indian people in large categories. Conversely, Debo contended that Wright wanted to preserve her Choctaw family history in an esteemed way, and that she did not want to contend with some of the negative aspects that primary documents revealed. By examining the origins and development of this relationship between two historians bent on accuracy and preserving Oklahoma's place in national history, we witness the early development of Oklahoma historiography and a particularly striking example of historians and contested places at the state and local level.

State and local history is commonly prone to personal disputes. Wright, as a confident and controlling editor at the *Chronicles of Oklahoma*, asserted authority over Oklahoma history, and in this way her interpretation of Oklahoma history became institutionalized in the historical society. Although she made claims that she did not "own" Oklahoma, she did control what the journal published, which historic sites would be sponsored by the historical society, and how the inscriptions would read on historic markers.

This proprietary impulse often prompted Wright to act as the gatekeeper of a carefully crafted narrative of Oklahoma history. For example, what Oklahoma historians know as the "Battle of Round Mountain Controversy" has served as an intriguing reminder of lively debate and feuding parties within the historical profession at large.[2] In this case, two groups squared off over the location of the first battle of the Civil War in Indian Territory. Muriel Wright commanded an active historic sites marker program on behalf of the Oklahoma Historical Society. Angie Debo, prominent historian of American Indians, also worked in historic preservation with the Payne County Historical Society. Both historians agreed that the first battle of the Civil War in Indian Territory occurred on November 19, 1861, between the Union Creeks headed for Kansas and Confederate troops, including a Creek regiment, Choctaw-Chickasaw and Creek-Seminole regiments, and a detachment of the Texas cavalry. The point of contention, however, pivots over place. Documentary evidence corroborates the correct date of the battle, but exact location within the territory remains ambiguous. In fact, two markers presently exist, at the "Keystone site" near Tulsa and the "Round Mountain site" near Stillwater.[3]

During the 1940s most Oklahoma historians agreed that the Battle of Round Mountain site was located in the Keystone area between the confluence of the Cimarron and Arkansas rivers. The Payne County Historical Society revisited the issue in 1949, when an amateur historian, Stillwater real estate agent John Melton, revealed new evidence supporting the Yale site. Melton collected battlefield artifacts and affidavits from older Yale residents.[4] In addition, Berlin Basil Chapman, Oklahoma State University history professor, and Angie Debo, both active members of the Payne County Historical Society, secured a photocopied statement made by Confederate Creek leaders in 1868 regarding the events of 1861 and 1862, from the National Archives in Washington, D.C.[5] Debo reviewed the battle in light of this new information and in the early 1960s wrote an article in support of the Yale site for the *Chronicles of Oklahoma.* Debo closed the article with the following statement: "To this one historian at least, the evidence is conclusive."[6] In a *Chronicles* article written one year before the Debo piece, Muriel Wright continued her support for the Keystone site, declaring that the Yale site "has never been accepted by the Oklahoma Historical Society in its statewide program of marking historic sites" since 1949.[7] Thus began the battle of the historians of Round Mountain.

To commemorate the Civil War centennial both Wright and Debo produced articles on the Battle of Round Mountain for the *Chronicles*. Not much new evidence emerged as a result, and the stalemate persisted. Wright used her editorial authority to reject Debo's article, only to be overturned by the OHS Board of Directors. The location of Round Mountain remains unconfirmed to this day. In an effort to end the controversy, National Park Service historians and local historians held a conference in 1993 but unfortunately reached no consensus regarding the exact location of the battle. Thus the two markers in Keystone and Yale remain intact, and the Battle of Round Mountain controversy continues to divide local historians.[8]

In this public controversy, Wright and Debo touched the public pulse and engaged their audience in the narrative. Both historians, in fact, presaged the "new" Indian history, carving a distinct place for themselves in Great Plains and American Indian history. Both women chronicled the history of Oklahoma, particularly American Indian topics, with scholarly rigor and ingenuity. Their passion for recording Oklahoma's past stemmed in part from their strong ties to the region.

This spirited difference of opinion between Oklahoma historians originated with the publication of Debo's *The Rise and Fall of the Choctaw Republic* in 1934. When approached by Grant Foreman to review Debo's work for the *Chronicles of Oklahoma*, Wright replied that she might not like the book, but Foreman insisted she write the book review anyway. "There were a lot of angles in the background because the Wright family and many other Choctaw families who were well known," Muriel Wright explained in the early 1950s, "were up-in-arms and almost ready to sue Miss Debo for statements she had made in the book."[9] When pressed to write the review, Wright defended her family history and that of many other elite Choctaw families. At the same time, she did not identify herself as the granddaughter of Principal Chief Allen Wright in the review. Wright's thirteen-page review, a very long review when compared to the typical two- to three-page review, established her reputation as "a very severe critic."[10] Because of "errors in statement, half-truths and refutations,"

Wright argued in the review, the work could not be called an "authentic history" of the Choctaws. Continuing in this vein, Wright attacked Debo's "hurried research" and "prejudiced viewpoints," making for a "superficial" study of Choctaw affairs.[11] Even the title was problematic, Wright argued, because the "Choctaw republic rose but it did not fall."[12] Wright's review caused "quite a stir," although no one approached her disputing the points she made in her critique. Wright reported in 1952 that she and Debo were on "friendly" terms, having met for the first time long after publication of Debo's book and Wright's book review. They never discussed the book or the book review with one another.[13]

At the center of Wright's fury was the notion that her grandfather, Allen Wright, accepted a kickback—or a treaty fee or a rebate—as tribal national treasurer and delegate of the Choctaw Nation negotiating the treaty of 1866 with the U.S. government following the Civil War.[14] In *Peter Pitchlynn: Chief of the Choctaws* (1972), W. David Baird supports Debo's findings. Chief Pitchlynn orchestrated these negotiations and directed Wright's dissemination of funds. John H. Latrobe, attorney for the Choctaws and Chickasaws, issued kickbacks to the Choctaw delegates. Debo discovered no evidence that implicated the Chickasaw Nation. Congress appropriated $300,000 to the Nations as payment for the Leased District and to influence the tribes to include their freedmen, or former slaves, in their tribes. The Choctaws received $150,000 for their portion. Wright paid Latrobe and the other attorneys their $100,000 fee, half of which was returned to him. Wright distributed $10,000 to the other delegates: Alfred Wade, John Page, James Riley, and Robert M. Jones.[15] "When the transaction became public, and the Choctaw people realized that Latrobe's fee had been inflated to the extent of $50,000 to benefit the delegates at the expense of the Nation," Debo argued, "it created a tribal scandal, and it seems to have ruined the political career of Allen Wright."[16] Debo does not elaborate on the notion that this rebate injured Wright's political career, for he served as principal chief of the Choctaws from 1866 to 1870.

These transactions turned scandalous when Pitchlynn, not an official delegate, claimed Jones's $10,000 because he served in his place. Pitchlynn further justified this fee by claiming it was an advance for his later work in prosecuting the net proceeds cases. Jones conceded. Wright explained that his payment was for services to Latrobe and for personal expenses. This reasoning proved questionable because the Choctaw Nation and the federal government reimbursed the delegates for their work.[17]

Muriel Wright did not dispute that Allen Wright accepted the payment, but she viewed it as reimbursement, as her grandfather indicated. For example, with regard to Allen Wright's compensation for treaty negotiations in Washington, D.C., Wright states that he received $2,968, and so did the other three delegates. This amount included travel, salary, and expenses. Upon ratification of the treaty, all delegates received $9,583.33 from the Choctaw Nation for their services.[18] She did not know her grandfather personally; he died before she was born. But the family stories, and Choctaw history in general, were personal, coveted matters to her. In addition, Wright recounted her grandfather's political achievements in the review:

> As for Allen Wright, one of the younger men on the delegation, his personality, ability and educational advantages won for him recognition as a leader during his sojourn at Washington. A man of principle and honor, he considered it his duty to apply himself energetically to each task that he was called upon to perform in furthering the welfare of his people. During the period of one year (1865–6), he served as treasurer of the nation, delegate to Fort Smith, delegate to Washington to negotiate a new treaty, was specially employed to assist in securing its ratification, and just before returning home, received word he had been elected principal chief. He served two consecutive terms (four years) in this position and remained to the end of his life beloved by a host of friends and a respected citizen of his nation, whose advice and counsel, due to his ability and experience, were sought by leaders among his people and in the States. What he accomplished in the educational and governmental

affairs and in the mission field was outstanding in the
history of the Choctaws and of the Indian Territory.[19]

Upon reading the evidence, it appears that Wright and Debo
interpreted the same event differently. Debo viewed Allen Wright's
payment as a delegate as a "kickback," and Wright viewed it as
services rendered. According to historian LeRoy Fischer, kickbacks
of this kind were routine matters; county commissioners received
them as well.[20] The remarks Wright made in her book review to
uphold the honor of her grandfather border on hagiography and
demonstrate Wright's passionate moments when her objectivity
unravels. Insistent on protecting her family history, Muriel Wright
approached Grant Foreman, historian and lawyer, about a potential libel suit against Debo. Foreman responded that the documents relating to the treaty negotiations and the kickbacks were
court records and available for scholarly and public use.[21]

By the early 1970s new Choctaw leadership disagreed with
Wright's evaluation of the book. Principal Chief Harry J. W. Belvin
praised the book as "one of the most inspiring and accurate histories of the Choctaws that I have ever read."[22] Commenting on the
incident in the early 1980s, Debo said, "Miss Wright would never
have known how shocked and distressed I was when I found out"
that Allen Wright did, in fact, receive kickbacks as part of the attorney's fees.[23] This episode was the genesis of the professional
conflict between Wright and Debo, even before the Round
Mountain controversy.

During the interwar period, women's access to professional
advancement was linked to academic credentials, networking, and
a variety of tangential qualifications. Wright considered herself a
professional historian but was aware that she lacked the academic credentials, especially the doctorate, that Debo possessed. With
reference to the scathing book review, Baird has commented that
many reasons explain the animosity. "Wright believed she was
most qualified to deal with Choctaw, almost family matters," Baird
explained, "and she was probably a bit intimidated by Debo's academic credentials."[24] Although Wright attended East Central State
and completed a teacher education program in 1912, she did not

receive a bachelor's degree. She pursued course work at Barnard College and, had the war not interfered with her studies, Wright has maintained, she would have completed both the bachelor's and master's degrees at Barnard. She realized the significance of academic credentials for professional advancement, and petitioned East Central State to grant her a degree based on completed course work there and at Barnard. She had also considered attending the University of Oklahoma to complete her degree. In 1968 she received an honorary doctorate from Oklahoma City University and she assumed the title Dr. Wright.[25]

Even without the academic credentials, Wright wielded tremendous power from her editorial position at the Oklahoma Historical Society. Of the three writers surveyed in this study, only Debo held the doctorate. Alice Marriott's work in anthropology was professional, but she did not hold advanced degrees. The authority of Wright and Marriott came from their practical experience on the job—Wright as editor of the *Chronicles of Oklahoma* for thirty years and Marriott's government employment with the Indian Arts and Crafts Board. They were considered experts in their respective professions. And in Debo's case, her doctorate did not guarantee academic posts or even an inviting response from the historical profession. Some historians still did not consider her a professional historian even with the degree and the Dunning Prize for her published dissertation.

And although local public memory and storytelling would disagree, correspondence between Wright and Debo as well as their oral histories and other writings indicate that, historical interpretation aside, they were on cordial terms and respected one another's professional work. Their different historical interpretations have much to do with religion, social status and economic background, regionalism, race, and academic credentials.

Religion was an important component in both Wright's and Debo's identities as scholars and community leaders. Wright's mother and paternal grandmother had been Presbyterian missionary teachers in Choctaw Nation, and Wright was raised and remained Presbyterian. Both of her grandfathers had been ministers. Wright's paternal grandfather and several of his sons, including Wright's father, attended Union Theological Seminary in New York.[26] For example, Frank Hall Wright, Muriel Wright's uncle, became a licensed Presbyterian minister and served as a missionary to the Indians of western Oklahoma in the 1890s.[27] Debo went one step further during World War II and served as the lay pastor of the Marshall Methodist Church when the congregation lost its minister.[28] Wright called Debo "very religious," and argued that her religious convictions dovetailed with her fight for social justice.[29]

Both deeply religious individuals, Wright and Debo held divergent views regarding issues of race and class. For Wright, social status was a leading factor in her Indian identity. She identified with affluent Choctaws who grew up in prominent families comprised of politicians, religious leaders, and professionals. Debo, on the other hand, did not share this privileged background and identified her settler background with that of American Indian people from a more modest socioeconomic background. Wright's family had once been slaveholders and prominent statesmen for the Confederacy. She was a member of the United Daughters of the Confederacy and had difficulty reconciling racial equality for African Americans with her Confederate tradition. In a 1945 letter to J. Bartley Milam, principal chief of the Cherokee Nation, she wrote: "Now as Southerners, you know and I know that there are some good, old darkies who do know local lore and some stories about former days whose reminiscences do have a place in history, but recording their accounts, the investigator has to take into consideration the reliability of the individuals giving the information."[30] In contrast, Wright described Debo as extremely critical of Confederate history. She viewed Debo as a liberal who "'bends over backwards' in favor of Negro racial problems, and evidently follows in the strain (*I think*) of Elinor [*sic*] Roosevelt."[31] In the late 1940s, the Oklahoma Pen Women's Association, a group that excluded black writers, invited Debo to join. She declined and explained to Wright, a leading member of the organization, "I object to racial bars in cultural and intellectual organizations."[32]

When Debo's *And Still the Waters Run* appeared in 1940, once again Muriel Wright took a strong position against Debo's work—this time by refusing to acknowledge it. While national journals such as the *American Historical Review*, the *Mississippi Valley Historical Review*, and the *Journal of Southern History* reviewed Debo's book, the *Chronicles of Oklahoma* did not.[33] The name of the president of the Oklahoma Historical Society, Robert Williams, former governor of the state and federal judge, appeared in *And Still the Waters Run* as an associate of "grafters," or land speculators capitalizing on Indian allotments. Perhaps Wright did not review it in the *Chronicles* out of deference to Judge Williams.[34]

Although Wright and Debo did not usually agree, to say the least, they did respect each other's work as historians. Mutual professional respect emerges within their limited correspondence. For example, in a letter addressed "Dear Angie," dated May 3, 1950, Wright referred to the Mississippi Valley Historical Association conference that they both attended in Oklahoma City. In a session on American Indian history, Debo presented a paper on the social and economic conditions of Oklahoma's Five Tribes, and Wright was in attendance. Other panelists included Wilbur R. Jacobs of the University of California, Santa Barbara, and Dwight L. Smith of The Ohio State University. Howard H. Peckham of the Indian Historical Bureau served as chair. Conference notes suggest that these papers generated lively discussion. Anna Lewis (Choctaw) of the Oklahoma College for Women, Muriel Wright, and other "persons of Indian blood" apparently reacted to the views of Peckham and other politicians. The consensus of the session was that "the United States has not yet discharged its obligations to the red man."[35] At the session, Wright had tried to seek out Debo before she left. In her letter, Wright elaborated, "I hope that I did not seem critical in my remarks for I did not intend them that way. But somehow those politicians 'kinda roused' me; they always have the same 'poor Indian' story but never seem to get anywhere except to be on hand at campaign time."[36]

Debo and Wright both published significant texts on American Indians in Oklahoma in 1951: Debo's *The Five Civilized Tribes of Oklahoma: Report on Social and Economic Conditions* and Wright's *A Guide to the Indian Tribes of Oklahoma*. Debo's report was steeped in the rhetoric of poverty, "backwardness," and the plight of Five Tribes full-bloods under meager rehabilitation programs.

Wright's *Guide* surveyed Oklahoma's fifty-seven federally recognized tribes and reported on the resilience, strength, and leadership of Indian people. Evaluating them as a pair, they are very much polar opposites—one framing despair and the glimmer of hope through reformist rhetoric and the other highlighting the positive contributions Indian people, mostly progressive elites such as politicians and businesspeople, have made to the state. Debo's discussion of mixed-blood elites placed them in company with other despoilers, profiting at the expense of full-bloods.

Beginning in 1949, at the request of the Indian Rights Association, Debo surveyed and conducted interviews of full-blood communities in eastern Oklahoma for eight weeks. A decade earlier in the preface of *And Still the Waters Run*, Debo had posited the question, "Could the lost fullbloods of the Five Civilized Tribes be saved?" She responded to her question in *The Five Civilized Tribes of Oklahoma: Report on Social and Economic Conditions*, arguing that many full-bloods struggled at mid-century, with chapter headings such as "Poor Indians on Poor Land" and "Weighing Imponderable Assets in Rehabilitation," following a declensionist vein.[37] *Indian Truth*, the Indian Rights Association's journal, lauded her study, which served as a precursor to the expanded program for the Five Tribes.

Wright's handling of the Debo report reflects her political maneuvering and ability to use the historical society to champion her causes. In a letter to Debo she praised the text, calling it a "fine report" that demonstrates "insight and knowledge on the subject."[38] Wright continued, "You have done a wonderful piece of work in this report and I hope that much good will come in solving the problem of our full-blood Cherokee and Choctaw who are in the main worthy of consideration and trust."[39]

At the same time, Wright used the *Chronicles of Oklahoma* as a platform to advance issues of importance to her family. Debo's report launched a fury of press attention and in turn incited some Five Tribes people to respond to both the report and Oklahoma newspapers' spin of the report. Wright's uncle, J. B. Wright, a Choctaw and field clerk for the U.S. Indian Service in Oklahoma for sixteen years, reacted negatively to the report, in an open letter to

W. O. Roberts, U.S. Indian Service area director at Muskogee. Muriel Wright published his letter in the "Notes and Documents" section of the *Chronicles*, "for both its historical and contemporary value."[40]

J. B. Wright called Debo's report "fairly good" but was greatly troubled by her sweeping generalizations without qualification such as "Most Oklahoma Indians live in appalling poverty amid disease, crime and general moral delinquency."[41] He was equally concerned about the press coverage. "Conditions are not as discouraging as one is lead [*sic*] to believe from reading the newspaper excerpts," he notes, "but it is already apparent that more people have read the newspaper article than have read the full report."[42] He criticizes Debo for her generalizations and choice of words and expressions that often lead to "wrong impressions." For example, he challenges Debo's claim that "Disease, drunkenness, crime and general moral delinquency exist to an appalling extent in the full-blood settlements."[43] He calls this a "reckless statement." He also disputes her conclusions of high illegitimacy rates among the Five Tribes and moral laxity in the churches. He concludes by stating that Debo may have received assistance from Indian Service employees in the Muskogee office, but he is convinced that "any conclusions reached by her in her report, that might be derogatory to the Indians under your jurisdiction, were not authorized by them."[44] Congressman W. G. Stigler read Wright's letter several times and noted that it "truly reflects living conditions among our Indians of the Five Civilized Tribes more than the report of Miss Angie Debo."[45]

Muriel Wright agreed with her uncle that Debo's careless statements and sensationalist rhetoric did not represent the majority of Five Tribes people. "If all persons of Indian descent in Oklahoma—full blood to the smallest quantum by blood identified as Indian—were placed together, the very poor hill country or rural group would be comparatively a small percent," she indicated in personal correspondence. "There are many, many good, Christian families who live quietly, have modest homes, send their children to school and can be counted among the Indian population of Oklahoma whom we do not read about."

Those people, as well as the leaders of the Five Tribes, were the stories Wright selected to preserve in public memory under her guidance at the historical society. Those who did not agree with her, such as Debo, were publicly criticized.[46]

Deeply concerned by Wright's decision to publish a letter from a nonhistorian rather than a book review from a historian, Debo responded to the *Chronicles of Oklahoma*:

> In all my career as a writer I have never replied to a review of one of my books. A reviewer is supposed to be a scholar in his own right, and his judgment is entitled to respect. If he makes a mistake, it is his own reputation that suffers. Thus if Miss Wright had reviewed my Report unfavorably, I should have made no objection, because she is a distinguished historical writer who has earned the right to criticize. But this is different. It is simply a letter from an individual correspondent.[47]

In short, Debo respected Wright's opinion as a historian—Wright had earned her right to critique the work of others in Debo's opinion. But by publishing this particular response to Debo's report in the *Chronicles*, written by an "individual correspondent" (not to mention a family member), not a historian, Muriel Wright tacitly supported her relative, without raising the issue herself. In private correspondence, she was freer and openly critical of Debo's work. "Miss Debo has been accepted in the state historical field," Wright wrote, "but she has her critics for some of her opinionated and rash statements. She is a good woman but unbending."[48] Many of Wright's colleagues at the historical society probably would have said the same about her.

Wright's most challenging research project occurred in the late 1940s when approached by E. E. Dale, professor of history at the University of Oklahoma and OHS board member, to write a handbook on the Indian tribes of Oklahoma. With funding from the Rockefeller Foundation, Wright took a six-month research leave from the historical society to concentrate on the research and writing for the project.[49] Wright's *A Guide to the Indian Tribes of*

Oklahoma (1951) has become a standard reference among historians studying Oklahoma's American Indian people. Surveying each of the fifty-seven tribes living in Oklahoma during the 1950s, Wright discusses each tribe's location, number of members, tribal history, government and organization, contemporary life and culture, and ceremonials and public dances. In the preface, Arrell Morgan Gibson maintains that Wright demonstrates "nonpareil credibility as spokesman" for Oklahoma's native peoples.[50] Wright's Indian identity and her stature as an authority on the history of Indians in Oklahoma, Gibson states, make this work "authentic," reminiscent of Thoburn's claims of Wright's authenticity in the late 1920s. Gibson, in fact, calls Wright's *A Guide to the Indian Tribes of Oklahoma* "an Indian viewpoint."[51]

In *A Guide to the Indian Tribes of Oklahoma*, the recurrent theme of the positive effects of assimilation is clearly at work. Wright selects themes that join the tribes together such as their common removal experiences and how the tribes adapted to changes in Indian Territory. For example, in her introduction she wrote, "The unique experiment of the removal of the Indian tribes to Oklahoma by the government, begun under inauspicious circumstances in the eighteen thirties, has resulted in a degree of mutual tolerance, understanding, and affection between two races which has no counterpart elsewhere in America."[52] She identified the positive manifestations of these changes and did not spend much time explaining loss—human, property, or otherwise. Indian people, in general, manipulated the land into productive farms, tribal governments resumed, and towns, schools, and churches were established in Indian Territory. As Gibson indicates, Wright portrays the Native Americans who settled in Indian Territory as "carriers of American civilization to this new land" as seen in their adherence to constitutional government, education, Christianity, law enforcement, and participation in the market economy.[53]

Rennard Strickland describes Wright as an "assimilationist historian," upholding the popular notion that Oklahoma's assimilationist program worked. This type of Oklahoma exceptionalism pervades Wright's work and is her major weakness as a historian. Oklahoma is a place where diverse American Indian peoples coexist alongside descendants from the land-run days and earlier, and that part of Oklahoma's story is unique. But such an emphasis on the positive aspects of Oklahoma's story without a critical evaluation of the underside of such a story is selective and objectionable. For instance, in her interpretation of the Choctaws she emphasizes successful leaders such as her grandfather and father as examples of assimilation into the larger society. Strickland and others, but particularly Angie Debo, have noted this selectiveness. In her review of Wright's *Guide*, Debo critiques Wright's selective interpretation:

> Not all Oklahoma Indians have been able to make a successful transition from a tribal to a composite society. Very little mention [is made] of the social degradation and poverty of many fullblood settlements.... This omission is not only a disservice to these Indians—victims of a too violent policy of disruption—but a serious gap in an otherwise complete coverage.[54]

Wright's interpretation of the Choctaws did not attempt to portray an image of Indian "pristineness" devoid of forms of cultural incursion. Her approach was selective—she chose examples of successful Choctaws as representative of all Choctaws—neglecting those who were suffering and propertyless. This is not to imply that Debo was not also selective; however, she was willing to be more critical of her native state than Wright.

Focusing on the positive aspects of Five Tribes history was a deliberate interpretive move on Wright's part. She maintained that there have been too many books written about the Five Tribes from the "poor Indian" angle, specifically the books of Grant Foreman and Debo. She wrote the *Guide* "from the positive, constructive point of view, at the same time giving facts and keeping a balance for all Indian types." Wright admitted that the *Guide*, a combination of anthropology, history, and "reporting the modern scene," was difficult to write. She included ethnic origins, name meanings, comparative population, and development for each of the fifty-seven tribes.[55] In his review of the book, Leslie Hewes found it "somewhat uncritical in anthropological matters." Hewes also criticized Wright's population figures as "exaggerated" and vague regarding blood quantum.[56]

Wright never wavered from her positive interpretation of Oklahoma history and the Five Tribes' central role in the narrative. She identified with affluent Choctaws who grew up in prominent families comprised of politicians, religious leaders, and professionals. Therefore, class was inextricably bound to her identity. In her own historical research she chose to focus on the largely mixed-blood progressives rather than on the traditionalists.

When Debo taught a special course on Oklahoma Indians to secondary schoolteachers at the University of Oklahoma in the 1960s, Wright's *Guide* was on her required reading list. In other words, although Debo was critical of Wright's text, she understood that the *Guide* remained the best handbook of American Indians in Oklahoma in the 1960s. No historian has attempted to revise this handbook, so it stands as the source historians and others often consult first.

Conflicts continued to brew between Wright and Debo, as their mutual interest in Oklahoma's American Indians clashed over interpretation. According to Debo, while the majority of Oklahoma's Indian population was receptive to her work, Wright was not. In an interview, Debo commented that Wright's heritage and class status helped to explain this position:

> [P]erhaps I don't know of anyone except Miss Wright and her relations, but perhaps there might have been other Indians like her, who were extremely successful leaders of the white man's society, who resented any allusion to the unhappy situation of the full-bloods who were cheated out of their property and who lived in remote places, on land that nobody wanted, who suffered from actual hunger and lack of educational opportunities, and everything else. Miss Wright resented that; and I know that some of her relatives did.[57]

Personal disagreements between Wright and Debo became public knowledge through public discourse regarding the Battle of

Round Mountain. Round Mountain enthusiasts dismiss it as an academic duel; several historians who knew Wright and Debo point to personal jealousy, and milder interpretations call it a difference of opinion.[58]

The controversy, now as then, was more than a historical turf war. Two women historians played central roles in this local battle. Muriel Wright headed the charge for the Tulsa County Historical Society under the auspices of the Oklahoma Historical Society. Angie Debo defended the Yale site on behalf of the Payne County Historical Society. Although both historians recognized the larger goal of educating the public on serious historical issues that held personal meaning for them, at times their personal differences and strong convictions interfered with their professional responses. Their differences, however, do not diminish their contributions to Oklahoma history. Perhaps the competitive spirit between them, combined with historical inquiry, spurred them on to seek regional and national recognition for their respective talents. Regardless of the reasons, Wright and Debo represent state and regional women historians who produced invaluable history texts laying claim to American Indian history and its significance to the development of Oklahoma.

PART TWO
Angie Debo
(1890–1988)

Figure 15.
Angie Debo (1890–1988) in 1935 (Courtesy of Angie Debo Papers, Edmon Low Library, Oklahoma State University, Stillwater).

Chapter Four

Angie Debo

"To Discover the Truth and Publish It"

ngie Debo fought against the injustices of American Indians at the hands of the federal government through the power of the written word. "I have written the worst things about Oklahoma that anybody else has ever written that ever touched a typewriter," she said during a 1981 interview at home in Marshall, Oklahoma, "and yet nobody seems to blame me for it. Nobody seems to hold it against me."[1] As a historian, she did not hesitate to expose prominent citizens who exploited American Indians for their own gain if that was what the historical records revealed. Courageous and perhaps naïve, her stalwart position on the history of Indians in the United States, particularly in Oklahoma, uncovered the darker side of American history that many other historians were reluctant to pursue.

During her professional writing career, Debo wrote nine books, coauthored one, and edited three. In addition, she published over one hundred articles and book reviews on American

Indian history and Oklahoma history. "In a real sense, [Debo] invented the 'new' Indian history," historian Richard White posits, "long before there was a name for it."[2] Debo studied American Indians in light of ethnological studies and oral histories to present what she believed to be more accurate narratives, and in many ways has served as an intellectual precursor to scholars who utilize a wide array of source material—including oral tradition—in their studies of American Indian history to get at what some call "the Indian perspective."[3] While this is rather extraordinary praise to laud one historian as a forerunner of the "new Indian history," it is just as dismaying to examine the flip side of her career as a historian. Although Debo published both her master's thesis and her doctoral dissertation, she never held a tenure-track position as a history professor. This failure to achieve university status as an academic early in her career was not through a lack of will or ambition. During the Depression years, Debo continued applying for academic posts without success and turned her attention toward a career as a professional writer. She supported herself through part-time employment and grants, and by living within limited means with her parents in rural Oklahoma. In a back room of the family home, Debo would pound out the stories of Oklahoma's Indians and pioneers on her typewriter. The controversy that swirled around her was at times quite contentious, but reliance on her personal mantra, "to discover the truth and publish it," provided Debo with the ability to tell the stories of Oklahoma's people.[4]

Shirley A. Leckie argues that Debo heard native voices more clearly because white women were professionally marginalized. Debo would not speak out on behalf of gender discrimination, but she would write quite passionately about injustices to American Indian people. Debo had experienced gender discrimination in the historical profession, but she did not complain about it. "Stoic cheerfulness" is Leckie's interpretation of Debo's activism on behalf of Indian issues. "Imbued with her parents' stoic attitude towards hardship and their dedication to maintaining the 'Oklahoma spirit,'" Leckie explains, "Debo could express her outrage over the treatment of others in a way that would have been unacceptable for herself."[5] What is this "Oklahoma spirit"? Leckie describes it as "cheerful equanimity in the face of hardships."[6] Keeping both of these terms in mind, "stoic cheerfulness" and the "spirit of Oklahoma," Debo demonstrated perseverance and steadfastness that bordered on stubbornness in her writings and career path, and an inherent kinship with those suffering or abused at the hands of imperialist forces or objectives.

During the late nineteenth century, many white families living on the frontier shared the desire for land and frequent moves in the name of upward mobility. The Debo family participated in this frenetic lifestyle and, like many families, was trying to escape tenancy. Married in 1889, Edwin and Lina Debo celebrated the birth of their daughter, Angie, on January 30, 1890, on their rented farm in Beattie, Kansas. Their son, Edwin, was born twenty-two months later. In spite of the 1893 depression, the Debos managed to purchase railroad land in Welcome, Kansas, twenty miles south of Manhattan. They sold this land four years later for a profit and moved to Oklahoma Territory.[7]

Angie Debo experienced the quest for land settlement and opportunity firsthand in her family's relocation to Marshall, Oklahoma, some sixty miles north of Oklahoma City. She arrived in Oklahoma Territory by covered wagon in 1899 with her family, ten years after the famous land run that opened the region to settlement.[8] "We arrived on November 8, 1899," Debo wrote, "and I have a distinct memory of the warm, sunny day, the lively little new town, and the greening wheat fields we passed as we lumbered slowly down the road to our new home."[9] She came of age in Marshall, and her identity was inextricably linked to this developing pioneer community. Notions of the "pioneer spirit," homesteading, and the desire for economic opportunity and land pervaded Debo's upbringing in Oklahoma Territory and would shape her later historical writings.

Growing up in a developing pioneer community had its benefits as well as its drawbacks. The sluggishness of the educational system in Marshall—the community did not have a high school, forcing Debo to wait for one to open—hindered Debo's intellectual development, and she has called this waiting period

Figure 16.
Debo family portrait, ca. 1898. From left to right: Edward, Edwin, Angie, and
Lina Debo (Courtesy of Angie Debo Papers, Edmon Low Library, Oklahoma
State University, Stillwater).

her "wasted years." Her educational experience began in rural one-
room schools in Kansas and Oklahoma. At the age of twelve, Debo
received her common school diploma and waited for the next four
years to become a teacher. She has looked back with regret on this
time as something that was beyond her control: "But for those four
years in there I really could have had the equivalent of four more
years to live if I hadn't wasted those four years in futile unhappi-
ness, and almost despair, in my inability to get anywhere at all
educationally."[10] At the age of sixteen, Debo received her teaching
certificate and taught in the nearby rural schools of Logan and
Garfield counties. She continued teaching in rural schools and
waited in anticipation for the new high school to open. She graduated from Marshall High School with the first graduating class in
1913 at the "advanced age" of twenty-three.[11]

   After two more years of teaching, Debo attended the University
of Oklahoma and majored in history. She studied history because

Figure 17.
Teacher and students at the Rosenberg School, District No. 97, southwest of
Marshall, Oklahoma Territory, about 1901. On the right, Angie and her brother
Edwin stand on either side of their pony, Queen (Courtesy of Angie Debo
Papers, Edmon Low Library, Oklahoma State University, Stillwater).

of Edward Everett Dale's enthusiasm as an instructor and his
interest in teaching historical writing to his students. Dale had
received his bachelor's degree in history from the University of
Oklahoma in 1911 and continued his interest in history as a graduate student at Harvard, working with Progressive historian
Frederick Jackson Turner. After completing his master's degree at
Harvard in 1914, Dale was appointed instructor of history at the
University of Oklahoma. Five years later he returned to Harvard
for his doctoral training under Turner, which he completed in
1922. Dale then resumed his position at OU, becoming chairman
in 1924, a position he held for eighteen years, and he remained in
the department until his retirement in 1952. Dale was the first professor in the history department at OU to add a course on
American Indian history to the course offerings. He also encouraged his graduate students to pursue Indian topics for their seminar papers and dissertations.[12]

There were many parallels between the lives of Dale and Debo that produced a natural kinship between them. For example, both were from rural families—Dale was raised on a north Texas farm, worked as a cowboy, and later owned a ranch in southwestern Oklahoma with his brother—and both experienced the limited educational opportunities of rural life. As Debo has commented,

> I suppose it was true that I had somewhat the same kind of background that Dr. Dale had had—of course, his was of the cow country, and mine was of the homesteaders, but both of us had been unable to pursue our education. Both of us had read every book we could get hold of, which were not very numerous. And both of us had gone to a country school, and learned whatever we could learn.[13]

In Dale's case, few of the local school districts could afford to hold class for more than three to five months per school year, and children were expected to work alongside their parents on the family farm. In addition, Dale and Debo taught in the rural schools. Lastly, they attended college at a more mature age, with Dale entering college at the age of twenty-six. In assessing Dale's contribution to western history, Arrell M. Gibson writes, "[Dale's] social milieu more than his academic training shaped his values, commitment, writing bent, and productivity as a professional historian."[14]

In his book *On Turner's Trail: 100 Years of Writing Western History*, Wilbur R. Jacobs argues, "the bole and root of western history is the sturdy Turnerian tree."[15] This is hardly an overstatement about the historian who could be called the first great promoter of western history. As Turner stated in his 1893 essay "The Significance of the Frontier in American History," "The existence of an area of free land, its continuous recession, and the advance of the American settlement westward, explain American development."[16] Essentially, Turner constructed a sweeping theme of American development and justified American greatness through the movement westward. In a masterpiece of synthesis, Turner brought significance to western history. The frontier thesis was at once a challenge and a call. It challenged the prevailing notion that American expansion was an extension of the European tradition. It called for historians to search for the larger meaning of the American West in national history. In short, Turner's thesis became the new paradigm.

It is instructive to follow Turner's interpretation of western history through Dale and then Debo. Dale absorbed Turner's frontier thesis into his own work and considered Oklahoma within the Turnerian framework of westward expansion. As Richard Lowitt puts it, "Turner wrote about it; Dale lived it."[17] In turn, Debo would be considered an intellectual grandchild of Turner through her studies with Dale. In her assessment of Dale as a teacher, Debo referred to the influence of Turner:

> To Turner's thesis that American history furnishes a concrete illustration of social evolution through various stages from savagery to a complex industrial civilization, [Dale] added from his own experience this significant particular: that only in Oklahoma was the process rapid enough to take place within the memory of one still living generation.[18]

But this statement could also be read as Oklahoma exceptionalism, the notion that Oklahoma is unique and merits a special place in historical study, for both Debo and Dale contend they witnessed Oklahoma's rapid development during their lives. Waves of settlement and the civilizing process, what would usually take several generations to develop, they argued, unfolded before their eyes in Oklahoma's rapid development. Throughout her writings, Debo has returned to this theme of Oklahoma as a microcosm of the frontier experience, as in *Prairie City* (1944), which demonstrates Dale's and Turner's lasting influence on Debo's work.[19]

In fact, both Dale and Debo viewed Oklahoma history as a microcosm of the larger narrative of American history, but the parallels ended there. For Dale, Oklahoma history told a story of "the conquest and development of the American Wilderness."[20] At times Debo inverted the Turnerian education she had received from Dale in her writings on American Indians and Oklahoma history. Where Dale saw a wilderness to be tamed and developed, Debo saw instead the "wilderness of civilization," or white settlement on Indian lands, as the burden of Oklahoma history.[21]

Debo attributed her research methodology to the training she received from Dale during an undergraduate history course. It was in his class that Debo discovered historical writing, and she would return to Dale again when pursuing the doctorate. In class, Dale would check his students' notes every week, inspecting citations and pointing out sloppy note-taking techniques. Debo utilized these meticulous research methods throughout her career.[22] In 1925, while working at the demonstration school at West Texas State Teachers' College, Debo commended Dale for taking the time to teach his students proper research techniques: "I have always been glad that you took the time to supervise our note taking and organization of material when you asked us to write a term paper." She also noted that as a graduate student at the University of Chicago, she appeared to be the only one who had been taught how to conduct historical research.[23]

Dale was an optimistic instructor who believed that the story of American history was one of progress. In one of his early seminar papers as an undergraduate at OU, Dale wrote that the territorial expansion of the United States was a "very wonderful story." And yet Debo's critique of this position represents a departure, though slight, from her advisor. "It is refreshing if one is sympathetic toward his viewpoint of joyful interest in American achievement," Debo writes in her examination of Dale in a graduate seminar paper, "but painful in the extreme to the writer who has subscribed to the orthodox creed of historical methodology."[24] According to Debo, only later in Dale's career would he conclude that the story of American expansion was a far more complex, "mixed" story.[25]

As Shirley Leckie and Richard White have both indicated, Debo moved beyond both Turner and Dale, becoming a precursor to the "new Indian history." Whereas Dale remained within the Turnerian tradition over the course of his career, Debo wrestled with this framework and wrote on the periphery of what was considered traditional historical writing of Indian-white relations. Although she never lived among American Indian communities as a participant observer like Alice Marriott, Debo did incorporate anthropological research in her writings and utilized oral tradition and oral history. This being said, Turner's influence remains apparent in her work.

Debo graduated from the University of Oklahoma with a bachelor's degree in history in 1918. During the next five years, she was employed as village principal at North Enid for one year followed by a four-year teaching position at Enid High School, with the hope of saving enough money to attend graduate school.

Encouraged by Dale's enthusiasm for historical research and writing, Debo sought entrance into two of the top graduate programs in history in the United States during the 1920s, the University of Chicago and Columbia University. She concentrated on these schools because she wanted to experience urban living in contrast to her rural upbringing.[26] She selected Chicago because it was "at the very height of its influence at that time," boasting a faculty that included Avery Craven, William E. Dodd, and J. Fred Rippy.[27]

At Chicago, Debo studied U.S. foreign policy, particularly the question of isolationism, with Rippy. On the heels of World War I, the United States turned inward and withdrew from international entanglements. President Woodrow Wilson failed to win congressional approval for the Treaty of Versailles and the United States was not a member of the League of Nations. Debo's master's thesis, *The Historical Background of the American Policy of Isolation*, explored these current issues within a historical context. Many historians argued that American isolationism began with President George Washington's Proclamation of Neutrality in 1793, in response to war between France and England. Debo argued instead that isolationism had earlier roots as evidenced in the writings of William Penn and then John Adams. With Rippy's encouragement and coauthorship (although it was Debo's manuscript, Rippy's name was listed first), Debo's thesis was published in 1924 in the *Smith College Studies in History*.[28] Coincidentally, this was Rippy's first publication.

Graduate programs in history at the time prepared women for historical writing and a future in women's colleges.[29] Although

Debo claimed she experienced no discrimination while attending Chicago, the job search clearly sent the message that university teaching positions were for men. History departments actively solicited male students from Chicago, but they politely did not request women. In fact, twenty-nine of the thirty colleges and universities requesting Chicago history graduates would not consider women applicants.[30] This surprised Debo. With the publication of her thesis, Debo expected to be competitive in the job market. When Debo realized that she would not secure the university position she desired, she consulted a woman on the history faculty at the University of Chicago:

> "Women are sometimes on history faculties. How do they get there?" She said, "When in time of war or some other situation where it's impossible to get a man they had to take a woman—temporarily." And then she acquitted herself so brilliantly that they had to keep her. And so that's the only way that a woman ever does get a position.[31]

During the early twentieth century, the percentage of women receiving doctoral degrees in history remained minimal; however, it grew after World War I. From 1920 to 1930, 131 women received their Ph.D. in history. From 1931 to 1935, 122 additional women received their doctorates in history.[32] Debo was among these 122 women. Between 1893 and 1935, women received 16 percent of doctoral degrees in history—a slender fraction of the total number of degrees awarded.[33] The dramatic disparities along gender lines increase when one considers that the majority of these women historians did not obtain tenure-track positions at the coeducational universities in which they were trained. Most of these women, like Debo, were relegated to teacher training colleges, women's colleges, museums, and government employment.

After Chicago, Debo received two offers from teacher training schools and selected West Texas State Teachers' College at Canyon, Texas. Founded in 1910 with student enrollment of 2,000 by the late 1920s, West Texas State maintained a demonstration school that served neighboring communities by providing teacher training and a lab school for children from kindergarten to tenth grade. Debo preferred West Texas State because it was in the Texas Panhandle, and it was the familiarity of this "pioneer situation," according to Debo, that attracted her to the area.[34] "I had grown up in a pioneer Oklahoma," she recalled, "and here was another pioneer place."[35] Whereas her upbringing in Marshall was one of homesteading, she believed the "pioneer spirit" of Canyon's cattle country was similar. During the next ten years in Canyon, Debo "absorbed this pioneer spirit" and shifted her historical focus from foreign policy to local history.[36]

Debo secured employment at West Texas State through the "old boys' network." The department chair at West Texas, Lester Fields Sheffy, had attended the University of Chicago as a graduate student at the same time as Debo. In addition, Sheffy and Rippy, Debo's advisor, were friends and Sheffy contacted Rippy regarding the position.[37] Although Debo was thankful to have employment after completing her graduate work at Chicago, the limited status and limited mobility were disheartening. Sheffy placed Debo in the demonstration school, only ancillary to the college, and she had no faculty rank in the history department. In fact, from 1924 to 1929, Debo was listed in the college bulletin as a high school faculty member of the training school, demarking the limited status of her position. For example, the teachers at the demonstration school did not march in the graduation procession. The demonstration school, then, not only trained college students to become teachers, but also enrolled high school students to complete their studies and begin college.[38]

Rather than dwelling on Sheffy's placement decision, Debo focused her attention on teaching and her commitment to students. For example, she would often take students on camping trips to Palo Duro Canyon, a picturesque canyon near campus, recalling the days of the "Old West." She also served as faculty advisor for the Young Women's Christian Association and taught Sunday school classes in the Methodist Church. But her enthusiasm waned over the next few years as Sheffy promoted other demonstration teachers to the history department. Most of Debo's colleagues held bachelor's degrees while she possessed a master's degree and a significant publication.[39]

Figure 18.
Automobile loaded with sleeping bags and other supplies for one of Debo's camping trips with students to Palo Duro Canyon during the late 1920s and early 1930s (Courtesy of Angie Debo Papers, Edmon Low Library, Oklahoma State University, Stillwater).

Many teachers at the demonstration school sought jobs at the college level for promotion and increased pay. With a full load of courses at the demonstration school and little spare time for research, Debo became increasingly frustrated as she watched other demonstration teachers promoted to the history department as college professors. Mary McLean, for instance, taught in the demonstration school her first year, and then Sheffy promoted her to the history department as associate professor when she completed her master's degree from Columbia University. Similar promotions included Hattie Anderson, J. Evetts Haley, and Geraldine Green.[40] Passing over Debo for promotion cannot be explained away by gender, for Anderson and Green were women. In other words, although Debo received positive teaching evaluations and had a master's degree from Chicago as well as a book, she was barred from promotion to the history department. Leckie offers some clues to Sheffy's unwillingness to promote Debo:

Figure 19.
Angie Debo with students at one of the camping trips at Palo Duro Canyon
during the late 1920s and early 1930s (Courtesy of Angie Debo Papers, Edmon
Low Library, Oklahoma State University, Stillwater).

> Possibly her assertiveness struck him as improper for a
> female. Businesslike and professional in all aspects of
> her life, she spoke out fearlessly on issues. Her forthright
> demeanor undoubtedly antagonized those who expect-
> ed females to be compliant and outwardly subservient
> when dealing with men in positions of authority.[41]

During the fall of 1932, Debo served on the college faculty for the
first time while a tenured professor took leave. But the dramatic effects
of the Depression quickly turned this temporary promotion sour. With
funding for higher education reduced, teachers suffered a pay cut, as
teachers' colleges slashed their budgets by 25 percent. There was even
talk of West Texas scaling back to a two-year school. Debo's workload
increased to six days per week, while her smaller salary pushed her
frugality to its limits. She found it increasingly difficult to support herself and pay for her graduate enrollment at OU.[42]

Working on her doctorate at the University of Oklahoma with Dale in the early 1930s, Debo examined the history of the Choctaws from the perspectives of Choctaw people. At a time when most historians of American Indians wrote from a non-Indian perspective based largely on government documents, Debo utilized these sources but also incorporated oral history, tribal records, and anthropological studies.[43] In selecting a topic, Dale had pointed her to the university's recent acquisition of the Choctaw Council manuscript collection dating from 1869 to 1910, sources that had never been previously examined by researchers. Admitting that she "didn't know anything about the Choctaws," Debo began pouring over the council papers and learning the intricacies of the Choctaw national history and its relationship to the federal government.[44] By using the manuscript collection, Debo was able to reconstruct the history of the Choctaw people through their documentary record.

In examining the correspondence between Dale and Debo during the dissertation draft process, one quickly learns of Debo's stubbornness and defensiveness, which may provide insight into her later difficulties with collegiality and the job market. Her incorrigible attitude may have also played a role in her troubles with Sheffy at West Texas. For example, Dale advised Debo not to rely too heavily on secondary sources and *Chronicles of Oklahoma* articles, but to cull more primary source materials. The authors of *Chronicles* articles, he cautioned, possess "little historical training and unless the article in question is a contemporary document, I would use it with a good deal of care."[45] He also suggested less use of *Oklahoma: A History of the State and Its People* (1929) by Joseph B. Thoburn and Muriel H. Wright.[46] "You must remember that while Mr. Thoburn and Miss Wright are both well informed on the history of Oklahoma," Dale cautioned Debo, "neither of them apparently has had very much historical training and their book is not in any sense a contemporary document." Dale continued that "[i]f Thoburn and Wright can find these sources, it seems to me that you should do the same." He had less trouble justifying Debo's reliance on Annie Heloise Abel, a historian noted for her three volumes on the Five Tribes during the Civil War era, because, he noted, "Miss Abel is a woman who had a very rare opportunity to secure material and is, of course, very well trained in historical research."[47] In response, Debo defended her position point by point. "Please do not think the vigor with which I am defending myself indicates any lack of appreciation for the kindly criticisms which I have received," she wrote. "It is only that I have the whole study in mind, while naturally all you have upon which to base your judgment is the beginning."[48]

One can almost hear a concerned sigh as Dale shared with Debo his experience directing another "mature" student's dissertation—Debo was forty-two—with each suggestion or criticism becoming "a protracted argument which eventually took many hours of time and in every case seemed to end with each of us feeling exactly as we did before." Dale thought that perhaps his informality with students was to blame. "I cannot imagine my arguing very much with Professor Turner, the director of my thesis," Dale wrote to Debo, "in regard to his suggestions and criticisms."[49]

Several issues are at play in the correspondence between professor and graduate student. First, Debo did not appear to accept the traditional role of deference to her dissertation advisor, and instead battled his suggestions with her own justifications. Second, some scholars may be quick to lump all of her troubles in securing academic posts with her headstrong personality, although I maintain this is only one part of the whole, which also included American Indian history as a field of study. American Indian history was a neglected field of study during the 1920s and early 1930s, although it was gaining attention. In addition, many of the topics Debo selected positioned some Oklahomans against others in serious legal matters, and this too may have played a political role and barred her from some academic posts. The issue of being a woman academic during the early twentieth century, and one who did not choose to express ideals of deference and was in fact unwilling to court opposing opinions at all, was surely a contributing factor.

But Debo's lack of deference within the constraints of academia continued and even intensified. Debo asked Dale in October 1932 if she could avoid going to Norman for her written examinations. She expressed concern for the cost and the fact that she would also have to go to Norman for orals and commencement. Her first suggestion was to bypass the written examination, "since my work all along has shown that I am not in danger of failing it." Her alternative plan was to take the written examination in Canyon. Her final suggestion was to take the written examination on the morning of her oral examination. "If the committee who is to give me the orals could meet a little early to pass on the other," she suggested, "perhaps it could be done."[50] Those involved in academic committee work and the procedures of the examination process know that proper evaluation and time are required, not a quick read of the written examination and on to orals. "I should not ask any of these favors if I have not complied so fully with every other requirement, and if there had been any weak place left over from my preliminaries. It is not that I mind taking the exam, but I do not seem able to budget an extra trip to Norman this winter," she told Dale.[51] Dale anticipated that graduate procedures would require Debo to take her written examinations and take them in Norman, but on a personal note, Dale added that he did not believe in the written examination. He advised her:

> Of course, you must not think of taking the written examination on the morning before you take the orals. In the first place, sufficient time must elapse between the writtens and orals to enable your committee to look over your writtens and in the second place, I would not give it to you on the same day that you take the orals. The oral examination for the Doctor's degree is a pretty serious undertaking and you will need all your strength to go through with it without being worn out by writing in the forenoon.[52]

Dale suggested that Debo ask West Texas for support in this matter, providing a week of release time for her Norman trip. "If they are unwilling to do so," Dale wrote, "it seems that they do not appreciate the importance of the Doctor's degree or the hard work which you have done in order to prepare yourself for it." He noted that two male professors at OU were preparing for their final examinations at the University of Chicago, and the department would provide support "to take care of their work for any time necessary for them to make the trip in comfort and give them ample time to rest a bit before coming up for the examination."[53] After consulting the dean, who was reluctant to establish the precedent of giving the written examination in absentia, Dale suggested Debo take the written examination Saturday, rest Sunday, and take the oral examination Monday.

During the winter of 1932–33, Debo looked for other teaching positions. With the severity of the Depression, teaching posts were extremely limited. Dale instructed her not to leave West Texas "until you are positively certain that you have something better elsewhere."[54] She defended her dissertation at the University of Oklahoma in May 1933. Shortly after her defense, Debo learned that West Texas would not renew her contract. Another reduction in state appropriations for higher education resulted in the elimination of many positions, while the remaining faculty took another pay cut. Faced with budget cuts, Sheffy eliminated Debo and actually kept Ima Barlow, her less-experienced replacement while she had briefly attended courses on the Norman campus. Twenty years later, Sheffy and Barlow wrote a textbook on the history of Texas. Debo met with S. A. Hill, president of West Texas, and protested Sheffy's mistreatment. In response, Hill appointed Debo part-time curator at the new Panhandle-Plains Museum on the West Texas campus. The job as curator was not necessarily a lofty position for a new Ph.D., but it would allow Debo time for research.[55]

There is also evidence that apart from a clash of personalities, Debo's Ph.D. may have threatened Sheffy. Sheffy received an honorary doctorate several years later from Austin College in 1937, and from then on he preferred to be addressed as Dr. Sheffy, which, as Leckie points out, indicates the importance of the title to him.[56] Muriel Wright also received an honorary doctorate and preferred to be called Dr. Wright as well. Following Debo, other women at West Texas, however, had received their terminal degrees, but did not experience tension similar to Debo's in their relationship with Sheffy.

The year 1934 was critical in Debo's professional life, for she received national recognition for her first monograph and ended her decade-long connection with West Texas. *The Rise and Fall of the Choctaw Republic*, an outgrowth of her dissertation, offered the first study of the Choctaw Nation from the end of the Civil War to the close of the tribal period and the beginning of statehood in 1907.[57] In consultation with the University of Oklahoma Press, Debo added three chapters at the beginning of the manuscript that provided the reader with the ethnology of the Choctaws, relying heavily on ethnologist John R. Swanton's *Source Material for the Social and Ceremonial Life of the Choctaw Indians* (1931). This insertion proved highly significant for a historical work, for Debo was creating one of the first representations of ethnohistory. Ethnohistory offers the interdisciplinary approach of history and anthropology to the study of American Indians by combining the documentary evidence of the historian and the fieldwork of the ethnologist in an effort to tell a fuller, more complete story by using a variety of sources and methods. As Debo described it, this was a story that should be "told from the inside, from the Choctaws' own account."[58] At the time Debo did not think of her treatment as something new, but later researchers point to *The Rise and Fall of the Choctaw Republic* as one of the early examples of an ethnohistorical approach.

The Rise and Fall of the Choctaw Republic received the John H. Dunning Prize of the American Historical Association as the most important contribution to studies in American history in 1934. Rennard Strickland has pointed out that although Debo was the only professional historian in Oklahoma to win the prestigious Dunning Prize, she never obtained a tenure-track position.[59] Debo noted this discontinuity between her publishing record and lack of professional status in 1981, asserting, "Whatever discrimination I have had was in getting a position in a history department at a college or university."[60] This statement was as close as Debo ever came to explicitly citing gender as a limiting factor in her career.

In general, *The Rise and Fall of the Choctaw Republic* received positive reviews with the exception of Muriel Wright's review. In her review in the *American Historical Review*, Five Tribes specialist Annie Heloise Abel called it "most illuminating and instructive and, to American national pride, not at all flattering." Abel questioned the title's usefulness. "The end is what the author has chosen to designate the fall of the Choctaw Republic. It was no single, isolated occurrence, unless the organization of the State of Oklahoma be given that distinction; but the steps leading to it were many and gradual, allotment in severalty the determining," she wrote.[61] Anna Lewis of the Oklahoma College for Women, in her review for the *Mississippi Valley Historical Review*, noted, "Miss Debo's observations show a sympathy and a realization of the vital problems of the Choctaw." "Had she known more about Choctaws," Lewis stated, "her volume would have been a more comprehensive history of the Choctaw people. The Choctaws are one of the proudest and most gifted of the Five Civilized Tribes."[62]

While Debo was receiving national recognition for her first book, her problematic work environment with Sheffy at West Texas continued during Debo's museum post. When Warren K. Moorehead, a well-known archaeologist and member of the Board of Indian Commissioners, attended the museum as a guest lecturer, for example, Debo was not invited to attend. She later received a letter from Moorehead, who complimented her on her book. As Petrina Russo Medley indicates in her study of Debo, Sheffy barred Debo from important lectures and meetings with visiting scholars who would be important contacts in her effort to secure employment. Debo's insularity within the museum on the fringe of West Texas's history department, and her discontent with Sheffy, were humiliating experiences.[63] After a one-year position, Debo returned to her home in Marshall in the summer of 1934 at the age of forty-four.[64]

Correspondence between Debo and Dale indicates that she continued to pursue teaching positions without much success. In 1934, Debo wrote to Dale asking for his recommendation for a position in the history department at Western Reserve University. "They want a woman," she stated in her letter to Dale.[65] The next day Debo wrote another letter to Dale regarding her strong desire for this teaching position. The letter clearly indicates Debo's frustration with the job market in the 1930s:

> I hope they will not think I have been too eager, but they
> ought to realize how desperate one feels when he is out

of employment. This is the first vacancy I have discovered during the two years I have spent all my spare time hunting for work. I did learn of the death of two history teachers, and though I felt like a ghoul I wrote the minute I heard the news before they had time to be decently buried. But one place was already filled when my letter arrived and they distributed the work of the other among the other members of the department and did not employ a new teacher.[66]

During the depths of the Depression Debo returned to her parents' home in Marshall, set up her work space in the back bedroom, and labored to produce another manuscript.

Examining Debo's crushing experiences at West Texas in balance with her commitment to writing is a complicated and nuanced endeavor. "At critical points in her life," Leckie observes, "when faced with the decision to devote her energies primarily to teaching or to writing, she invariably chose the latter. She never fully acknowledged that fact to her interviewers. Very likely, she never admitted it to herself."[67] Perhaps this preference is the case; however, I am not convinced as I pour over her letters to Dale during the Depression years. She wanted a teaching position, but the jobs were few and far between. During this period, Debo supported herself through grants from the Social Science Research Council, the Federal Writers Project at the Oklahoma Historical Society, and part-time teaching positions during the summer months at Steven F. Austin State Teachers College and Oklahoma A&M.[68]

Debo continued her tenure-track pursuit throughout the late 1930s and early 1940s. In addition to her requests for recommendations from Dale, Debo also contacted Rippy at the University of Chicago to assist her in job placement. In a letter to Dale in 1938, Debo wrote of her recent visit with Rippy at Chicago regarding the "very vital matter of getting a job before I starve."[69] Three years later, Debo asked Dale to consider her when he received the latest job postings. The following rambling plea to Dale indicates Debo's desperate desire for a teaching position:

When you go to the Mississippi Valley meeting, won't you please keep a look-out for a teaching position for me? You enjoy your classroom work and your association with students so much that you can understand how seriously and definitely I chose teaching as a profession and how satisfying it was to me. I was so completely happy at Canyon—expecting to stay there the rest of my life—that I specialized unwisely in Southwestern History, and came for my graduate work to Oklahoma where I could obtain the best courses in that field. Then when I lost my position, the very specialization that would have made me more useful if I had remained there, proved to be my greatest handicap.[70]

And she continues:

The successful books I have written have typed and labeled me still further. I have really done better work in other history fields than many of the people who have specialized in them, but because my books about Indians have been so outstanding, people assume that I am ignorant of all other subjects. I am writing so fully because I hope you can help me. I know that people who can hold the attention of a college class and inspire students to enter into research and writing are not too plentiful even in the overcrowded history field, and it seems to me there should be a place where my talents could be used. I am not desperate or discouraged, for I can always find things to do, but I am not satisfied to waste the best of my gifts.[71]

Debo's situation was typical among women academics during the Depression. For the first time, women's colleges began hiring men over women with the prevailing notion that men had families to support. In order to keep their faculty positions, women often remained single. Furthermore, Jacqueline Goggin contends that prior to 1940, white male historians offered little support to women colleagues. "In

Figure 20.

During the late 1940s and early 1950s, Angie Debo worked as curator of maps at Oklahoma A&M (later Oklahoma State University. In this image, Debo stands in front of the new Edmon Low Library at Oklahoma A&M, 1956 (Courtesy of Angie Debo Papers, Edmon Low Library, Oklahoma State University, Stillwater).

fact," Goggin maintains, "the records of the American Historical Association and history departments, and the personal papers of male and female historians reveal that discrimination against women deterred them from realizing fully their scholarly and professional potential as historians."[72] Debo's historical reputation relies almost exclusively on her scholarly publication record. One can only imagine the possibilities if she had trained graduate students and they in turn continued her work.

In correspondence between Dale and Debo regarding the job market, he did not assure her a position and he did not provide her with temporary employment in his own department. As mentioned earlier, one factor was Debo's lack of deference to Dale and the other factor was gender. Debo wrote Dale asking to be considered for one such vacancy, acknowledging her "one disqualification" was her gender. In simple, painful language, Debo told Dale that she hoped that *The Rise and Fall of the Choctaw Republic*'s national recognition and her teaching experience "might serve to balance this defect."[73] In response, Dale promised her nothing, as he recruited other former OU students such as Arrell Morgan Gibson and Morris Wardell to join his department. By the mid-1940s, only one woman, Margaret June Mitchell, a Chicago Ph.D. in education, had taught in the OU history department. Debo's awareness of her "defect" is a telling example of the gender inequities among history departments throughout the United States during the first half of the twentieth century.[74]

Although she was a productive scholar, she therefore had difficulty securing a position as a history professor. After years of struggle, Debo decided to pursue a career as a professional writer and keep the hope of an academic position within view. With many academics splitting time between a challenging teaching schedule and publications, Debo "severed [her] institutional connection" and focused exclusively on her research and writing. "I didn't do anything except write," she reflected in 1983, "except once in a while if I needed money and had to work for a time to earn a little."[75] Debo continued publishing other important studies on American Indian history, including the controversial and, to Debo, "most important" work, *And Still the Waters Run*.

When comparing herself to her mentor Dale, Debo stated that Dale had more opportunities than she did because he was a man. "It was blocked for me," she said in 1981.[76] Gender discrimination within the patriarchal structure of the historical profession was certainly one overriding factor that prevented Debo from receiving a professorship, but it was not the only one. As stated previously, Debo lacked the political desire to defer to her mentor or to others in positions of authority, which often sabotaged her opportunities for professional advancement. Moreover, Debo's commitment to social justice and her selection of controversial historical subject matter coupled with her disbelief in acquiescence to politicians or administrators marked her as a potential threat to her contemporaries. They did not embrace her as a colleague; therefore she forged her nontraditional career path on the fringe of the academic world.

❧ Chapter Five ❧

The "Odd and Uncomfortable" Marriage of Angie Debo's *And Still the Waters Run* and *Prairie City*

In a public ceremony in the capitol of Guthrie in 1907, residents of the new state of Oklahoma witnessed the marriage of Indian Territory and Oklahoma Territory. Within this symbolic gesture, the primarily Five Tribes lands and the settler and Plains tribes lands became one. This notion of Oklahoma as "Native America" remains pervasive in popular culture. It has become a storytelling device when describing Oklahoma's development and uniqueness.

Patricia Nelson Limerick, author of *The Legacy of Conquest* (1987), finds problems with this conception of Oklahoma history. In this landmark challenge to Turnerian thought, Limerick turns the

Turner thesis on its head and discusses westward expansion in terms of conquest, imperialism, and plunder—talking about the negative aspects of western history and grounding the argument in the West as place. She argues that the notion of a closed West in 1890 must be removed from current historical discourse and replaced with her version of the West as a continuously evolving place. Over a decade later, Limerick admits oversight in failing to mention Debo among others such as Bernard DeVoto as major influences in her own work, as historians who were engaged in this treatment of the American West, this declensionist vision of the West, long before her "New Western History" of the 1980s.[1]

"This may well be the moment that sums up Oklahoma's dilemma with history," Limerick argues in her study of Debo.

> If you have a state that originates in the marriage of Indian Territory to Oklahoma Territory, you have a paradox that no one is going to resolve. That will be, unmistakably and unchangeably, an odd and uncomfortable marriage. Nothing in the way of creative analysis and interpretation is going to reduce its oddity or its discomfort. Thus, if you put *And Still the Waters Run* on your bookshelf, and then you put *Prairie City* next to it, then you have created an effective and comprehensive display on the subject of Oklahoma history. The books are not going to merge and reveal a concealed harmony, but if you shift your attention back and forth between them, you get a telling glimpse of Oklahoma.[2]

The pairing of Debo's *And Still the Waters Run* (1940) and *Prairie City* (1944) offers a lens through which to examine the complexities and nuances of western regionalist writers during the first half of the twentieth century.

Debo was a regionalist writer working to politicize the injustices to some American Indian people because of federal Indian policy and Oklahoma statehood. Debo analyzed primary documents and concluded that many Native American people suffered in the name of American imperialism, progress, and conquest. The complexity she revealed in the case of the Five Tribes was that many Five Tribes leaders also participated in graft and other forms of corruption for their own gain in Indian Territory.

During the 1930s there was a general lack of interest in the history of American Indians. Historians who researched American Indian history tended to approach their topics largely from a non-Indian perspective, concentrating on federal Indian policy. Long before the New Indian scholars or the New Western historians published the revisionist histories of the 1970s and 1980s, Angie Debo was involved in the process of "self-criticism." As an Oklahoman, raised in the homesteading tradition and schooled in Turnerian thought, Debo sought detachment from some aspects of her heritage. Rather than writing laudatory histories of Oklahoma and its people, Debo observed the damaging effects that the conquest of the American West had left in its wake. As Howard Lamar indicates, Debo was consistently critical of political corruption, grafters, Sooners, and the mistreatment of American Indians throughout her writings. This criticism is her greatest legacy. Debo systematically examined power, state development, and abuse within her own region and wrote about it with a critical eye.[3]

But such a legacy is not without its own set of problems. The road to publication for *And Still the Waters Run*, an examination of the effects of forced liquidation of tribal lands and government on Oklahoma's Five Tribes, provides a telling example. Debo considered it her "most important" work.[4]

Debo enjoyed researching topics in which she had limited knowledge and was curious about the dissolution of Five Tribes lands. She insisted that she did not select this topic for a "romantic reason"; rather she needed a topic and viewed this one as a natural extension of her first book on the Choctaw Nation. According to Debo, she began her research rather innocently and was shocked at what she uncovered. "I didn't know that all of eastern Oklahoma and Oklahoma in general," Debo later recounted, "was dominated by a criminal conspiracy to cheat these Indians out of their land after their own tribes were broken up into individual allotments." She claimed that had she known about these injustices from the outset, she probably would not have tackled the topic.[5]

CHAPTER FIVE

Debo surveyed the history of the Five Tribes in Oklahoma from 1890 to 1936, and specifically discussed the events leading to the termination of tribal governments and allotment of tribal lands. She referred to the "orgy of exploitation" by whites as "almost beyond belief" and concluded that the policy of the United States in liquidating the Five Civilized Tribes was a "gigantic blunder."[6] Such was the Progressive rhetoric she used in *And Still the Waters Run*, following the tradition of other Progressive historians, including Turner, Vernon Parrington, Charles Beard, and John Hicks, who also focused on economics and conflict in American society.[7] Yet Debo moves beyond these historians, questioning the notions of progress in American history and the celebration of westward expansion, by considering that history from the perspectives of American Indians. Debo's reading of the evidence called the Progressive historians' own notion of progress into question, in Robert L. Dorman's words, "equating assimilation not with Progress, but with power."[8]

Debo wrote *And Still the Waters Run* during the depths of the Depression. The narrative clearly defines the winners and the losers. She juxtaposes the financial greed of the grafters, those involved in illegal land speculation and real estate transactions, with the tremendous economic and political loss of the Five Tribes. Dorman views this book as a "depression-era parable of the systematic exploitation of the powerless by the powerful."[9] On one side were influential whites and a few assimilated or mixed-blood Indians representing the powerful grafters, and on the other, the powerless victims, traditional Indians of the Five Tribes, who sold their allotments to grafters for a fraction of their value. The grafters upheld a philosophy, according to Debo, "in which personal greed and public spirit were almost inextricably joined. If they could build their personal fortunes and create a great state by destroying the Indian, they would destroy him in the name of all that was selfish and all that was holy."[10] She called this effort to strip the Indians of their surplus lands following allotment a "criminal conspiracy."[11] Again appealing to Depression-era rhetoric, Debo argued that the once prosperous Five Tribes "were almost stripped of their holdings and were rescued from starvation only through public charity."[12]

Grant Foreman, a lawyer turned historian and friend of Debo's, witnessed the events of land speculation in eastern Oklahoma as a longtime resident of Muskogee and a former employee of the Dawes Commission, but he would not tackle this subject in print.[13] Not only did Debo expose the schemes of grafters to profit from the Five Tribes' resources, but she went one step further and "named names" of the grafters.[14] She used the word "grafter" to describe those who had participated in illegal transactions of Indian lands. Foreman corroborated her use of the term "grafter." "The disgraceful exploiting of the Indians became so common," he maintained, referring to his experiences working for the Dawes Commission during the late nineteenth century, "that the term 'grafter' almost ceased to be a word of opprobrium."[15]

Like Foreman, E. E. Dale, Debo's advisor at the University of Oklahoma, did not want to offend prominent Oklahomans in his publications, as Richard Lowitt has indicated. Dale's selective interpretation of history differed from Debo's need to "discover the truth and publish it." For instance, in 1923 when the Agricultural History Society actively solicited his manuscript on the range cattle industry in Oklahoma, Dale was reluctant. Many of the cattlemen in his narrative were still living at the time and their "curious intrigues and diplomatic struggles for grazing rights in the Indian Territory" included graft and corruption. Dale agreed to publish the manuscript only after consulting several cattlemen and revising the manuscript to their satisfaction.[16] This type of historical writing, specifically Dale's reluctance to offend prominent Oklahomans, deeply conflicted with Debo's approach to research and writing. Although a strong mentor-student relationship existed between Dale and Debo, major differences in their approach to history may help to explain Dale's reluctance to promote Debo's career in the profession.

Debo submitted the manuscript to Joseph A. Brandt, director of the University of Oklahoma Press, in July 1936. D'Arcy McNickle, administrative assistant to Commissioner John Collier and author of *The Surrounded* (1936), reviewed the manuscript. "Nothing quite so ambitious has been attempted," McNickle wrote in the reader's report; "it is a real joy to come across a work of such competence."[17]

He recommended publication although he encouraged her to shorten the text. Encouraged by this positive response, Debo spent the remainder of the year reducing the manuscript by a third.

Although Brandt's initial response was favorable and publication had been scheduled for October 1, 1937, following a favorable second reader's report, his staff had learned of the possibility of cuts in the press budget if the manuscript went forward due to its potential libelous nature. Concerned about possible libel suits and the damaging repercussions it could have on the young press, Brandt sent the manuscript to a University of Oklahoma law professor, Floyd A. Wright, in June 1937. Wright called it a "masterpiece" and recommended publication, but cautioned that the book's contents could produce some libel suits. Given such news, Brandt sent the manuscript to William Bizzell, president of the University of Oklahoma, for his review.[18]

Politics, power, and censorship serve as major roadblocks in publication with a potentially explosive book like *And Still the Waters Run*. Many of the men and women mentioned as grafters in Debo's book had attained high social status, becoming prominent politicians, businesspeople, and community leaders—in other words, Oklahoma's elite—by the 1930s. These people had helped contribute to the state's development, not to mention the fact that many of them were major donors to the University of Oklahoma. A book calling into question the moral standing of former governor Charles N. Haskell and former senator Robert L. Owen and others among Oklahoma's elite triggered alarm in the university administration.

Two factors resulted in the cancellation of Debo's contract with the University of Oklahoma Press. First, President Bizzell and his assistant, Morris L. Wardell, a member of the history department, considered the threat of libel very real. Wardell called the manuscript "fearlessly written" and his primary criticism was that it would offend "friends of the university."[19] One such "friend" was former Bacone College president B. D. Weeks, who apparently had utilized some questionable fundraising practices with American Indian donors. "Why should we go out of our way," Wardell wrote to Brandt, "to rehash something that [Weeks] no doubt would like for the public to forget?" Wardell criticized Debo's use of the term "grafter," arguing that the name had a different connotation during the first decades of the twentieth century than in the late 1930s. These criticisms aside, the following statement encapsulates Wardell's prevailing argument: "The book is history, and the facts are there," he stated, "but it is dangerous to write in a book about it."[20] Wardell and Bizzell both encouraged Brandt not to publish the manuscript.

Second, Brandt believed that political groups inside the university and in the state legislature would shut down his young press if he published this controversial manuscript. Debo shared such concerns, although she remained convinced that the manuscript needed to be published, if not at OU Press then somewhere else, so that the truth would be known. By mutual agreement, Brandt and Debo terminated the contract.[21]

Threatened by libel suits from prominent Oklahoma business-people and politicians mentioned in the manuscript, the University of Oklahoma Press deemed publication too risky. Debo maintained that one of the most unhappy experiences in her life was the time she spent conducting the research for *And Still the Waters Run*. It seemed as if everything she uncovered, all of the available evidence, was "slimy." Furthermore, as the story unfolded, Debo discovered how her childhood role model, Kate Barnard, the commissioner of Charities and Corrections from 1908 to 1914, was destroyed by influential Oklahomans bent on profiting from the allotments of Indian orphans.[22]

The decision not to publish *And Still the Waters Run* under the Civilization of the American Indian series also devastated Brandt. He felt a moral obligation to publish the manuscript. In a letter to President Bizzell in July 1937, Brandt maintained that the manuscript "is honest in intention and execution, it is history and not exposé, although its dealing with recent events sometimes gives it the appearance of exposé. It has all moral right on its side."[23] When Brandt left Oklahoma to become director of Princeton University Press in 1938, he immediately contacted Debo and asked to publish the work.[24]

Committed to publishing scholarly American Indian history texts at all costs, Debo's situation was compounded further as she waited for publication of *And Still the Waters Run*. She had completed the manuscript in 1936, but Princeton University Press would not publish it until 1940. During the latter part of the 1930s and early 1940s, Debo worked on two Works Progress Administration projects. The first project, Grant Foreman's "Indian and Pioneer Papers," as mentioned previously, was a compilation of oral history interviews from Oklahoma's older Indian population and early homesteaders. Debo had met Grant and Carolyn Foreman, both contributors to the *Chronicles of Oklahoma* and avid Oklahoma history enthusiasts, while working on the research for her Choctaw history. "I was badly in need of work back in those depression days," Debo recalled. She contacted Grant Foreman and asked if he had any employment opportunities for her on his WPA projects. He responded affirmatively and she began working as an editor of the Indian-Pioneer Papers beginning in January 1937.[25] Many of the oral interviews conducted under this project became the primary source material for her later study of the Creeks.

Debo accepted the second of her WPA jobs as director of the Oklahoma guide under the Federal Writers' Project in 1940.[26] The guidebook series was a nationwide effort by the WPA designed to stimulate travel. In Oklahoma, the project enabled professional writers like Debo to participate in a New Deal program along with other researchers. Although Debo was probably grateful for the position, she was quite critical of the Federal Writers' Project:

> They were creative projects of the depression. But I do not think that they were as effective in helping people as some of the other white collar projects because it assumed there were unemployed writers over the country. Actually, there aren't any unemployed writers. Everybody that can write writes. It might be the depression period when they can't get anything published, but anyhow he writes, and when he wants a job he has to take a job at something else besides writing.[27]

Her work with the guidebook series resulted in the publication in 1941 of *Oklahoma: A Guide to the Sooner State*, coedited by John M. Oskison.[28]

The "Odd and Uncomfortable" Marriage

While Debo awaited publication of *And Still the Waters Run*, she received another grant from the Social Science Research Council to write a history of the Creeks and quit her WPA job. She selected the Creeks because they were the most conservative people of the Five Tribes and, she claimed, other historical accounts were largely inaccurate. Debo wanted to write an accurate history of the Creeks. She called it *The Road to Disappearance: A History of the Creek Indians*. "If I had called it the History of the Creeks," Debo recounted, "nobody would have been interested in it at all."[29] To select a title for marketability is one thing, but to use one implying the decline of a people as a marketing ploy is an egregious transgression. Although an expert in American Indian history, Debo's weaknesses were her sweeping generalizations and her penchant for flamboyant language—in other words, all the criticisms Wright purported. Debo's titles indicating decline, as in *The Rise and Fall of the Choctaw Republic* and *The Road to Disappearance*, are offensive renderings to many American Indian people. Although her research was impeccable, the language and blanket statements in the texts are serious shortcomings in her otherwise sound scholarship.

In her Creek history Debo recorded the "internal life of the tribe," to examine Creeks from the inside, a recurring theme that set Debo's work apart from that of her contemporaries. She acknowledged the work of Grant Foreman, who studied the removal of the Creeks to Indian Territory, and of Annie Heloise Abel, who examined the Creeks during the Civil War, but her source material offered a new glimpse of this "internal life." Debo relied again on Swanton's ethnological work to describe the Creeks, joining it to other sources, including tribal records, Creeks newspapers such as the *Indian Journal* and the *Muskogee Phoenix*, government documents, court records, and travelers' accounts. Of particular importance was her use of the elderly Creeks' oral histories recorded during the WPA project.[30]

In her interpretation of the Creeks, Debo pairs seemingly contradictory statements of spiritual collapse and persistence of the Creek spirit in order to tease out the subtle ways of culture. Although the Creeks had achieved some degree of "civilization," she argued, "their greatest strength always lay in their native steadfastness." The Creeks successfully adopted Anglo ways with respect to attire, agriculture, livestock, education, and Christianity. But, Debo argued, "the attempt to replace their group loyalties with the white man's individualism brought a [spiritual collapse] from which they never fully recovered." She concluded that after all of the civilizing efforts made by missionaries and Indian agents, the Creeks "remained to the end [essentially unchanged], and their hope of survival still rested upon the unyielding tenacity of their native traits."[31] These arguments by Debo regarding the Creeks seem contradictory—statements regarding the sustenance of the Creek spirit and yet a spiritual collapse—but they speak to the complexity of Indian-white relations. Mary Jane Warde explains in her biography of the late nineteenth-century Creek diplomat George Washington Grayson that Creeks often adopted food, clothing, religious beliefs, and language from other Indian and Euro-American cultures. These cultural borrowings did not make Grayson or others any less Creek. In fact, Warde argues, Grayson assumed many aspects of white culture as a strategy to maintain Creek community.[32]

Reviews commended Debo's use of Creek oral history. LeRoy R. Hafen praised *The Road to Disappearance* as "the first complete history of the Creeks." Hafen added, "She tells the Creek story with deep sympathy."[33] For example, in her description of creating allotments in severalty, Debo writes, "No white man ever fathomed their mystical love of the soil that made them regard its division into metes and bounds with a horror of dismemberment."[34] Richard L. Power responded similarly in his evaluation that Debo was "at her best when describing the everyday life of the Creeks."[35]

In 1966, when the University of Oklahoma Press reissued *The Road to Disappearance*, Debo remarked that this book represented her most difficult research. Whereas other, in her words, "more articulate tribes" she had researched had more visible histories, the Creeks were "a conservative people" who kept to themselves. "Their inner history was hidden until I uncovered it," she boasted.[36] Michael D. Green praises Debo's study. "One cannot begin even a peripheral study of Creek history," Green states, "without early and continued excursions into Angie Debo's *The Road to Disappearance*. Her analysis of Creek history...remains the standard by which other scholars must measure their work."[37]

Debo was disappointed with the lukewarm reception for *And Still the Waters Run* in 1940. The delay in publication extinguished any hopes Debo had of attracting a wide readership for her book. With the onset of World War II, the liquidation of the Five Tribes— and Indian topics in general—did not capture the country's interest. Perhaps if the book had been published during the mid-1930s as expected, during Commissioner John Collier's "Indian New Deal," the public response to this work would have been greater. She had hoped more people would want to learn about injustices that Indians faced in the development of the United States, a theme repeated throughout American history: "Break up their land so that you can get it in shape [so] that the white people can grab it."[38] Debo recognized the failure of the Dawes Act of 1887 and its efforts to divide Indian lands into individual allotments and sell the surplus lands to white settlers. Such recognition was emerging as federal Indian policy under Collier and other New Dealers' plans to end allotment and emphasize increased native landholdings, tribal organization, revival of native arts and crafts, and revitalization of languages and religious ceremonies: in other words, a reversal of almost fifty years of the "civilization" or assimilation program under Dawes.

Scholarly reviews were favorable and lauded her negative assessment of allotment policy. Debo's findings, Dan E. Clark contended, are "all the more devastating" because of her "complete objectivity." He called the book "unemotional" and applauded Debo's "painstaking research." "The author shows no disposition to censure government officials, either Federal or state," Clark observed, "except in cases where they were proved to be in league with the despoilers."[39] Grant Foreman called the book "one of the most comprehensive and convincing indictments that this reviewer has ever read. It is not an indictment only of the people first attracted to the Indian country that is now Oklahoma to exploit the immigrant Indians, at the opportune time presented by the allotment of their lands and the relaxing of federal supervision, but it is an indictment of the white race, for the reader will recall similar exploitation in every state where the interests of the whites conflicted with those of the Indians."[40]

With reviews of *And Still the Waters Run* appearing in national historical journals, a review from the *Chronicles of Oklahoma* was glaringly absent, as noted previously. One explanation for this omission is that Robert Williams, president of the Oklahoma Historical Society, former governor and federal judge, appeared in *And Still the Waters Run* as an associate of grafters.[41] A second explanation is that Muriel Wright chose not to review the book because she did not agree with the historical interpretation. In general, Oklahoma's American Indian population reacted favorably to *And Still the Waters Run* and Debo's other books. But there were some exceptions. Debo called Indian people who disputed her interpretation of Indian history and the development of Oklahoma, including Wright, "successful Indians, leaders of the white man's society."[42] According to Debo, they resented "any allusion to the unhappy situation of the fullbloods who were cheated out of their property."[43] But overall, Oklahomans accepted the claims made by Debo in *And Still the Waters Run* as part of their history. "A good many Oklahomans will accept severe criticism if it's true," she stated.[44]

Debo expected to receive criticism from the grafters themselves, but Oklahomans in general remained quiet—perhaps because many Oklahomans did not read the book. She thought she "wouldn't have a friend in Oklahoma" when the book appeared. Instead, she heard not one word of criticism. "I still don't know whether grafters don't read," she mused, "or whether they were afraid to tell the whole story, and tell a lot more than I had space to tell in the book."[45] Coincidentally, Debo met Charles Haskell's daughter once, but the book was never mentioned because she had not read it and did not know Debo had written about her father.[46]

Of all the books she had written, Debo contended that *And Still the Waters Run* was her most important book. The sensitive subject matter needed to be researched, interpreted, and published so as to make the historical events surrounding allotment available for public consumption. In addition, Debo was attracted to subjects that other Oklahoma historians did not want to tackle, and this surely was such a topic.[47] Rennard Strickland, of Cherokee and Osage descent, describes Debo's treatment as "piercingly honest." Most shocking in her research, he notes, was that "otherwise honest and law-abiding judges, public officials, and citizens silently stood by and watched when their action might have saved a significant portion of the Indians' patrimony."[48] Debo wanted the public, particularly Oklahomans, to read this book and become informed on injustices made against native peoples as part of the legacy of Oklahoma history. She did not want another generation of Oklahomans to remain passive; rather she called for an educated public who would become aware of the darker aspects of Oklahoma's past.

Following publication of *And Still the Waters Run* and *Road to Disappearance*, Debo published a steady succession of books, articles, and book reviews on Indian history and Oklahoma history. Her books included *Tulsa: From Creek Town to Oil Capital* (1943), *Prairie City: The Story of an American Community* (1944), and *Oklahoma, Foot-loose and Fancy-free* (1949).[49] Debo's reputation as a popular historian of Oklahoma history grew during this period because many of her works appealed to the general public rather than to an exclusively scholarly one. Moreover, her book reviews for the *New York Times Book Review* supplemented her income and increased her national visibility.

Prairie City and *Oklahoma, Foot-loose and Fancy-free* demonstrate Debo's versatility as a writer of subjects other than American Indian history. Written in a casual style and intended to appeal to the general reader, Debo describes in both texts what it means to be an Oklahoman. Debo's *Prairie City*, a fictional city based on her hometown of Marshall, located in the northern part of Old Oklahoma near the Cherokee Outlet, tells the story of the initial development, sudden rise, and eventual decline of an American farming community from the 1890s to the 1940s. Debo's life is interwoven in this rural story. As mentioned earlier, she and her family arrived in Oklahoma Territory by covered wagon in 1899. They came to Oklahoma for the chance to farm their own land. Debo began teaching in rural schools at sixteen. As a result, the life of the pioneer was deeply imbedded in her own life experience. Today the Marshall community gathers annually to celebrate "Prairie City Days," to honor both the town and Debo. Debo was the grand marshal of this celebration until her death in 1988.

This book represents a departure from Debo's usual historical treatments, in this case entering the realm of historical fiction. "The whole epic sweep of American history," Debo posited in the preface to *Prairie City*, could be recovered in the story of this frontier community.[50] Twenty-five years later, Debo remained convinced that Prairie City's history "is the history of the United States in microcosm," adhering to the Turnerian tradition of Dale.[51] This beautifully written narrative covers the land runs with cities growing overnight, the importance of the railroad, the development of government and statehood, the Depression years, and World War II. This story also encompasses the full range of pioneer life, from times of prosperity, such as the discovery of oil and increased land value, to times of depression, such as when family farms were forced into foreclosure. *Prairie City* is based on research ranging from county records to census statistics to oral histories.[52]

Dale reviewed *Prairie City* for the *American Historical Review*, calling it "an excellent portrayal of the pattern of American life as it has been lived in the small towns on our western prairies for the past half century." His notion of American exceptionalism, particularly as it relates to the frontier, comes across in the following statement: "Here also is depicted the formation and development of civic, economic, and social consciousness of a typically American community," Dale writes, "during a generation marked by greater and more rapid changes than can be found in any other similar period of years in the history of the world." *Prairie City* is not the story of a single town, Dale concludes, but the story of every western prairie town.[53]

The second work, *Oklahoma, Foot-loose and Fancy-free*, again is a departure from Debo's more scholarly works. This book is an interpretation of the Oklahoma spirit written in an engaging style. During the 1940s, Debo was extremely critical of Edna Ferber's *Cimarron* and John Steinbeck's *The Grapes of Wrath* for their inaccurate, if not stereotypical, portrayals of Oklahomans. These two books, according to Debo, "are only the most conspicuous of the books named for Oklahoma, but rooted in nowhere."[54] In this work, funded by the Rockefeller Foundation, Debo critiques Ferber and Steinbeck and counters with her more accurate depiction of the character of Oklahoma's people. In order to describe this character, she covers topics ranging from physical geography to agriculture to athletics to oil to artists. Debo insisted that the Oklahoma character was different from the character of neighboring states such as Kansas, Texas, or Colorado. She argued that the state's historical experience, which included both the legacies of Oklahoma's Indian history and the "pioneer spirit" of the land run years, influenced the character of the people. Debo established Oklahoma history as America in microcosm in *Prairie City* and reiterated here the theme that "all American traits have been intensified in Oklahoma," as America's last frontier.[55]

Two reviews of *Prairie City* offer both praise and skepticism of Debo's examination of community-building, boosterism, and Oklahoma exceptionalism. "Coming to Miss Debo's book cold— that is, without having lived in Oklahoma," Paul B. Sears of Yale University writes in his review, "one might easily make the fatal mistake of assuming that it is merely an expansive and literate country column such as used to record the homely doings of crossroads and neighborhoods. Many of the names and events seem at first to have only local interest. Many of course do not, for the impact of Oklahoma and Oklahomans on the nation has been considerable."[56] In a more critical review, taking to task Debo's advocacy of Oklahoma exceptionalism, or the notion that Oklahomans are unique because of the blending of American Indian and pioneer history, George L. Anderson of the University of Kansas contends that Debo's evidence is "not always as adequate as some readers would like to have."[57] In a departure from her more critical works, Debo supports Oklahoma boosterism while pointing out the strengths and weaknesses in Oklahoma character.

While *Prairie City* and *Oklahoma, Foot-loose and Fancy-free* are different from her more scholarly texts, they expose Debo's inheritance of the Turnerian model, discussing waves of settlement and

Figure 21.
Charles Banks Wilson painting Debo's portrait that currently hangs in the
Oklahoma Capitol Building, 1985 (Courtesy of Angie Debo Papers, Edmon Low
Library, Oklahoma State University, Stillwater).

the importance of the frontier. Although *Prairie City* does not contain much discussion of American Indian history, *Oklahoma, Foot-
loose and Fancy-free* includes American Indian history and American
Indian participation as essential components of statehood.

In reconciling what Limerick calls "the two Debos"—the critical Debo attacking the despoilers of American Indian lands and
the booster Debo lauding the pioneer spirit of Oklahoma—I am
inclined to select Limerick's third option, that these divergent perspectives of Oklahoma history should not be forcibly joined.[58]
Rather, they stand symbolically much as the marriage of the twin
territories—as a reminder of diversity, variety, and what Debo
called "the pursuit of truth." According to Limerick, "[Debo]
extended to white pioneers the same historical courtesy she
extended to Indians."[59] Debo was Turner's intellectual grandchild,
producing texts that told stories of westward expansion, imperialism, and conquest. She also took Turner in a different direction by

presenting American Indian history from Native perspectives. Her portrait hangs in the state capitol in Oklahoma City as a reminder of the complexities of writing accurate if painful histories of Oklahoma's development and her own marginalization from other academics who would not tackle such political and controversial subjects in their own published texts.

PART THREE
Alice Marriott
(1910–1992)

Figure 22.
Alice Marriott (1910–1992), ca. 1948 (Courtesy of Alice Marriott Collection,
Western History Collections, University of Oklahoma, Norman).

❧ Chapter Six ❧

Alice Marriott

Field Specialist for the Indian Arts
and Crafts Board in Oklahoma

Many women during the early decades of the twentieth century were drawn to anthropology for the freedom it promised. Fieldwork provided the opportunity for women to travel alone, work independently, and assume the identity of a participant-observer in other cultures. For those who selected this profession, museum work and popular writing were the common means of support. The reality was that only a small percentage of women anthropologists could secure tenure-track positions at the university level.[1]

Alice Marriott was an ethnologist who enjoyed the independence of her profession. Completing a bachelor's degree in anthropology from the University of Oklahoma in the early 1930s, Marriott spent the next seven years driving from town to town in Oklahoma and frequently living in hotels as part of her job with the Indian Arts and Crafts Board (IACB). She was the field representative for Oklahoma's markedly diverse Indian population, and her job required her to canvas the state as the liaison for the board—a monumental mission for one person. This would be one of the only "regular jobs" she would hold. The remainder of her life would be spent as a freelance writer whose finances were linked to successful book sales and fellowships. She lived on the margins of traditional society, and she preferred it that way.

Marriott was a good storyteller. Her books on American Indian people in Oklahoma and the greater Southwest read like fiction, separating her writing style from some other anthropologists' drier narratives. This style was an intentional move on her part. She wanted to reach a broad, general readership with her stories of American Indians, both to educate readers about Native communities and to interest them in anthropology.

In 1986, Barbara Babcock and Nancy Parezo at the University of Arizona sponsored a public conference and exhibit highlighting the early work of women anthropologists in the Southwest, specifically those women who were active from the mid-1870s to the end of World War II. Entitled *Daughters of the Desert*, the project began with women such as Matilda Coxe Stevenson and moved chronologically to women born after 1910 and academically trained as anthropologists. As an ethnologist from Oklahoma, Marriott attended the conference and represented some sixteen hundred women who had conducted fieldwork with American Indians in the Southwest. Babcock and Parezo called such women "hidden scholars," for their scholarship was voluminous but the threads of their personal stories remained hidden. Today, we continue the project of collecting their biographies.[2]

Marriott was born to a middle-class family in 1910 in Wilmette, Illinois, a Chicago suburb. Her first distinct memory of her interest in American Indians began at age six with her English paternal grandfather at Chicago's Field Columbian Museum, a natural history museum featuring anthropological exhibits from the 1893–94 Chicago World's Fair. Marriott's grandfather had studied law at Oxford, and one of his favorite pastimes in Chicago was to visit the curator of Egyptology at the museum. Rather than finding interest in her grandfather's passion for Egyptology, Marriott had wandered off to the basement and found herself amid some enormous totem poles. When her grandfather went looking for her, he finally found her sitting at the base of one totem pole, looking with awe at another. This was the earliest event that Marriott remembered as her initial connection to anthropology. "If you found something like that, in very unusual circumstances, in childhood, you would just go on following it," she later recalled.[3]

In 1917, at the age of seven, Marriott and her family moved from Chicago to Oklahoma City in search of economic opportunities. Her father, Richard, had accepted a position as the treasurer of an insurance company and her mother, Sydney, worked as a certified public accountant. As Marriott reminisced about the move to Oklahoma, she also noted that her family traditions became more pronounced in a new region. Her English grandfather and her father's family grew up in that tradition. Her mother's family was from Virginia and had operated a station on the Underground Railroad. When these two traditions, one English, the other Southern, came together within the Marriott household, confusion sometimes reigned, according to a variety of different accents and regional dialects: "We grew up at home speaking two different languages really. Then we went to school in Oklahoma and we learned a third. Nobody, but nobody could understand anyone of us when we spoke as we would have at home. We just had to switch tracks and learn Oklahoman."[4] This adaptability and interest in exploring new environments and people proved beneficial for Marriott as her interest in anthropology grew.

The Depression of the 1930s had dramatic consequences for Marriott, as it did for Angie Debo and Muriel Wright, guiding career choices, education, and relationships. In order to save money, Marriott lived at home as she pursued her college degree at near-by Oklahoma City University. In 1930, she graduated magna cum laude with a double major in English and French. For the next two years she worked as a cataloger for the Muskogee public library, where the second significant event that stimulated her interest in anthropology occurred.[5] The Depression's economic impact was extensive in Oklahoma, and the head librarian did not want to fire anyone. Instead, Marriott's employer organized numerous cataloging projects for her younger employees. "The head librarian had a passionate interest in history and genealogy," Marriott later wrote in one of her autobiographical accounts, *Greener Fields: Experiences Among the American Indians* (1953), "which expressed itself in the form of a collection of books on local history, which in that town meant Indian history. It fell upon me to catalog the books, and subsequently, to index their contents. The indices completed, I discovered in myself an interest in the subjects [they] covered."[6] This cataloging project familiarized Marriott with the essentials of Five Tribes literature. Marriott's interest in studying American Indians emerged from this time-consuming, yet informative, project. She had always wished to return to graduate school, and she became fully committed to anthropology after her library work in Muskogee.

With bachelor's degree in hand, Marriott believed she could attend the University of Oklahoma as a graduate student, only to discover that the new program in anthropology did not have a graduate program. Without prior experience in anthropology, her advisor, Forrest Clements, a Berkeley graduate who had studied with Alfred Kroeber, a Franz Boas student, enrolled Marriott in Anthropology One, the freshman course. Marriott attended the University of Oklahoma "out of sheer necessity," she later stated, in order to study anthropology and remain at home for financial considerations during the Depression.[7] During her first year of study, in addition to her entry-level courses, Marriott conducted laboratory work in pottery restoration and intensive library research on the archaeology of eastern Oklahoma, with a view to proving, through material culture, the relations of pre-Columbian and historical tribes in the region.[8] She received her second B.A. in 1935, as the first woman graduate of the University of Oklahoma's anthropology program.

During the second year of her training at OU, in the summer of 1934, Marriott received a fellowship from the Laboratory of Anthropology in Santa Fe, to study the Modocs in southern Oregon as a fieldworker under the direction of noted Columbia anthropologist Leslie Spier. This annual summer program provided graduate students from across the country with the opportunity to learn field methods under the guidance of experienced anthropologists. This became Marriott's first major trip in the field, as one of twelve fieldworkers and one of two women. The field experience introduced Marriott to the value of gender in anthropological work. "As I predicted," Marriott wrote to her mother in July 1934, "we two girls are working together, and on the women."[9] She described to her mother her first encounter with Modoc respondents, a scene she had been told was "typical" by the more experienced anthropologists:

> We drove up to the house, and discovered our informant at dinner. With her was her daughter, her cousin, who was a much older woman, and the cousin's granddaughter, a child about seven. The woman to whom we were [to] talk was perfectly friendly, but the cousin announced that "I do not like to talk to white people." We sat down while they finished dinner, and got scraps of conversation. Among other things we learned that white women should stay home and mind their own business, and that the woman was not to know anything until she found out what we were going to pay![10]

Marriott and the other woman researcher returned the next day and discovered that the cousin of the original respondent, Mrs. Walker, had the information they needed on medicinal roots. That afternoon the three of them journeyed through the hilly country among the pine and juniper in search of roots. The two fieldworkers discovered that by gaining the interest and, to some degree, trust of Mrs. Walker, she became willing to act as a respondent herself.[11]

Marriott's work with Modoc women also focused on place names and kinship. On another excursion, Marriott, the other woman anthropologist, and two Modoc respondents went to Clear Lake, just south of the California border, in pursuit of place names. "Goodness knows these trips are not for pleasure only," Marriott reported to her family, "they are real work."[12] After the long drive to California, the four women hiked to various sites, drew maps, and recorded place names in their notebooks. Marriott quickly learned that fieldwork required extreme concentration, and she also discovered that the work agreed with her. Writing home, she revealed her enthusiasm for fieldwork:

> The thing that amazes me about myself is the amount of patience and self-control I have developed, apparently from nowhere. I can sit for hours, repeating kinship terms over and over and over, and not only not lose my temper or my grip, but actually be fresh at the end of the session. It was particularly noticeable at the end of three hours of this sort of thing yesterday afternoon. Evaline and Mary were completely worn out, and I was only annoyed because I couldn't type my notes up then and there. And that it wasn't nervous energy is proved by the fact that I was going strong all evening.[13]

This research trip served as a catalyst for Marriott, reinforcing her desire and interest in anthropology. She began to chart her professional course while in Oregon, acutely aware of her role as a woman ethnologist and of the value of studying American Indian women's communities. She also became cognizant of the contributions she could make to the discipline of anthropology by producing readable texts for public consumption.

As a bridge between her academic study and her future career as a writer, Marriott worked for the federal government as a field representative for the newly established Indian Arts and Crafts Board (IACB). A discussion of the IACB and Marriott's work in the field demonstrates the important changes occurring in federal Indian policy during John Collier's tenure as Commissioner of Indian Affairs during the 1930s and early 1940s.

As Commissioner of Indian Affairs beginning in 1933, Collier actively campaigned for economic revitalization among American Indian communities through the production and sale of native arts and crafts. The IACB served as a component of Collier's larger "Indian New Deal," a program planned to halt the longstanding policy of assimilation in favor of a return to semisovereign tribal status through communal land tenure, traditional religions, ceremonies, and arts and crafts. Under Franklin D. Roosevelt's administration in

1934, Secretary of the Interior Harold L. Ickes formed a committee to investigate the issue of Indian arts and crafts and the promise of economic growth among American Indian people. With a favorable committee report, Congress enacted the Indian Arts and Crafts Act in 1935 and Rene d'Harnoncourt became General Manager of the IACB in 1937. Under d'Harnoncourt, the IACB encouraged the production and marketing of Indian arts and crafts. "The primary purpose of the board," as Susan Labry Meyn indicates in her study of the Indian Arts and Crafts Board, "was to promote the economic welfare of Indians through the development and expansion of their arts and crafts."[14] The board placed representatives such as Marriott in the field to improve the quality of Indian goods and to broaden the market.

The IACB sectioned the United States into five geographical regions: the Northwest, the California-Great Basin, the Southwest, the Great Plains, and the East. Within these regions lived approximately 350,000 Indians, and some 200 Indian nations. In developing a strategy, the board realized that each tribe had specific needs, and that these needs must be respected according to religious beliefs and heritage. The board concluded that each local group or tribal subdivision must be treated individually. Although time-consuming, this method was necessary in order to treat Indian groups on a case-by-case basis rather than employing a general plan that would cut across all tribes nationwide. Therefore, as part of the preliminary research, the board conducted surveys of the arts and crafts of each Indian nation, with the intent of developing traditional and marketable native arts.[15]

Oklahoma proved a special region, in the board's view, for a variety of reasons. First, during the 1930s, Oklahoma had the largest Indian population in the United States, followed by Arizona and New Mexico.[16] Second, the diversity among Oklahoma's native peoples would be challenging, with fifty-seven federally recognized tribes living in the state. An additional challenge was the general public's lack of awareness of Indian arts and crafts in Oklahoma, in comparison to the arts and crafts of Indians of the Southwest, particularly Pueblo pottery and Navajo weaving, which had gained a high degree of visibility among the American pubic beginning in the late nineteenth century with the rise of the tourist industry.

Gender assumptions undergirded the structure and strategies of the IACB. First, the board assumed a basic association between women and arts and crafts. The board also argued that most Indian women could not be employed outside the home, but they could supplement household income through the production of arts and crafts. Marriott agreed with this approach based on her experiences in the field: "The work of the Indian Arts and Crafts Board in Oklahoma has been principally concentrated on the development of home industries; both in traditional tribal crafts and in introduced handicrafts. We find that the majority of the crafts workers are women, who are anxious to earn extra money at home in their spare time."[17] Given the board's initial awareness of the role of women in native arts and crafts, it is no coincidence that the first field representatives for the IACB were all women anthropologists.

The IACB's simple solution, Marriott wrote in an unpublished manuscript on the Indian Arts and Crafts Board in 1986, "was to bring together females who had acquired a certain familiarity with Indians, and the lives and work of Indian women, [and then] put them under a male supervisor (naturally...)."[18] The number of IACB field representatives remained small throughout the board's seven-year existence. At the outset, the board hired three women field representatives. Marriott and the other women anthropologists were aware that anthropology was traditionally a male profession. On her list of "men's professions" she included medicine, dentistry, social reform, banking, law, architecture, and, of course, anthropology. "These women felt discriminated against," Marriott wrote, "especially when they tried to get equal pay for equal work from their male colleagues. Salaries were lower all across the board."[19]

The first three women anthropologists assigned as field workers were Marriott, Gweneth B. Harrington, and Gladys Tantaquidgeon. The board assigned Harrington, a Harvard graduate, to the Pima and Tohono O'odham areas in southern Arizona. Harrington's prior work with the Soil Conservation Service in southern Arizona had familiarized her with the local conditions. The board instructed her to revive basketry in the region. The board assigned Tantaquidgeon, a Mohegan Indian from Norwich, Connecticut, to Lakota lands in the Dakotas. She was the adopted daughter and former student of Frank Speck, a professor of anthropology at the University of Pennsylvania.[20] The board assigned Marriott to the Oklahoma-Kansas-Texas area, an unwieldy region, she soon discovered: "I found myself with fifty-seven tribes and languages and a territory that eventually included everything Indian from the western Great Lakes to Florida."[21]

In the unpublished manuscript Marriott indicated the difficult employment situation anthropologists, particularly women anthropologists, faced during the Depression era. Marriott commented that she was fortunate to have her position with the IACB: "a single woman in the 1930's could live well and dress smartly on a salary of $1620.00 a year. She was lucky to get that much, and to have additional travel money, which meant that clothes that were new when they were first bought, if they wore well, could survive many changes of seasons and places. Nobody but the wearers knew the difference."[22] Prior to receiving the permanent position as Specialist in Indian Arts and Crafts for the IACB in August 1937, Marriott's temporary position title was Arts and Crafts Investigator. The temporary position paid $1,620 with per diem for travel expenses. The permanent position paid $2,000.[23]

Working as a field representative for the IACB required self-motivation, enthusiasm for the work, and a belief that one's efforts would assist in the economic improvement of American Indian communities. The field representatives' duties, as Meyn indicates, "largely consisted of surveying the history of an Indian group, assessing the activities related to obtaining a livelihood, looking for surviving cultural traits, attending arts and crafts meetings and related activities, and writing reports to d'Harnoncourt."[24] In reviewing Marriott's travel logs, one quickly realizes the fast pace of the work, the long hours, and the grueling lifestyle of living out of a suitcase. She would drive from town to town, talking to Indians and non-Indians about the importance of reviving Native arts and crafts and the additional need for markets.

Marriott's position with the IACB began in February 1937. Initially, her assignment was to research the Cheyenne women's crafts guild, as part of the preliminary research for the Oklahoma region. Later, her study, *The Trade Guild of the Southern Cheyenne*

Women, became the board's first "purely ethnological paper."[25] During the first six months of her employment, as part of the board's preliminary survey of American Indian communities in Oklahoma, Marriott also conducted extensive research concerning the material culture of the following tribes: Kiowa, Cheyenne, Kickapoo, and Sac and Fox, and, to a lesser degree, Arapaho, Kiowa-Apache, Comanche, Cherokee, Choctaw, Creek, and Seneca. Her reports detailed not only arts and crafts, but also the tribes' living and economic conditions, customs, traditions, and beliefs.[26]

Following these initial surveys, the board decided to begin its work with Kiowa, Cheyenne-Arapaho, Shawnee, and Five Tribes people. For example, the IACB encouraged the Kiowas and Shawnees to pursue silver work, especially jewelry. Marriott and other field representatives relied on contacts or respondents within the tribes to serve as intermediaries to promote and implement the federal government's plan to revive Native arts and stimulate tribal economies. Furthermore, the board employed only respondents who were over sixty years old and had some knowledge of traditional arts and crafts.[27] The notion that older Indians equaled traditional, or "real" Indians, was the prevailing view of many anthropologists and Interior Department employees during the early twentieth century.[28] With the board's assistance, as one example, the Kiowas received a loan from the Anadarko Chamber of Commerce to purchase supplies for the production of silver jewelry and then the superintendent displayed the finished products in his office. "'They have been making this beautiful silver work for years and years,'" Marriott commented in the *Anadarko Daily News*, "'but they have done so, largely to make gifts for their friends. It is quite as traditional to their culture as bead and leather work, yet they are not remembered for it.'" The article also reported, "It is Miss Marriott's belief that the best and biggest market in the east will be for silver jewelry, because it is more adaptable for personal use than the beadwork and leather work."[29] The board, Marriott claimed, did not attempt to influence their Indian contacts' conceptions of good arts and crafts, but tried to focus on products that the board considered marketable. Eastern markets, through the Department of the Interior, the Department of

Agriculture, and department stores, art galleries, and gift stores, proved the most reliable.[30]

In addition to stimulating the production of arts and crafts among the aforementioned tribes, Marriott also researched stores that sold Indian-made goods. Oklahoma stores that sold products identified as Indian-made, Marriott soon learned, stocked shelves primarily with items from the Southwest, almost exclusively Arizona and New Mexico. These products, the storeowners and managers maintained, were better known in Oklahoma than products made by local tribes. Even the Indian agency stores carried such goods from the Southwest.[31] Marriott was reminded of such Southwestern commodification at the IACB-sponsored Oklahoma City Christmas sale in 1938. Prospective buyers attended the sale expecting to find Southwestern products such as Navajo weaving and Pueblo pottery. Without these items on display, the largely non-Indian public had a difficult time associating the local arts and crafts, largely ribbon work, silver work, and weaving, as "Indian" art.[32] Oklahomans needed to be educated regarding arts and crafts made by Oklahoma's American Indian people. As Marriott reported to d'Harnoncourt following the Christmas sale, "Indians in Oklahoma are so largely accepted as a part of the general population that the idea of being different in any way, even in traditional crafts, does not occur to many persons."[33] In this statement, Marriott articulated an interesting facet of Oklahoma's distinct identity. Oklahomans, during the 1930s and presently, identify with a state heritage that combines strands of American Indian settlement and land run settlement. These notions of blending American Indian and "pioneer" settlement together have been so strong in Oklahoma, even during the 1930s, that the state's citizens often overlooked Native crafts in Oklahoma in favor of the romanticization of American Indian arts and crafts from the Southwest, especially from tribes in Arizona and New Mexico.

Adding to the challenge of educating potential buyers to identify local Indian arts and individual artists, Marriott faced an additional roadblock: lack of markets for Oklahoma products. Through public exhibits like Tulsa's American Indian Exposition in 1937 and later the San Francisco World's Fair in 1939, the IACB labored to generate greater public awareness of quality Indian arts and crafts. By showing potential buyers—and the implication here would be largely white, middle-class buyers—how to use these arts and crafts as decorative accents in the home, the IACB hoped to stimulate market demand. These goals returned to the board's central premise, according to Meyn, "that it was possible to alter the nation's mindset and improve the Indians' income derived from the sale of their artistic creations."[34]

Marriott brokered the specialty items made by Oklahoma Indians. She found work for Indian artists, and at the same time, she found markets for their products. For example, in a letter to Mary Inkanish, a Cheyenne woman from Anadarko, Marriott offered the artist a position demonstrating her skill at moccasin making at Oklahoma City's Indian Fair for one month. As Marriott suggested to Inkanish, "You could sell the moccasins that you made while you were here, and we would furnish food and living-quarters for yourself and Mr. Inkanish."[35] Marriott was keenly aware of the importance of having Indian craftspeople demonstrating their skills at fairs and expositions. In addition to individuals such as Inkanish, Marriott arranged for Choctaw and Cherokee basketmakers to demonstrate their skill at expositions such as the Tulsa Exposition. Marriott concluded through experience that the public was receptive to demonstrations by Indian artists, and she continued to use this approach in preparation for the San Francisco Exposition.

Perhaps one of the largest projects Marriott organized in Oklahoma was the Choctaw women spinners in McCurtain County. Initially, the board had instructed her to study women's basketmaking among the Choctaws followed by an evaluation of the market potential for the baskets. As Marriott has noted in *Greener Fields*, during the 1930s many Choctaws existed on a meager income—the average family income was less than fifty dollars per year—and lived in remote areas of eastern Oklahoma. In her unpublished manuscript on the IACB, Marriott commented on these desperate times: "Anything, however far-fetched, that could increase the Choctaws' standard of income and living, would be a gain. All you had to do was find a traditional craft that was marketable, and urge the

Choctaws on, into production."[36] During Marriott's visits with Choctaw women, she learned that hand-spun yarn might also serve as a viable IACB-sponsored product. Three hundred Choctaw women were interested in the project and, although many of them were not familiar with the work, they wanted to learn how to spin. In addition, these women could be organized into a production and marketing cooperative, one of the board's objectives. "Here was the very thing we were looking for," Marriott stated emphatically in *Greener Fields*, "a product with an almost unlimited market."[37] The Choctaw yarn, although uneven and lumpy at first, became a success. By the end of the project's second year, the average annual family income of participants had increased 400 percent, according to Marriott.[38]

Marriott received the board's approval for the Choctaw spinners' project and it began in earnest in late 1937. Mabel Morrow of the Education Division of the Bureau of Indian Affairs taught Choctaw women the necessary skills and evaluated their final product. Some Choctaw men also grew increasingly interested in the project and contributed by carving some spinning wheels by hand or by learning how to spin wool.[39] Similar projects had been attempted by the Works Progress Administration and the Indian Emergency Conservation Work, but they did not sustain themselves. The IACB contended that it was essential to teach the spinners how to acquire the wool, presumably by raising their own sheep, and how to market their final product. McCurtain County in southeastern Oklahoma was often damp, and sheep tended to suffer from hoof rot. The Department of Agriculture helped with drainage, and the sheep flourished. "Even the incidence of malaria and hookworm among the spinners and their families declined," Marriott noted.[40] Local interest continued to grow, and by early 1938 the women organized a spinning association and expressed the desire for a spinning contest. In February, the Choctaw Spinning Association held its first spinning contest at Broken Bow, Oklahoma. Judges evaluated the yarn on fineness, length, cleanliness, and evenness of twist. The participants were pleased with the results and scheduled another contest for the fall.[41]

The Choctaw project was one of many. Marriott continued to encourage the production of specific crafts from each area. For instance, she worked to organize the Plains tribes into a beadwork cooperative. Intricate beadwork was often used for decorative purposes on moccasins and other leather goods. Other production projects that Marriott observed included Cherokee baskets and Creek baskets, and local artists teaching ribbon-work to the students at the Pawnee Indian School. In her 1938–39 report to d'Harnoncourt, Marriott listed the numerous Indian events she attended as the IACB field representative: the Seneca Blackberry Dance at Grove in July, the Kickapoo Harvest Dance at McLoud in August, the Cheyenne Sun Dance at Catonment in October, the Kiowa Christmas encampment at Rainy Mountain Church in December, and the Shawnee Ceremonial Ball Game in the Big Jim Territory in April. "Probably not more than five hundred personal interviews with workers took place during the year," she modestly mentioned in the report. To be one person acting as field representative for Oklahoma obviously required an individual with stamina, perseverance, and a keen interest in economic revival in American Indian communities through the production of arts and crafts.[42]

In preparation for the World's Fair in San Francisco in 1939, Marriott traveled to the Great Lakes area and Florida to meet Indian artists and to collect arts and crafts for the Indian exhibition in the Federal Building located on Treasure Island in San Francisco Bay. The American Indian exhibit was one of ten sponsored by the federal government.[43] During much of 1938 and 1939, the IACB channeled the majority of its energies into this "grand endeavor," which attracted some 1,500,000 visitors. "The exhibit depicted Indians as vital and dynamic," as Meyn describes it, "not as dying or vanishing people, by showing their cultural products as art."[44] Indian artists demonstrated their talents before the visitors, and arts and crafts were also available for purchase. "d'Harnoncourt reasoned that the public, through this exhibit in the Federal Building at the fair, would learn that Indians and their artistic creations were more than curiosities," Meyn maintains in her study.[45]

From May to September 1939, Marriott worked in the exhibition and sales rooms at the world's fair with Indian artists, including Mary Inkanish from Oklahoma. There were approximately forty Indian demonstrators ranging from a totem-pole carver from

British Columbia to Julian and Maria Martinez, the couple from San Ildefonso Pueblo, New Mexico, who were famous for their black-on-black pottery. Indian demonstrators came to San Francisco for a specified length of time, and usually at Indian Service expense. Marriott drove Mary Inkanish and her husband from Oklahoma City to San Francisco to attend the world's fair as demonstrators of moccasins and beadwork.[46]

Marriott worked as a Specialist in Indian Arts and Crafts for the IACB from 1937 to 1942 when, due to U.S. involvement in World War II, the field operations of the board were suspended and only nominal work continued at the Washington, D.C., office. Marriott evaluated the work of the IACB and her participation in it as a success. "As nearly as we could estimate," she claimed, "the Indians were doing a two million dollar a year business in fine arts—instead of twenty thousand a year in curios."[47] Marriott considered her job with the IACB to be "heaven," and maintained that her position with the board never took her away from anthropology, as she continued to use her training as an anthropologist in the field.[48]

❦ *Chapter Seven* ❦

Alice Marriott's
The Ten Grandmothers
and the Pursuit of
Ethnographic Authenticity

Marriott distanced herself from professional anthropologists, preferring to call herself an ethnologist who wrote for the general public. Her formal education as an anthropologist ended with a bachelor's degree in anthropology from the University of Oklahoma, and she deliberately chose to spend her time in the field rather than pursuing advanced degrees. In the following passage from her experimental ethnography *Greener Fields* (1953), her explanation regarding who should study ethnology also provides a telling glimpse of the way Marriott perceived herself:

> All your accomplishment depends on your ability to
> detach yourself from your own culture. In fact, it is safe

to say that you would not be where you are, doing what
you are doing, if you easily found a satisfactory niche
within your own culture. Mentally, emotionally, or in
some other inner way you are a displaced person, or you
would not have found interest in or satisfaction from the
study of other cultures. This is your lack—or your great
good fortune. Face it squarely, admit it honestly, take
advantage of it.[1]

Marriott was a "displaced person" who lived quite contentedly on
the margin of what was considered acceptable behavior for women
during the first half of the twentieth century. In her private life she
established long-term relationships with women partners. In her
research, she employed American Indian women interpreters, collaborators, and respondents, and consciously sought out and
wrote women's narratives.

In 1934, Marriott returned to the University of Oklahoma after
her summer fieldwork with Leslie Spier's team in Oregon among
the Modocs. This experience renewed her enthusiasm for ethnology, particularly working with Indian women. As Marriott
explained in *Greener Fields*, "I am a woman and I talk to women."[2]
Her approach to gender could be seen as her greatest contribution to anthropology. Her interest in American Indian women,
being a woman herself and employing Native women collaborators
as interpreters and respondents, culminated in numerous books
and articles on American Indian women. During this time, male
anthropologists generally did not utilize women respondents or
study women's community among Indian people.

Marriott's *The Ten Grandmothers*, published by the University of
Oklahoma Press in 1945 as the twenty-sixth book in the Civilization
of the American Indian series, became the book for which she is
best known.[3] This book tells stories of Kiowa life spanning almost a
century from the buffalo days of the mid-1840s to World War II.
These stories expose the intense cultural incursions Kiowa people
faced: the federal government's presence and the transformation
of Plains landscape, the decline of the buffalo and encroaching
westward settlement, reservation life and assimilation policies such

as Christianity and boarding schools. But throughout these changes, as Marriott insists, the grandmothers, or ten medicine bundles, remained a stable force among Kiowas.

Marriott's intention was to write an accessible text with popular appeal for general readers. She was successful in this regard, for the book has gone through numerous printings. According to Marriott, the Kiowa people with whom she collaborated on this project supported her research and viewed *The Ten Grandmothers* as a way of preserving their stories. In addition, Marriott considered this book an ethnological achievement because, she argued, younger members of the tribe consulted it to learn more about their history. By utilizing *The Ten Grandmothers* and *Greener Fields* as well as correspondence and field notes, we have a window through which to view the ethnographic process between anthropologist and collaborators and the published text as the tangible product of that process.

When it came to selecting a research topic, in consultation with her advisor Forrest Clements, Marriott narrowed her choices to the Kiowa or Arapaho communities. Of the fifty-seven Indian tribes in Oklahoma, according to Clements, these two had not received adequate ethnological attention since James Mooney, government ethnologist for the Smithsonian Institution's Bureau of American Ethnology, in the 1890s. Mooney's classic text, *Calendar History of the Kiowa Indians* (1898), represents an early example of "salvage ethnography," the effort to recover "disappearing" American Indian cultures.[4] With the idea that older generations of Kiowas were dying, anthropologists sought to record their stories before they perished. This method was still at work when Marriott took to the field in the 1930s.

Marriott indicated the "chance" nature of her selection of the Kiowa project: "I remember sitting in the office talking to Clements, and he was reaching for a pipe and then he reached for a cigarette. He went back and forth between the two things on the desktop and I made up my mind: if he picked up the pipe, it would be the Kiowa, and if he picked up the cigarette, it would be the Arapaho. It was the Kiowa. I've never stopped with it since."[5] Although her initial introduction to the Kiowas may appear arbitrary, her work and relationships with Kiowa people lasted from the mid-1930s until her death in 1992.

In preparation for fieldwork, Marriott first examined the existing literature on Plains Indians' material culture. She became particularly interested in Kiowa social structure. As her reading of the secondary literature deepened, she grew disturbed by what was left out of the narratives—principally American Indian women's stories and activities. She attributed this oversight to the fact that male anthropologists using male respondents had conducted past studies. She commented on this omission in the scholarship in *Greener Fields*:

> The life pattern of Plains Indian men had been, by the time I came along, recorded thoroughly by several competent observers. The literature concerning the lives of Plains Indian women was less complete, and it seemed thoroughly natural and right for me to try to bring it up to date. After all, being a woman myself should give me a slight edge over the previous, masculine, field workers.[6]

Thus began Marriott's pursuit to collect Kiowa women's narratives. She focused on "women's life, women's ways, women's tricks" when she interviewed Kiowa women.[7] But she did not believe that her research was exclusively about Indian women, but rather the missing link to a fuller study of the social structure of Kiowa culture. "I just felt that the audience for anthropology was going unsatisfied, so to speak," Marriott maintained. "Because half of everything was being left out. It became a kind of challenge, as 'I'm as good as you are' way of proving to everybody I knew that women did have a life."[8] After only one year of anthropological study, Marriott had located an important untapped resource in the lives of women; she uncovered material that had been invisible in prior anthropological research. Marriott became committed to working with women respondents and women interpreters in order to reveal women's culture within Kiowa society.

After Marriott had received permission from the superintendent of the Kiowas at the agency at Anadarko, Marriott began her initial acquaintance with the tribe during Thanksgiving in 1934. The superintendent and his staff recommended a few people as good respondents. "I found out afterwards," Marriott reflected, "we had different standards."[9] She set out in her car—she had recently learned to drive—for the first respondent's house. A violent November storm forced her car into a ditch. As Marriott recalled,

> I turned off the motor—I assumed that was as sensible as anything I could think of—and sat there and looked out of the window on a lower level. There was a house with a road going up to it. I got out of the car and started walking to the house. If you got to a house, they'd certainly take you in. About midway along the driveway, I bumped into a nice, square, chunky Kiowa gentleman who put a blanket around me and said, "Come on in the house and get warm." So we went in, and that was the beginning of what has been a lifelong and wonderful friendship.[10]

This hospitable man was George Hunt. Marriott's recollection of her initial encounter with Hunt gives the false impression that their meeting was kismet on a blustery day, but this was no random encounter, for Hunt was a historian himself and worked as an interpreter for other scholars working with Kiowa people.

With interests in Kiowa and frontier history, Hunt was a tribal historian who both worked as an interpreter and secured respondents for historians and anthropologists. Hunt worked as Wilbur Sturtevant Nye's principal respondent and interpreter for two texts, *Carbine and Lance: The Story of Old Fort Sill* (1937) and *Bad Medicine and Good: Tales of the Kiowas* (1962).[11] Orphaned as a boy, Hunt lived with his uncle, I-see-o, an Indian scout at Fort Sill, and attended school there. Hunt learned to speak and write English at school and from people stationed at the fort. Equipped with his mastery of languages, including sign language, Hunt served as interpreter for I-see-o and the Indian troop, "Troop L," of the 7th Cavalry.[12] In his youth, Hunt was "perhaps the only Kiowa," according to Nye, "then able to interpret properly for James Mooney" during the 1890s.[13]

In 1897, George Hunt eloped with Julia Given, daughter of Kiowa chief Sitting Bear, also called Satank. They married according to Kiowa custom and later became the first Kiowa couple married in a Christian ceremony at Rainy Mountain. Given received her early education at Fort Sill and then attended Carlisle Indian School in Pennsylvania, where she became a Christian and studied domestic arts as part of the federal government's larger assimilation program. Her brother, Joshua, also educated at Carlisle, became an Episcopal priest and returned to his tribe in Oklahoma, but died shortly after from exposure and tuberculosis. After ten years away from home, Julia Given returned to Rainy Mountain as an interpreter and missionary helper for the Woman's American Baptist Home Mission Society. At Rainy Mountain, she taught missionaries the Kiowa language and also translated portions of the New Testament into Kiowa.[14] George Hunt worked as farm agent for the Indian Service conducting business from the Anadarko office and dispensing annuity checks to the Kiowas.[15] The Hunts remained active church leaders at the Rainy Mountain Baptist Church. For example, George Hunt and their eldest child, Ernest, served as deacons there.[16] Marriott's contact with the Kiowas was through the Hunt family. Their Baptist commitment, experience with boarding school education, and willingness to welcome Marriott into their family influenced the ethnographic process and the production of *The Ten Grandmothers*.

George Hunt welcomed Marriott into his home that Thanksgiving weekend and proved a vital resource for her ethnological work by introducing her to potential respondents. In fact, he first suggested that Marriott talk to older women and preserve their stories for young members of the tribe.[17] By this time, Hunt had remarried following Julia's death after a long battle with tuberculosis. His second wife, Lillian Goombi, was the daughter of Millie Durgan, a white captive who had been taken from her home in Texas by Kiowas. Durgan was adopted by a Kiowa family, raised within the community, and had two marriages to Kiowa men.[18]

George Hunt and his family were Marriott's point of contact with the larger Kiowa community. He even recruited his daughter, Ioleta Hunt McElhaney, the first Kiowa woman college graduate and a Christian missionary, to become Marriott's principal interpreter. In addition McElhaney's sister, Margaret Tsoodle, and their father introduced Marriott to other potential respondents, all drawn from the older members of their family, a common practice in ethnographic fieldwork situations.

These relationships are important to establish at the outset, for Marriott's interpreters and respondents are all drawn from Hunt's extended family. The Hunt family commitment to Christianity, education, and Kiowa history influenced the production of Marriott's texts as well as her ability or inability to access certain Kiowa people and tribal information. In evaluating *The Ten Grandmothers*, then, one must bear in mind that Marriott relied on Hunt and his family's stories to represent "Kiowa culture," even if she posits otherwise. This reliance is problematic from an ethnographic point of view. For example, the Hunts were Christian missionaries, which inevitably shaped their view of Kiowa history and the way they were perceived in their community. For example, during the summer when McElhaney and Marriott would arrive in a university vehicle at a farmhouse or brush arbor to inquire about a possible respondent, Marriott observed, "decorum immediately reigned over all who saw us. Conversation became correct to the point of being stilted, table manners became finical, and we were surrounded with an atmosphere of well-doing and good behavior that transfigured everyone around us."[19] Such observations indicate that the ethnographic experience was influenced not only by Marriott as an anthropologist with a university car; McElhaney's presence also altered people's normal behavior. McElhaney was an educated, religious Kiowa woman who was always looking for "possible converts."[20]

Marriott conducted the bulk of her research during the summers of 1935 and 1936, but she continued to return to Kiowa country throughout the course of her life. Initially, Marriott lived with the Hunt family in a room she rented while conducting her research. McElhaney's grandmother adopted Marriott in a ceremony attended by Marriott's parents. She continued to visit and correspond with the Hunts, joining them when they camped together at Kiowa gatherings and addressing her correspondence to George Hunt as "Dear Father." "If you establish that kind of relationship, a rapport, with an Indian group," she stated during an oral history interview in 1986, "it will spread from one person to another. You will eventually find that you have much more in common with them, than you have with people in your own age group, in your own culture."[21] Her emotional attachment to the Kiowa people, particularly the Hunt family, never waned throughout the course of her life.

Marriott learned to say a few Kiowa phrases, but she never pursued the study of the language. Marriott contended that the Kiowa language, a five-toned, pitch language was too difficult for her to learn, for, she said, "I have no ear, none whatever, for pitch."[22] Most of her respondents were older people who only spoke Kiowa. Therefore, Ioleta Hunt McElhaney's work as interpreter was essential to Marriott's fieldwork.

McElhaney was Marriott's age, in her late twenties, and had just graduated from college with a degree in sociology.[23] She spoke English and Kiowa. McElhaney became, in Marriott's words, her "dearest friend," and for the next three summers, they did everything together. Marriott commented on her relationship with McElhaney: "She was the interpreter, I was the recorder, and anybody we could put our hands on, our four hands, was the informant! Most of them were in the family."[24]

In tracing the life of Ioleta Hunt McElhaney, a teacher and social worker for the Indian Service, one quickly finds that she was an exceptional individual. Born near the Wichita Mountains at Saddle Mountain in 1908, McElhaney's father raised her to be mindful of Kiowa history and its ramifications. She had been born shortly after the cutoff date of the Jerome Treaty, and those born in 1908 or after would not receive an allotment of 160 acres. "Poor little Ioleta—no land," her father would say. So at an early age, Hunt reinforced to his daughter the importance of education as a tool of economic advancement and stability in her life, for she would receive no land. Educated in public schools at Rainy Mountain and Mountain View to fifth grade, she then attended Bacone College, the Northern Baptist school for American Indians at Muskogee in eastern Oklahoma through high school and two years of junior college. Her older sister had also attended Bacone and then married.[25]

For her final two years of study, McElhaney attended Keuka College, a women's college in upstate New York, and majored in sociology. She was the first Kiowa woman to receive her bachelor's degree. At Keuka College, McElhaney had her first experience living with white people. She recalled this experience in an interview in 1968:

"[Classmates] made it rather hard for me because they had never seen an Indian before. And they wondered if I knew how to sleep in a bed or knew how to eat with a knife and fork. They didn't know that my mother was a graduate of Carlisle and father had gone to school." Moving beyond the objectified "other" was complicated for McElhaney, and although she enjoyed her time at Keuka, misunderstandings continued as graduation approached and her parents made plans to attend. To finance their trip East by bus, her stepmother sold beadwork. "And when they were coming," McElhaney recalled, the other students were concerned about their journey. "'How will they come across country, not knowing how to speak English?' I didn't say they didn't speak English, I said. 'You just wait and see.' 'Will they have feathers on?' I said, 'You just wait and see.' And when he came he had on his suit and could speak English. They were surprised, but he had his bows and arrows with him and he taught them archery."[26] Again, although these were painful moments for Ioleta, she educated her Keuka classmates about her heritage and what it meant to be Kiowa.

For the next fourteen years during the 1930s and 1940s, McElhaney worked as a teacher and social worker for the Indian Service in eastern Oklahoma. She began teaching at a school north of Vian, in the Cookson Hills of Cherokee Nation, one of four government Indian day schools for underprivileged children living in the region. The work was emotionally trying, for McElhaney had a difficult time observing children without shoes and with inadequate health care, and the Depression only intensified the poverty of the communities she served. "And then, back of it all," she said, "I think there was this desire to be a full time missionary. But teaching was doing mission work and I thought being a social worker was doing mission work too."[27] During her second year of teaching, she married Robert Louis McElhaney, a Cherokee student she met while attending Bacone. After Bacone Robert McElhaney attended Haskell Institute in Lawrence, Kansas. During the early 1930s he worked for the Civilian Conservation Corps at the Five Tribes Agency in Muskogee.[28] McElhaney continued teaching for several years in eastern Oklahoma, among the Choctaws, Shawnees, and Delawares.

By the late 1940s, Ioleta Hunt McElhaney's dream of missionary work became a reality and she returned to Rainy Mountain to serve as a missionary helper and interpreter for the Woman's American Baptist Home Mission Society. She had been campaigning for this position for years, visiting churches in the East and lobbying for more missionaries among the Indians. McElhaney was continuing the work of her mother, who had also been a missionary helper at Rainy Mountain. One of her most thrilling moments in life, next to her graduation from Keuka and the birth of her daughter, Helene, was her appointment as missionary at Saddle Mountain. McElhaney was the first Kiowa woman to be commissioned by the Baptists. "I was appointed first,' she recalled, "because in our home mission society they did not appoint married women. So it was quite an experience."[29] Rainy Mountain also performed a special ceremony following her commission, giving her a license to preach there that was unprecedented for a Kiowa woman. McElhaney conducted her services in Kiowa and English and continued the tradition of sign language that her father initiated many years earlier. By the mid-1950s, her husband was also commissioned as a missionary.[30]

Marriott recognized the importance of securing McElhaney as her interpreter. "Getting a woman interpreter would not have been easy under ordinary circumstances," Marriott noted. "When one added [McElhaney's] background in sociology, and her thorough training in social work to the fact that she knew and liked the older members of the tribe, the wonder is that she did not do the research for me."[31] McElhaney called the work "fascinating."[32] "On Mrs. MacElhaney fell the burden of the work, not only as interpreter, but as contact woman," Marriott emphasized. "Her great knowledge of both English and Kiowa and her painstaking care in translation made it possible to be sure of accuracy of spirit, as well as meaning, throughout the work."[33]

The Ten Grandmothers is based on Kiowa oral traditions that were passed down through tribal members. Older Kiowas had lived as buffalo hunters on the Plains at one time. One of Marriott's principal respondents was McElhaney's grandmother and another was her uncle. During the mid-1930s these respondents were in their mid-nineties. Marriott considered herself fortunate to have had this opportunity to work with them, for within the next five years their entire age group had passed away.[34]

In her discussions with respondents and others, Marriott concluded that she could not make generalizations about the Kiowas during a period of "great stress" due to white incursion, from the buffalo days to acculturation. "While each person acted within the general pattern of the culture he knew," she states in the preface of *The Ten Grandmothers*, "the pattern itself was changing too rapidly and too radically to be absolutely defined."[35] Therefore, the sketches illustrate individual behavior rather than generalizations about all Kiowa people. However, she adds, "It is only that no one but a Kiowa would have behaved in that way, at that time, under those conditions, that links the sketches." And finally, Marriott notes that she did not embellish the stories: "I have tried to tell these stories as much as possible as they were told to me," she concludes in the preface.[36]

The Ten Grandmothers presents thirty-three short stories, each associated with a year in the Kiowa calendar. Beginning in 1832, the Kiowas kept a calendar that recorded the major events in the tribal year pictographically. Marriott consulted Mooney's *Calendar History of the Kiowa Indians*, a record he made from Anko's calendar. For comparative purposes at the back of the book, she placed Mooney's work alongside George Poolaw's continuation of the Mooney calendar to 1939, and George Hunt's and Mary Buffalo's respective calendars. She found some discrepancies in memory and interpretation, but similarities overall. Each summer and winter is named for specific events. For instance, the first sketch, "The Bear," corresponds with 1847, or in the Kiowa calendar, "The Year That Red Sleeve Was Killed."

The result is a series of chronological sketches under four headings: "The Time When There Were Plenty of Buffalo," "The Time When Buffalo Were Going," "The Time When Buffalo Were Gone," and "Modern Times." Although Marriott cautions the reader that she merely recorded these Kiowa stories, what she does not acknowledge is her crucial role as the constructor of the narrative. We should not cast too critical an eye on this practice, for she was following anthropological conventions of her time. For instance, like most anthropologists of the era, she frames the story along fairly rigid declensionist lines: good times, bad times, and modern times. The implicit argument is that for Indians, this decline was unavoidable, and that "modern times" are not as "Indian" as the good old days. Kiowas tend to talk about this process very differently. This is not a literal translation of stories—Marriott crafted them into her own sketches. Her role as the narrator must be understood. Although she is a sympathetic narrator, she is still positioning herself as the authority.

Two issues that arise in my study of *The Ten Grandmothers* merit lengthy discussion: first, problems with the title, and second, the limitations of using one family to explore a culture. The book's title refers to ten medicine bundles that, according to Marriott, the Kiowa tribe called the ten grandmothers.[37] These small, sacred bundles made of rawhide hold the "power" of the tribe and emanate that power among the Kiowa people. As Marriott explains in the preface, the bundles still exist but their contents are unknown. Even the guardians or the keepers of the sacred bundles did not open them. Once a year the ten guardians brought the ten grandmothers to a priest who had inherited his position. In his ceremonial tipi the priest opened the bundles, examined their contents, prayed and participated in ceremonial smoking, and closed the bundles. In the 1890s the last priest who had this duty died, and the bundles have remained closed.[38] One of the bundles perished in a fire in the late 1930s, and the other nine remain with their guardians who care for them. In the late 1960s, James Silverhorn, for example, was the keeper of four of the grandmothers and he kept them in his storm cellar.[39]

The title is problematic because it is misleading and offensive to some Kiowa people. By publishing her text as *The Ten*

Grandmothers, Marriott appropriated Kiowa religion for public consumption, even if unintentionally. Silverhorn argues that the sacred bundles should not have been disclosed to a general audience in the 1930s and 1940s. By the 1950s, he said, restrictions regarding talking about the grandmothers had been lifted, but Marriott and others used respondents willing to discuss religious information whether to preserve the information for the tribe or for other reasons. Silverhorn criticized Marriott's book for including many Kiowa names, and he thought she should have known better.[40]

In a separate study appearing in the late 1960s, Marriott pointed out several legends about the origins of the grandmothers. Some maintain that Sunboy, the original Kiowa, split and formed twins. One twin fell into a lake and the other fractured into ten pieces, becoming the ten grandmothers. Some anthropologists contend that the twins were rock formations.[41] During the late 1960s, Kiowa historian Guy Quoetone recounted the origin story of Spider Woman and the Half Boys: "After the flood and the earth destroyed everything except 'Spider Woman' and after this child disobeyed orders of the goddess, 'Spider Woman,' she was divided in half and made two boys instead of one. That's what we called 'Twin Gods,' the 'Twin Grandmother Gods.' They're kept by our people today."[42] Stories of the Half Boys or Twin Boys are part of the essence and power of the ten medicine bundles, or ten grandmothers.

What becomes clear in Marriott's work with Kiowas, and also a point of criticism, is that her research was based largely on the stories told by one Kiowa family, the family of George Hunt. Many of the respondents had been buffalo hunters on the southern Plains and were in their eighties and nineties during the 1930s. Marriott encouraged them to tell their stories. She told them that she was interested in learning about their lives as buffalo hunters and recording their stories so that other people could remember the days of the buffalo.

The explanation Marriott offered to the older Kiowa respondents was typical of the "salvage ethnography" of the era, or as Louise Lamphere defines it, "the collection of myths, tales, details of kinship and social organization, items of material culture, details of phonology and grammar, and accounts of ritual practices and

Figure 23.
Alice Marriott with Oscar Tsoodle in southwestern Oklahoma in the mid-1930s
during her early anthropological research with Kiowa people (Courtesy of
Alice Marriott Collection, Western History Collections, University of
Oklahoma, Norman).

belief systems before cultures 'died out.'"[43] Marriott told the older respondents, "think of the children who will grow up not knowing what their grandparents lived. It's cheating the grandchildren."[44] This approach proved effective, and Marriott marveled at their willingness to share their stories with her:

> Hour after hour it pour[s] out, as fast as I can write it, even when it goes thru [*sic*] the interpreter. If I can ever get my mind off the sign talk which accompanies the stories I shall do better, but it is fascinating. My pronounciation [*sic*] is, as usual, a huge joke, but they are willing to repeat words indefinitely, until I get them, which helps.[45]

Reflecting on her initial fieldwork experience with the Kiowas, Marriott expressed her good fortune in talking to elders during her research in the mid-1930s: "I was just unbelievably lucky in finding such people right at the beginning of the decade, because within five years all of that age group was gone. But I had got the essentials."[46] Again, Marriott's approach adhered to the tenets of cultural relativism made popular by Boas and his students at the turn of the century.

Working with Grandma Biatonma, McElhaney's grandmother, was one of the most memorable experiences for Marriott during her Kiowa research. "I wanted an old lady who could describe the life she had lived when she was growing up in the buffalo-hunting days," Marriott noted decades later.[47] Biatonma was an "easy and willing informant" who was "pleasantly excited" when she discovered that she would be paid to tell Marriott about the stories of the old days.[48] During hot summer days, Marriott, McElhaney, and Biatonma would meet together under the shade of the Hunt family arbor. Biatonma preferred that Marriott suggest a topic, and she would follow it to the end. At times, McElhaney would raise her hand and would translate to Marriott. "I would write down her words, she would lower her hand, and Grandmother would continue from exactly the point where she left off, without, apparently, missing a beat or losing a thread from the train of thought."[49]

In a sketch from *The Ten Grandmothers*, "Hanging the Red Blanket" in the Year of the Power Contest (1881–82), Spear Woman contemplates the changes in Plains life and thinks to herself, "It wasn't so much having the soldiers come that changed things . . . as having the buffalo go."[50] Altering the Plains landscape beyond the point of sustenance was a tragic transition for Kiowa people. Their notions of land use and buffalo hunting worked as long as others did not alter the landscape. When white encroachment invades the land and changes it, the Kiowa people must accommodate the changes and alter their ways. So as Spear Woman says, the departure of the buffalo herds was the painful separation, for much of their culture revolved around buffalo.

Another theme includes the shift from "old ways" to the ways offered by the federal government, missionaries, and reformers. For example, Spear Woman and Hunting Horse marry in the mid-1860s and have a baby. Marriott discusses Spear Woman's toilsome days caring for the baby and maintaining her household, which lead to unhappy times between the couple:

> Spear Woman had cleaned up the breakfast things after she had fed the baby. She had cleaned the tipi and had put the bedding out to air, washed her face again, and was sitting down making her husband a pair of moccasins. Life was strange. Only a short year ago she had been running around like a young girl, going to dances with him and having a good time, and now look at her. The only times she ever sat down were when she was going to make something. She was always busy, and much of what she did turned out like the breakfast in the morning. She did many things at once, and nothing was done right.[51]

Spear Woman asks Hunting Horse to take the baby for a while so she could have some time to herself. He takes the baby to Little Bluff's wife, an adopted sister of his mother. Through a telling exchange, Marriott explains polygamy and the notion of women's labor among the Kiowas. Little Bluff's wife explains: "A woman takes care of herself and her own things. When there are three women, each one just takes care of her things for herself. But a man doesn't take care of anything. The woman has to look for things for him and cook for him and clean up after him, while all he has to do is go hunting."[52] When you have two men, meaning Hunting Horse and his son, she said, you need two women.

Hunting Horse thought this over, the idea of marrying Spear Woman's younger sister, and then discussed it with Spear Woman. He suggested that she would be less lonesome, could share the work with her sister and have more fun. Spear Woman agreed, "Now we have two men, we need two women."[53]

This storyline continues throughout the narrative. In "Allotments" (1900), Marriott discusses the family's encounter with the assimilative process at the turn of the century—missionaries at Rainy Mountain and Saddle Mountain, "taking the Jesus road," education, and the federal government's policy of dividing reservation land into individual allotments in severalty. A missionary asked Hunting Horse if he was ready to follow the Jesus road. He responded that he was following it now. The missionary shook his head and told Hunting Horse that he could not follow the Jesus road with two wives. Hunting Horse needed time to think this over.

In masterful fashion, in the same sketch, Marriott adds a discussion of selecting allotments. It is an insightful section, for it conveys the emotion that goes into such acculturative decisions. Hunting Horse wanted to follow the Jesus road but what about his two wives, Spear Woman and Bow Woman? All three started to cry and through the weight of his tears, Hunting Horse said: "I want to take the Jesus road. That's the only way to go. It's what we know all our lives is right. But it isn't right to hurt somebody, even to take that road. . . . Seems like I'm being pulled in two, two ways at once."[54]

Spear Woman decided to make it "easy" for Hunting Horse and Bow Woman. She told them in a cross tone—Marriott implies that she is sounding cross deliberately to convince herself and convince them—that she would leave the marriage. "I've had all of it I can stand," she hastened. "I was married to you at first, and I've had to stand it longer than my sister has." They would each receive an allotment and select them side by side, ensuring water at the creek and limited fencing. In Marriott's subtle way at the end of the sketch she adds the response to Spear Woman's decision: "They were understanding what she was saying, all right. In another moment they would understand what she wasn't saying, and then the worrying would start all over again. She turned her back on them and walked off, leaving husband and wife alone."[55] Within this short, six-page story, Marriott conveys the powerful forces of the assimilation process at the individual and family level. She indicates how their lives change from the "old ways" of polygamy and the days of following the buffalo, to the Jesus road and allotments.

A team of three women working as respondent, interpreter, and recorder was rare in ethnological work. This scene was reminiscent of anthropologist Ruth Bunzel's earlier work with two Zuni women in 1926. Bunzel recorded seventy-year-old Lina Zuni's life story, while her daughter, Flora Zuni, a thirty-six-year-old woman who spoke English and Zuni, served as interpreter.[56]

And a special sense of women's community was developing during the interview process. Marriott's pleasant demeanor and her interest in Biatonma's stories prompted a special message from Biatonma: "I am a shy woman, and have always been afraid of white people, and especially of white ladies, because they laughed at me and my old clothes. But I know you are honest and do not laugh at me, and I talk to you as if you were my own daughter."[57]

By the end of the second week, Biatonma was just as interested in learning more about Marriott's family and her background as she was in telling Marriott her stories. Biatonma wanted to know if Marriott's parents knew where she was and what she was doing. Marriott assured her that they did. Biatonma wanted to know if Marriott's parents were concerned that she spent so much time with Indians. Biatonma suggested that her parents come to Mountain View to check on their daughter and for a chance for everyone to meet. Marriott contacted her parents and they agreed to come.

What followed was an adoption ceremony under the Hunt family arbor. Biatonma donned her special white buckskin dress and moccasins, parted her hair in the middle and wore it loose down her back rather than in braids, painted red on her cheeks and yellow on her nose and chin, and wore many silver bracelets, rings, and earrings. The entire Hunt family was also present. Marriott introduced her parents to the Hunt family. Then McElhaney interpreted Biatonma's adoption ceremony message to Marriott's parents: "'[Biatonma's] first child was a girl that died. It was in the winter that the smallpox first came to us. That child would be a woman older than my father now. If that girl had children, one of them would have been a daughter, your daughter's age.'"[58] For that reason, McElhaney explained, Biatonma wanted to adopt Marriott as her own granddaughter, "'to replace the child that died and the children who died with her.'"[59] Biatonma requested the permission of Marriott's parents and they nodded.

Marriott's adoption ceremony strengthens her ethnographic authenticity and authority to her reading audience. Although "taking relatives" is common in many American Indian communities, new status as a daughter or granddaughter in a Kiowa family reinforced Marriott's position to non-Indian readers that she had expert knowledge. Luke E. Lassiter maintains that many ethnographers reinforce their association with a tribe according to two relationships: "I'm adopted" or "I've got Indian blood." Both of these statements are used within the context of American Indian studies literature to convey "insider status" to the reader.[60] Marriott often framed her writings according to this device in order to validate her authority and "expert voice" to readers.

In their collaborative work, the relationship that evolved between Marriott and McElhaney was one of mutual fascination, learning, and growth. McElhaney began borrowing Marriott's anthropology texts and started using terms such as "culture-pattern" in their discussions, as ethnographer and interpreter engaged in the fieldwork experience together. Marriott wrote home telling her family about the progress she and McElhaney were making interviewing respondents: "Isleta paid me a high compliment to-day [*sic*]. She said she didn't know which was the more interesting; what the old people have to say, or my questions."[61] Their relationship became one of sisters as the Hunts accepted Marriott into their family.

McElhaney also influenced Marriott. For example, Marriott had been reading ethnographies by Leslie Spier, wrestling with the notion of categorization. She contested some of Spier's categories and decided to create her own. Rather than adhere to categories such as social relations beginning with the tribe and working toward the family unit, Marriott reversed this and started with the family and worked outward. "I didn't realize how living with a sociologist had affected my point of view," Marriott wrote to her family in 1937. "I have started with the family, then friendship and hospitality, THEN the political structure; bands, chiefs, and the tribe as a whole." Marriott broke from anthropological conventions to create her own narrative, her own unfolding of the story. And she attributes this in large part to McElhaney's sociology background. "I think my method is quite logical," Marriott continued, "and a good deal more sensible, since the family is the real basis of all social relations."[62]

In part four, "Modern Times," of *The Ten Grandmothers*, Marriott again illustrates assimilation on a personal, individual level. This time, in "Back to the Blanket" (1928), it involves an educated Kiowa woman, Leah, returning to her home and her people after being away at an eastern boarding school. She intends to teach her people "civilized ways," the ways she learned back East, only to return to many traditional ways that boarding schools had tried to erase. This sketch is drawn from McElhaney's own experiences. Within the sketch, Marriott also explains the complexity of the experience for Leah.

The story begins with Leah traveling west by train in a first-class sleeping car. School administrators sent the students home in style and "people knew you amounted to something." What follows is a description of Leah's "civilized" attire: "Girdle, brassiere, bloomers, slip, blouse, skirt, jacket. Her hair braided, and the braids twisted around her head. A pin at the throat of her blouse, and then her hat and gloves. She looked at herself and pulled her veil down. The outfit really was stylish. Now that you couldn't see the color of her skin, she could pass anywhere for a white girl."[63] In this discussion of civilized ways and dress, Marriott is directing the reader to the subtleties and the overt displays of identity. In this attire, with her hat and veil covering her face and her gloves pulled up covering her hands, Leah's identity as a Kiowa woman was masked.

By extension, as the reader walks through this process, Leah's sense of identity is masked and she longs to recover it: "It was hard coming back to this life. The missionaries made it sound easy. You went away for most of your life and forgot your own language, but you learned lots of other things to take the place of it. Then you went back and taught all the new things to the people at home, and they did better and lived better, like you. There was just one danger that you had to look out for. That was going back to the blanket. If you ever went back to the blanket, you were lost. Then there was no hope for you any more. You would be just Indian all your life."[64]

Her father, stepmother, and sister, Jane, meet Leah at the station with their "ugly" wagon and their sluggish ponies. Leah climbs aboard the wagon and they head for home. She grimaces to herself as she looks in the wagon bed and sees a slab of beef, a sack of flour, and a can of coal-oil alongside her trunks. Seeing the beef "lying out like that with the flies all over it" especially pained her. She had learned at school the importance of cleanliness and the dangers of germs. She must tell her mother about the "proper" handling of meat. And didn't her parents know to keep coal-oil separate from the other items? One of the aims of her eastern education was to return home to educate her people on the domestic arts such as housework, mending, and food preparation.[65]

But on their day-long trip home in the heat and the dust from the red dirt, Leah started to get restless in her fancy clothes and longed for the comfort of a shawl and breathable cotton dress. She spoke more Kiowa to her parents and Jane. And when they stopped for lunch, she was impressed with her mother's deftness at preparing the beef, the fire smelled like perfume, the smoke smelled sweet, but as her eastern training taught her, she was still reluctant to eat the meat.

When they arrived at home after the long journey, Leah stripped off her fancy clothes and borrowed one of Jane's cotton dresses to keep cool in the summer heat. Her sister handed her the dress. "Sure is funny," Jane said. "You go away, learn to be white woman. First thing when you come back, you put on Indian clothes."[66] The missionaries arrived to check on Leah and to make arrangements for her work as interpreter at the church. The white woman missionary was horrified to see Leah wearing a "squaw dress." Jane defended her sister. "She's Indian," Jane said. "She's just educated Indian."[67]

The transition from eastern boarding school to home was far more complicated than Leah had imagined. "She thought she would come home, go to the mission, work to uplift her people. It would all be easy. Then she would marry some good young man, not an Indian, a missionary, and go away and do good all her life. And here was her own sister calling her Indian."[68]

Many themes are wrapped up in this short yet telling story. The most pervasive is Leah's struggle to find balance as a Christian missionary among her own people. The reader participates in Leah's internal struggle to at once reject Kiowa culture and participate in it. She thought she had immersed herself in the Christian ways of boarding school, only to find that many of her Kiowa ways—the cotton work dress, the language, curing beef over an open fire—made sense to her in this place. The story offers a glimpse into the life of an educated Kiowa woman and her personal conflict with her mission to "uplift" her people and, simultaneously, to defend her culture to white missionaries.

Sometimes Marriott's sessions with respondents would last all day, and only at night would she have a few hours alone to type her notes. She generally liked to keep a session limited to four or five hours, so as not to exhaust anyone. But sometimes sessions went longer. During one session, for example, Kiowa George Poolaw of Mountain View, Oklahoma, talked about the Sun Dance for six hours. At the time, Marriott reported: "[Kiowa George] talked for six hours, Isleta going like mad to interpret, and I scribbling notes that I can hardly read and that cover something like thirty pages. I haven't the nerve to count them. At four o'clock I stopped him, and he will begin where he left off tomorrow morning and go on till he comes to the end—I hope!"[69] Marriott called Kiowa George a "gold mine" of knowledge on the Kiowas. "Of course the wonderful thing about this culture," Marriott added in a letter home, "is that people who are old enough to have lived it are still young enough to remember it in detail."[70]

Many Kiowa respondents, particularly the men, had worked with other anthropologists. And most of the anthropologists were men. When a woman anthropologist and a women interpreter were added to the mix, interesting things happened, revealing latent cultural values and customs such as avoidance patterns. For instance, Marriott experienced the "father-in-law taboo" firsthand during her sessions with Henry Tsoodle, Margaret Tsoodle's father-in-law. Henry Tsoodle was a "gentleman of the old school," Marriott described, and he insisted that, according to the avoidance pattern, he could become Isleta McElhaney's father-in-law at any time. Out of respect for Tsoodle and for the custom, McElhaney could not speak to him, they could not look at one another, and she was always careful not to step into his line of vision. This custom affected the interviews however. The three of them reached a solution that would respect the custom and allow sessions to commence:

> Isleta and I sit in the middle of the arbour—at the east
> end—at a table, one on either side. The old man lies at
> the place of honour at the west end. We keep our backs
> turned to him, and he to us. We all keep up the polite
> fiction of the tabu by solemnly addressing the centre-pole
> of the arbour. When anyone comes in who is of a safe
> degree of relationship, we use him as a telephone, but
> when there is no one, the centre-pole does very well.[71]

This anecdote indicates the richness of Marriott's fieldwork and the empathy she brought to her work, not just as a recorder of words and stories, but as a sensitive, inexperienced anthropologist who is respectful of customs. As a family member, and out of respect for the father-in-law avoidance requirements, Marriott complied with these conditions, emulating McElhaney's demeanor with Henry Tsoodle. It also demonstrates how Marriott's role as a woman anthropologist and her added responsibility as a family member both increased and limited her access to information. A male anthropologist, for instance, would not have to adhere to this particular custom. In contrast, during her meetings with women such as Grandma Biatonma and others, Marriott discussed Kiowa women's culture with them and collected stories that may have been denied to men studying the Kiowa people.

A few days later Henry Tsoodle devised a plan to accommodate the avoidance requirements and also relieve some of the awkwardness surrounding their meetings. Tsoodle decided that it would be too odd for him to sit in the arbor and talk in the presence of the two young women, Marriott and McElhaney. Therefore, he insisted on bringing Joanna, his second wife, to these meetings. "She is not permitted to take part in the conversation," Marriott observed in 1936, "a sore trial to Joanna; she loves to talk—she must just bring her work and play propriety. So there we sit and talk to the ridge-pole, while Joanna makes moccasins for the children."[72]

Their initial meetings with Henry Tsoodle had been "ghastly," according to Marriott, because he was reluctant to volunteer any information. Tsoodle was holding back information, but Marriott did not know why. Marriott was almost ready to quit when Tsoodle's son, also called Henry, discussed the situation with his father. Marriott learned that Henry Tsoodle was following the structured interview technique utilized by Alexander Lesser, a prominent anthropologist from Columbia, whereby Lesser and his students would ask specific questions and Henry Tsoodle would answer them and wait for the next question. Marriott's technique was a type of "stream of consciousness" method, as she would later call it, posing a broad, general question and encouraging the respondent to discuss it at great length, often leading to a wide range of topics. This is called a semi-structured interview technique. Henry Tsoodle said that if Marriott just wanted him to talk, he would. They compromised. "He talks, and then I cross-examine," Marriott explained in a letter home. "It works very well, and saves a terrific amount of nervous wear and tear."[73]

In July 1936, Marriott attended a Kiowa dance in Carnegie, Oklahoma. Now, she was not only a guest of the Hunts, but a family member.[74] The dance took place outside under a big brush arbor. Kiowa participants granted permission to Marriott to photograph the dance. In a letter home, she indicated that there were "very few white people there, and no other cameras."[75] Her description of the dance continued:

> Most of the dancers were young boys, but two of the older men and any number of the older women took part. The men—all who danced—wore the most gorgeous costumes I have ever seen. Real, too; heirlooms, most of them. The women, of course, wore the usual Mother Hubbards and shawls. Most of them wore moccasins, but a few had on store shoes—too funny, in the general set-up. There were two drums and eight drummers, and only the old songs were sung. There was a give-away for one of the boys, with first two girl cousins, and then his mother and grandmother dancing behind him. They gave money, pop, and ice-cream cones, and pledged a feast.[76]

In addition, Margaret and George Tsoodle also took Marriott to several peyote meetings. She was grateful for this introduction and the opportunity to participate in a peyote ceremony. "I should not feel that I were qualified to write of the Kiowas unless I had attended at least one," she commented.[77] Based on her fieldwork, Marriott later testified in support of peyote and the Native American Church.

Perhaps the culmination of her fieldwork among the Kiowas came when Uncle Frank allowed Marriott into his tipi—a tipi containing one of the ten grandmothers, or sacred bundles. They entered the tipi and talked for one hour. "We had to leave our hats outside," she described in a letter home, "and sit at the east end, because the place of honour is all filled up with the grandmother, but we got in, and saw not only the wrapping of the god, and the altar, but the pipe that goes with it, and the preparation of the ceremonial tobacco."[78]

Marriott was filled with expectation at the news that McElhaney's uncle wanted to tell her stories of the grandmother gods. McElhaney translated to Marriott, "His grandmother god and his own power have told him to speak, and to speak to you. Once each guardian had a woman to help him; a young woman, of his own family. Now you are a member of our family, and he is getting old. The time has come for him to tell you what you are supposed to know."[79] He instructed them to come back the next day to hear the initial story. It takes all day to tell the story and the telling can only be interrupted once for the noontime meal.[80]

But things went awry the next day as McElhaney's uncle began telling children's stories instead of the promised religious stories. At first, Marriott thought that he needed another interpreter, a non-Christian. It turned out that Tsoodle's father-in-law, another medicine bundle guardian, had heard that McElhaney's uncle would reveal these stories to Marriott, so he called a meeting of all the guardians. The other guardians told him that they would put a fatal curse on him if he revealed those stories to Marriott.[81]

As she concluded her second summer of fieldwork with Kiowa people in 1936, Marriott paused to reflect on the wealth of materials she had collected. With great care she sent her notes back to the University of Oklahoma and her advisor, Forrest Clements. She believed that her field notes were "GOOD" and "worth every cent they are costing."[82] She had talked to Ioleta McElhaney, and they both agreed that the first summer's work provided a "solid and lasting foundation," but the second summer's work proved invaluable to her project, creating something, Marriott assessed, "better than I ever dreamed it could be."[83]

She intended for her story to be told as some Kiowas would tell it, and she explains this intention in a letter to her parents regarding her decision to send her future manuscript to the University of Oklahoma Press: "If I have anything to say about it, it will go as it is, literally transcribed, without any English to come between the real life and the reader."[84] This method was a recent trend, appearing first in Spier's *Yuman Tribes of the Gila River* (1933) and then in Ruth Underhill's *Autobiography of a Papago Woman* (1936). Marriott was influenced by these two texts and referred to the latter as her Bible.[85] In addition to literal translation methods, Marriott also altered traditional organization to her own style, emanating from the family to the larger community.

Although Marriott included her consultants in her texts, often giving the impression that they were speaking in the first person, she still arranged and edited the material into a book marketable to a primarily white general readership. She wrote the text in a "brief, Kiowa manner," as one reviewer noted, and reaffirmed her claims that she was merely the recorder of stories that were told to her. "Each sketch may be taken as an eye-witness account of the event related," she maintains in the preface, "and where the feelings of a person are described, it is only because he himself said that he felt that way that the feeling is put down. I have tried to tell these stories as much as possible as they were told to me."[86] Marriott and other anthropologists during the 1930s and 1940s may have claimed they were merely recorders of American Indian stories or autobiography; however, the final draft of the manuscript was often reshaped or modified by anthropologists to conform to their objectives.

Kiowa consultants often discuss anthropological texts by noting which Kiowas worked with the anthropologist. "They do not," Lassiter states, "talk about Maurice Boyd's *Kiowa Voices* (1981, 1983) or Alice Marriott's *Ten Grandmothers* (1945), for example, as a definitive representation of Kiowa culture. Instead, they explicitly point out that these books reflect the opinions and viewpoints of the particular Kiowa people who worked with the authors of those books."[87] In Marriott's case, she specifically worked with the Hunt family, and this family could not speak for all Kiowas and thus would not be representative of "Kiowa culture." Instead, *Ten Grandmothers* offers a family's account of their lives and connects their stories to the larger tribal experience from the times of the buffalo to World War II.

The Ten Grandmothers received praise from those close to Marriott. Her advisor, Forrest Clements, at the University of Oklahoma was one of the readers of the manuscript for the University of Oklahoma Press. Clements was quite pleased with Marriott's "brain child" and was particularly complimentary of the book's organization. "I think [the book's organization]," Clements wrote to Marriott, "gives the book a vitality which would have been absent had you followed the orthodox ethnographic report style and this method is particularly effective when dealing with a culture which is cracking up."[88] Clement's "cracking up" comment follows the lines of "salvage ethnography" and also indicates that he did not spend much time with Indian people. After reading *The Ten Grandmothers*, Ioleta Hunt McElhaney's husband, Louis, commended Marriott for "writing a book about Indians which is, so far as I can tell, utterly devoid of prejudice, and which reveals a genuine desire on your part to get at the simple truth." He admitted that he expected to read a "coldly-analytical, test-tube treatment" of the Kiowa people and was surprised that the book read like a novel.[89]

Some professional reviews were less favorable, as expected since she deliberately broke from scholarly conventions. For example, Ernest Wallace, a specialist in Southern Plains studies, commented that the "scholarly reader may be disappointed that the author has not cited her authorities as the story progresses, and consequently may wonder at times if there is any departure from fact to fiction."[90] Wallace's claim is valid, for Marriott did not document her sources. In addition, Marriott's writing style is fluid and fiction-like, which could cause people like Wallace to question the book's accuracy. Marriott assures the reader in the preface, however, that Kiowa respondents have told the stories to her and they have not been embellished. And Wallace concludes, "after a careful study and analysis of the work," that Marriott did present an accurate depiction of Kiowa life.[91] To Marriott's credit, she contended that the book was intended to appeal to a general readership, not necessarily a scholarly one. On the other hand, Angie Debo, who also targeted a broad audience for her books, sent Marriott a note of praise, stating that for her, *The Ten Grandmothers* was a "once in a blue moon" kind of book. "I have no words to tell you how much I enjoyed it. I read it slowly savoring every word to make it last longer," Debo wrote.[92]

Clark Wissler of the American Museum of Natural History in New York City found the book's greatest strength in the autobiographical narratives of Kiowa people. He applauded Marriott's effort to accept her respondents' interpretations of events "as realities in the sense that they express the reactions of the individuals concerned as they remembered them."[93] He concluded that the reader must evaluate the accuracy of Marriott's fieldwork experience, the ethnographic process, and the important role of the interpreter, for, he maintained, the book's integrity "hinges upon the fidelity which these autobiographies are rendered in English."[94]

Twenty years later, in the early 1950s, Marriott returned to Kiowa country at McElhaney's invitation to spend the week of Indian Fair with her family. McElhaney, quoted by Marriott in *Greener Fields*, comments on her reconciliation of Christian faith with the "old ways":

> I believe in all the articles of the Christian faith, as you say. But *still* I wouldn't like to offend the old gods. They were here first. People walked this earth believing in them for centuries. Belief is power. Some of it could be left behind. I don't believe in the old gods as living gods, no. But I wouldn't like to insult them. I wouldn't be afraid my children would die, or anything like that—nor my parents, if they were living—but I wouldn't want to break the old rules.[95]

A young Kiowa man decided to put on the Sun Dance at the Indian Fair, a dance that apparently had not been performed since 1892, the year the dance was performed at the Chicago World's Fair. The Sun Dance arbor is a circular arbor and should not be erected. McElhaney explains why:

> In the old days the Sun Dance was a healing rite, as well as one to bring food. If it were done properly, you made a vow that if someone in your family, very near to you, recovered from a sickness or returned from a war raid you would give the dance. And if the vow were fulfilled, you and your friends danced and fasted from food and water during four days and nights. Then you and your family and the whole tribe could look forward to a year of health and happiness and prosperity. But if anything went wrong—if there were any tiny slip in the dancing or

if your vow were not sincere—if anyone ate or drank and continued to dance—there would be a curse on everybody. Some person you loved would die, and the whole tribe would have a year of misfortune.[96]

The link here is that a week later, the father of the Sun Dance organizer died of pneumonia, having contracted it the night of the storm—the night the Sun Dance was supposed to be held. The Sun Dance organizer got the description of the Sun Dance from Marriott's book. He said that if the dance and the sacred ceremonies had been described to a white woman and she wrote it down, "then it must be dead, and perfectly safe for anyone to do."[97] But Marriott and McElhaney maintained that they did not record the secret ceremonies nor the Sun Dance legend. "Women didn't know those things," they stated, "and we didn't claim to."[98] McElhaney even referred to Marriott's text again, just to be sure that they had not revealed these things. McElhaney said, "You described just exactly what anyone walking around in the camp during the four days of the Sun Dance could have seen. Only, you described it so clearly, anyone who read the book would think you knew a lot you hadn't put down."[99]

Factions within the Kiowa community, Christian missionaries and those following the Jesus road versus practicing peyotists and powwow people, are no longer applicable, according to Lassiter. By the 1930s and 1940s what had once looked like remnants of the "old ways" were no longer viewed as hindrances to assimilation. Many Kiowas attend church services on Sunday morning and participate in powwows in the afternoon. "Contemporary divisions between activities like hand games, powwows, and churches," Lassiter finds, "have more to do with revolving and changing interests, choice, belief, and family background than with overt factionalism."[100] Although some Christian fundamentalists condemn these activities, Lassiter points out, other Christian congregationalists do not and instead opt for finding a middle ground.[101]

Marriott explains her relationship with Kiowa people in *Greener Fields*:

> The acid test of an ethnographer's relations with a tribe
> he has studied is whether or not he can go back. It has
> always been a matter of intense pride to me that I could
> return at will to the group of Indians whom I first stud-
> ied, and could come and go among them, at once an
> honored guest and a member of the family. This was true
> even after I had published two books on the tribe, a time
> when, if ever, I should have been cast with scoffing into
> outer darkness.[102]

In 1983, Marriott was an honored speaker at the dedication of
the Kiowa Cultural Center in Anadarko, where her fieldwork had
begun more than five decades earlier. The Kiowas were dedicating
the center to the "old people who were dead but not forgotten,"
Marriott explained.[103] In her dedication speech, she discussed her
initial work with the Kiowas:

> Perhaps they took pity on me and my open ignorance.
> I'm afraid I had no pity on them. I wanted to learn, learn,
> learn, whatever they were willing to teach me. I grabbed
> at every fragment of knowledge, and it all went into the
> scuffed stenographers note books in which I recorded
> everything. It is all still there, although most of it has
> been bound in books by this time, so that other people
> may know about the Kiowas.[104]

She again reminded her audience that the Kiowa Cultural Center
would encourage future generations of Kiowas to "learn what the
old people tried to teach, and wanted to have known."[105] She
viewed her presence in the Kiowa community as a collaborator, as
one who was always welcome to return and participate in community events. And this collaboration also adds to her authenticity as an anthropologist who could claim "insider" status.

✥❦❧ Chapter Eight ❧❦✥

The Tradition of
Women Public Intellectuals
in the American West

Women's presence in the American West has been coterminous with men's, but the professional writings of men have muted or overshadowed much of the professional writing of women. Matilda Coxe Stevenson traveled with her husband to Zuni in 1879 as a member of the first research expedition of the Bureau of American Ethnology. Scholars have called Stevenson the first woman ethnographer of the Southwest because of her collection of information on women for the bureau.[1] Despite this recognition, much of Stevenson's research appeared under her husband's name and therefore represents the submersion of women's presence in the fields of anthropology, ethnology, and western history. This is only one of many examples of women's presence as researchers, observers, and interpreters of the West overshadowed and rendered invisible by men's observations.

In the late nineteenth and early twentieth centuries, many women were studying American Indian cultures in the Southwest. Their work was part of a long reform tradition in the United States, dating back to pre–Civil War reforms such as abolition, which then served as a springboard for women to take up the cause of American Indian reform.[2] Lydia Maria Child, better known for her abolitionist novels, wrote her first novel, *Hobomok*, an American Indian novel, in 1824. Helen Hunt Jackson's *A Century of Dishonor* (1881) stirred national awareness on the need to reform federal Indian policy and bureaucracy, and helped to encourage passage of the Dawes Act, although this was not necessarily her intention. Passed in 1887, the Dawes Act called for the end of tribal landownership in exchange for individual allotments in severalty. Jackson was not necessarily a proponent of acculturation, but as Shirley A. Leckie maintains, "by publicizing the plight of Indians, Jackson's work helped Eastern humanitarians achieve passage of assimilationist policies."[3] Siobhan Senier adds complexity to the notion of assimilation by teasing out evidence of resistance within women's texts.

In *Voices of American Indian Assimilation and Resistance*, Senier traces the assimilation period of American Indian history from 1879 to 1934 through women's written and oral narratives. By offering a textual analysis of the works of novelist and reformer Helen Hunt Jackson, Paiute writer Sarah Winnemucca, and Clackamas Chinook informant Victoria Howard, Senier challenges the prevailing assimilationist discourse of the era in a more nuanced reading of these texts. Jackson and Winnemucca are often read as pro-assimilationist texts, although Senier disputes this reading. Although not Indian herself, Jackson was a self-identified voice for Indian people. In her reading of Jackson's *Ramona* (1884), a sympathetic account of California mission Indians, Senier finds a narrative supporting tribal sovereignty rather than assimilation. Jackson died in 1885, two years before the passage of the Dawes (General Allotment) Act, and Senier questions whether Jackson would have approved of such a policy and its devastating results. In Jackson's texts Senier finds "one of the very few recorded places where we can recognize the slightest resistance to or skepticism about the assumptions underlying the policy of allotment and assimilation."[4]

Winnemucca was a Paiute woman from Nevada who was educated in what Senier calls "white schools." She wrote what some consider the first Indian woman's autobiography, *Life Among the Paiutes* (1883). In the case of Winnemucca's self-representation, Senier portrays a Paiute woman maintaining her cultural identity while engaging in a complicated discourse with white audiences over what it means to be Paiute. As a child, Winnemucca traveled with her parents throughout California and Nevada performing the Pocahontas story. Then as a young adult she worked as an interpreter for the U.S. Army and negotiated Indian-white disputes. While other scholars have read Winnemucca as a cultural mediator and perhaps even a proponent of assimilation policy, Senier concedes that Winnemucca was a mediator but argues that she privileged cultural traditionalism over accommodation.

Senier's examination of Victoria Howard makes a significant contribution to the study of American Indian women's narratives. Howard lived on the Grand Ronde reservation in northwest Oregon. An informant for linguist Melville Jacobs in 1929–30, Howard's work demonstrates "the endurance of indigenous traditions while juggling her readers/listeners out of hierarchical positions into more, mutual and examined relationships."[5] Their collaboration resulted in Jacobs's *Clackamas Chinook Texts* in the late 1950s. Jacobs included Chinook and English versions of Howard's stories on the same page, which encourages the reader to engage in the production of the text. Again, Senier finds resistance in Howard's storytelling, which include allusions to sacred practices without further detail or abbreviated versions of a particular story or even self-concealment. In reading Howard alongside Jackson and Winnemucca, Senier demonstrates quite effectively the new ways scholars can utilize American Indian women's voices and oral tradition in the larger literature of textual resistance.

Such examples represent the many Indian and non-Indian women who participated in the tradition of American Indian reform. Alice Fletcher, as another example, supported the allotment policy alongside her ethnological pursuits. In the early 1880s, the commissioner of Indian Affairs appointed Fletcher as a special agent to the Omahas in Nebraska to survey and assign allotments. Her work continued with the allotment of the Winnebagos in Nebraska and the Nez Perce in Idaho in the late 1880s and early 1890s.[6] By the end of the nineteenth century, leaders of Indian reform organizations were often women. The Women's National Indian Association, for instance, which later became the National Indian Association, played an important advocacy role for Indian welfare in the early twentieth century.[7]

Recent studies situate white women's narratives of the American West as carriers of cultural assumptions and hegemonic power. In her survey of nineteenth- and twentieth-century women's writings on the American West, Brigitte Georgi-Findlay finds that "white women's western narratives do assume a role in the affirmation of cultural power and, in fact, establish materialist versions of an American West."[8] She interprets white women as agents of territorial expansion. Georgi-Findlay finds that women's accounts add complexity to the literature of westward expansion, empire building, and colonization, for women's texts at once participate in and reject the national narrative.

Although Georgi-Findlay had assumed she would find women's texts to be more "detached and critical" than the predominantly male national narrative, in fact she finds that "white women emerge as authors and agents of territorial expansion, positioned ambiguously within systems of power and authority."[9] Georgi-Findlay also finds commonalities among women's western texts. Most of the texts she considers describe the American West as an "extremely insecure terrain" where westward expansion maintains a tenuous position at best. Finally, these writers tend to link nature in the West with the Native American presence on the land. They do not see a pristine nature devoid of humans; rather they connect western nature with the Native Americans' connection to the land.[10]

Early women anthropologists and historians who studied American Indian communities in the Southwest were part of this larger tradition of writing about westward expansion and Indian reform. Whether as wives who assisted their ethnologist husbands in collecting data on American Indian women and children or as single women who perhaps discovered fewer gender limitations in the West than in the East, many women converged in the Southwest and explored their fascination with what they considered "primitive." Primitivism "is a source of authority," according to Leah Dilworth, "because the primitive is imagined as a state somehow previous to modernity and therefore more real, more authentic."[11] Women anthropologists and historians joined other writers, artists, and tourists in this search for the "primitive" and "authentic" among Native peoples in the Southwest.

Anthropology has been called the "welcoming science" for women, and women's community was stronger among anthropologists than historians.[12] Historian Frederick Jackson Turner and anthropologist Franz Boas trained women scholars for future work in the American West. Women ethnographers Matilda Coxe Stevenson and Elsie Clews Parsons provided the much-needed financial assistance to women anthropologists for field research in the Southwest, thus facilitating a women's community of anthropologists. Stevenson founded the Women's Anthropological Society to encourage and assist women in the field. Parsons also established an organization, the Southwest Society, which financed the fieldwork of both women and men anthropologists over three decades.[13] Turner, on the other hand, trained as many as eight women Ph.D.'s, including Louise Phelps Kellogg during the late 1890s, but the notion of a women's community within the historical profession was lacking during the early decades of the twentieth century.[14]

With the increasing participation of women in higher education beginning in the late nineteenth century, more women entered the professions of history and anthropology, but gender discrimination persisted in both disciplines. Many women scholars did not attain tenure-track university positions. As Barbara Babcock and Nancy Parezo indicate, "despite the quality of work they did, few women had 'official' academic positions, many of them spending their lives in museums, which work anthropologist Clark Wissler saw as fitting for women since it resembled housekeeping."[15] University employment tended to be a haven for men, with women's career paths destined for women's colleges, government, historical societies, museums, and freelance writing.

As a public historian, Muriel Wright worked as an institution-builder at the Oklahoma Historical Society, preserving both American Indian history and settler history through her active historical preservation program and role as editor of the *Chronicles of Oklahoma*. The *Chronicles of Oklahoma* served as Wright's vehicle through which to promote her interpretation of Oklahoma history, an interpretation emphasizing the positive aspects of state history and American Indian people's contributions and participation in it. Other women such as Ella Cara Deloria, Grace Raymond Hebard, Louise Phelps Kellogg, and Mari Sandoz also worked as public historians, protecting state and local history for future generations as leaders in their state historical societies.

Deloria (1899–1971), Yankton Dakota, grew up on Standing Rock reservation in South Dakota.[16] Her father had converted to Christianity and became an Episcopal priest. Educated in mission boarding schools in her youth, Deloria attended Oberlin College in 1911. She transferred to the teachers' college at Columbia University, took courses from Franz Boas, and completed her degree in 1915. She taught for a number of years at Haskell Institute, a Bureau of Indian Affairs school in Kansas.[17] Surveys of Deloria's life and writings do not indicate that she received advanced graduate degrees in anthropology, yet training with Boas and Ruth Benedict at Columbia, coupled with fieldwork, qualify her as an anthropologist, just as Alice Marriott's fieldwork qualified her.[18]

Ella Deloria was a cultural mediator, according to anthropologist Beatrice Medicine, who "stood within and outside her own culture."[19] A member of her Native community, Deloria deftly negotiated her role as a Native anthropologist and observer of her community. Deloria also assumed a rather precarious position in her relationship with Boas. She struggled to balance her identity as an anthropologist in her own right with her utility to Boas as a collaborator. The difficulty of Deloria's position becomes clear in a letter to Boas: "To go at it like a white man, for me, an Indian, is to throw up an immediate barrier between myself and my people."[20]

Deloria used her position as a Native anthropologist to educate the predominantly white general public. She viewed her "mission" in the following way: "To make the Dakota people understandable, as human beings, to the white people who have to deal with them."[21] As one example, Deloria wrote *Speaking of Indians* (1944) primarily for a white audience, according to Medicine.[22] In the text, Deloria displays her Christian beliefs, but she also discusses traditional Dakota spirituality, as seen in her discussion of the Sun Dance.[23] As Janet L. Finn argues, the intention of women like Deloria was "to write for cross-cultural understanding by writing against the grain of dominant representations of Native Americans."[24]

After resigning from Haskell, Deloria supported herself through part-time museum employment, small research grants, lecturing, and consulting work, as many women anthropologists and historians did during the first half of the twentieth century. She conducted interviews with elders at Standing Rock, Pine Ridge, and Rosebud reservations on Siouan language and culture. Her fieldwork resulted in *Dakota Texts* (1932), a collection of folk tales and legends, and *Dakota Grammar* (1941), which she co-authored with Boas.[25] The work was arduous, the pay was low, and recognition was not always forthcoming. Her novel, *Waterlily*, for example, the story of a young Dakota woman's experiences on the plains in the late nineteenth century, was completed in 1944, but not published until 1988.[26]

In a second example, Rachel Caroline Eaton (1869–1938), a Cherokee born in Indian Territory, graduated from the Cherokee Female Seminary in Tahlequah in 1887. She returned to Cherokee Nation to teach in the public schools and at the Cherokee Female Seminary before attending graduate school in history. She received her M.A. in 1911 and her Ph.D. in 1919 from the University of Chicago.[27] Unlike Angie Debo, who had also attended Chicago for her master's degree in the early 1920s, Eaton had no difficulty securing employment at the college and university levels. She was head of the history department at State College for Women in Columbus, Missouri; professor of history at Lake Erie College in Painesville, Ohio; dean of women and head of the history department at Trinity

University in Waxahachie, Texas; and superintendent of schools in Rogers County, Oklahoma. The majority of her publications focused on Cherokee and Oklahoma history. She is best known for *John Ross and the Cherokee Indians* (1910), her revised dissertation. Muriel Wright called Eaton the "first [Oklahoma] woman of Indian descent to achieve distinction as an educator and writer of history."[28]

As we examine the life of Muriel Wright and her efforts to promote and shape her narrative of Oklahoma history as a blending of American Indian and settler history, we can look one generation prior to Wright at an earlier advocate of state history, Grace Raymond Hebard (1861–1936). Hebard wrote "highly romanticized" books depicting Wyoming history that appealed to a statewide readership.[29] For example, *The History and Government of Wyoming* (1904) sustained eleven editions. Other works include *The Bozeman Trail* (1922) and *Sacajawea* (1933). Her career path as a civil engineer brought her to Wyoming, where she worked as a draftsman in the land office of the U.S. Surveyor General at Cheyenne in the 1880s. During this time, Hebard also actively campaigned for women's suffrage and was on the committee of three women that petitioned for women's suffrage in Wyoming in 1889. Two years later, she served as secretary and trustee for the board of trustees at the University of Wyoming. She taught courses in political economy, history, library science, and a variety of other courses, and served as department head of political economy until her retirement in 1931. Simultaneously, Hebard worked as the university librarian, and with this title she launched a campaign to collect materials relating to the history of Wyoming and the American West. Finally, Hebard was the first woman admitted to the Wyoming bar in 1898.[30] As Virginia Scharff argues, an evaluation of Hebard as a "good historian" is not the point. Undoubtedly Hebard romanticized her accounts, but she took a sincere interest in preserving the history of her state and shared this information with the public.[31] "When Grace Hebard wrote and spoke and marked Wyoming places in the name of history," Scharff explains, "she did so in an effort to engrave on the page and in real space the name of the American nation, and the values she believed it represented, including the cause of liberty for women."[32] Hebard exemplifies this tradition of "hidden scholars" throughout the American West, namely educated white women who enjoyed the western landscape and the opportunities to forge new careers in a region that seemed more accepting of those who stretched the boundaries of gender expectations than the more rigid East.

Grace Raymond Hebard represents countless women who preserved their state and local histories at the turn of the century. Hebard's varied careers and experiences represent many unmarried and mobile women who settled in the West during the early twentieth century. She took great interest in her genealogy, similar in many ways to Muriel Wright's interest in her family lineage. Both women were powerful forces in their state's efforts to preserve and promote state history. Both, in fact, worked tirelessly in historic preservation programs, ascribing meaning to historic sites and in turn interpreting their state histories. In Wyoming, Hebard researched and marked such sites as the Oregon Trail and Fort Laramie. In Oklahoma, Wright marked and wrote the text for more than five hundred historic markers. In both cases, these women were interested in marking and celebrating their state histories in the larger context of the national narrative.

Like Wright and Hebard, other women created careers for themselves in state historical societies. Frederick Jackson Turner described Louise Phelps Kellogg (1862–1942) as one of his most important students, yet her career remained in the State Historical Society of Wisconsin rather than academia. According to Dwight L. Smith, Kellogg was the mainstay in the development of the state's historical society and its journal. Her greatest disappointment, however, was that she never received an academic appointment at the University of Wisconsin.[33] If Kellogg was indeed one of Turner's most promising students, why were opportunities at Wisconsin or elsewhere denied to her? It would appear that gender played a role in this decision.

At Wisconsin, Kellogg received competitive graduate scholarships and worked as Turner's assistant. She received her Ph.D. in 1901. The American Historical Association published her dissertation, "The American Colonial Charter: A Study of English Administration in Relation Thereto, Chiefly After 1688," and awarded it the Justin Winsor Prize.[34] Upon graduation, Kellogg received a research post in the State Historical Society of Wisconsin. She served an important role at the historical society as so many other women did during this period. Kellogg, along with Grace Raymond Hebard and Muriel Wright, are only three examples of such women who collected, catalogued, and preserved state history. In addition to her interest in local history, Kellogg participated in national historical organizations. She became the first woman president of the Mississippi Valley Historical Association, now the Organization of American Historians, in 1930.

In another example, Mari Sandoz (1896–1966) worked as a researcher at the Nebraska State Historical Society during the 1930s and 1940s. This was a common avenue of employment for women who shared an interest in historical research and writing. Prior to her work at the historical society, beginning in 1922, Sandoz enrolled as a special adult student in creative writing at the University of Nebraska after several years teaching in rural schools and a failed marriage. In addition to research, she taught creative writing courses at the University of Colorado, Indiana University, and the University of Wisconsin.[35]

Again, the deep regional connection is evident in Sandoz's novels and illustrates her ties to the landscape of the Great Plains. Sandoz grew up on a farm in Nebraska, the eldest of six children. Like Angie Debo, Sandoz's upbringing was filled with the emotional joys of pioneering as well as the accompanying hardships. Sandoz's temperamental father, as described in *Old Jules* (1935), brought instability and abuse into their home, and Sandoz makes it clear that domestic violence against women was commonplace in frontier communities.[36]

Describing the regional setting was important to Sandoz, and the Great Plains remained the backdrop for most of her novels and nonfiction. During the research for *Crazy Horse* (1942), for instance, Sandoz visited Pine Ridge and Rosebud reservations and the battle sites to visualize the historical setting.[37] Similarly, Sandoz spent five weeks on the Northern Cheyenne reservation in Montana during her work on *Cheyenne Autumn* (1953).[38] When

Sandoz described the U.S. Army's effort to "tame" the American West and Native peoples from the 1860s to the 1880s, she tended to position herself on the Indians' side of the story and depicted U.S. military leaders as callous and inhumane. Although her works have enjoyed popularity among general readers, critics point to fictional embellishment in her nonfiction and the absence of documentation. Her literary success was not immediate. More than twelve publishers rejected *Old Jules*, for example, before Little, Brown accepted it in 1935.[39]

Many women from the 1920s to the 1940s wrote popular histories of the American West, particularly on American Indian topics, intended to appeal to the general public. Freelance writers such as Alice Marriott, Mari Sandoz, Angie Debo, and Eve Ball (1890–1984) were compelled out of financial necessity to attract a loyal public who would purchase their books. Most of the women writers surveyed here remained single throughout their lives, and those who married quite often divorced. In many cases, popular writers did not have the professional credentials that came with advanced graduate training in history or anthropology. Nonetheless, these histories contributed to the representations of American Indians during the early twentieth century.

As a public intellectual, Debo was part of this tradition. Her books from the 1930s and early 1940s, including *The Rise and Fall of the Choctaw Republic* and *And Still the Waters Run*, demonstrate Debo's role as a precursor of ethnohistory. Not only were her books readable and popular, but they also incorporated Debo's deliberate "Indian-centered" perspective. Many of the women under review here had a literary background that enhanced their popular appeal. Alice Marriott and Ruth Underhill, for instance, both received undergraduate degrees in English and English literature. Critics often discounted their texts as "too literary" and therefore unscholarly. In addition, both Marriott and Underhill made connections between Indian women and non-Indian women that made their works popular with a nonacademic audience.

Eve Ball took a different approach in her writings, utilizing oral history to present American Indian perspectives. She wrote six books and more than one hundred articles on frontier and Indian research in the Southwest for *True West* and *Frontier Times*, popular periodicals on the American West. Ball recognized the importance of oral history long before it became widely used by professional historians. She began interviewing the Mescalero and Chiricahua Apaches living on the Mescalero Apache reservation near her home in Ruidoso, New Mexico, in the 1930s and 1940s.[40] Prior to living in Ruidoso, Ball was a teacher, receiving her M.A. in education in 1934 at Kansas State University. She had always been intrigued by the Southwest and moved to New Mexico after a career in elementary and secondary education.

The process by which Ball first became acquainted with her Apache neighbors is telling. Apache women would pass Ball's home on their way into town and ask for water. Soon Ball provided lemonade and cookies for her guests along with a comfortable place to sit in the shade. Ball's hospitable reputation spread throughout the reservation, and as she gained the trust of her neighbors, she shared with them her desire to preserve Apache history through oral history interviews.[41] *Indeh, An Apache Odyssey* (1980) is a compilation of Ball's interviews with sixty-seven Apaches from the Mescalero Indian reservation. As Ball states in the preface, "this is not an attempt to write a definitive history— many people and events aren't known by informants—lost forever—nobody was sufficiently interested in securing it while there were living participants and witnesses to relate their experiences."[42] It took Ball several decades to get her books published, due to the reluctance of presses and academics to accept the inherent value of oral history. Only in recent decades has oral history become a more acceptable methodology. Ball's interviews with the nephews of Geronimo and Victorio inspired her to tell Apache history from *"their side of the fence."*[43] Prior to her work, most of the research on Apaches had been written from a non-Apache perspective.

Angie Debo had corresponded with Ball while researching and writing *Geronimo*. Ball provided helpful guidance and research materials to Debo. In fact, there are parallels between the two writers. Both writers positioned themselves as writers of "truth" and told their narratives, they claimed, from an Indian perspective.

Such dedication to the idea of an Indian perspective or voice emerges as a central theme in a comparative study of women writers who studied American Indians in the American West. If the writers were to speak to one another today, they would no doubt debate the issue of Indian voice. The majority of these writers are non-Indian, yet they claim to be writing from an Indian perspective. Others use ethnohistorical methods as a way of interpreting available evidence from a so-called Indian point of view. American Indian scholars in this survey, Muriel Wright, Ella Deloria, and Rachel Caroline Eaton, are members of the communities they study, so would they tell a more accurate account or portray a "purer" Indian perspective or speak more authoritatively with their Native voices?

Women writers including Angie Debo, Alice Marriott, Ruth Underhill, Eve Ball, and Mari Sandoz all claimed to be writing from an Indian perspective or voice. At the same time, American Indian writers such as Muriel Wright, Ella Deloria, and Rachel Caroline Eaton did not make such claims. They did, however, indicate that they often wrote about their cultures to educate the broader public and thus made claims for authenticity that resemble others' claims for the adoption of Indian voice. Recent studies from Devon A. Mihesuah and Craig S. Womack discuss the challenges and complications with making claims to an "Indian perspective" or a "Native voice." As Mihesuah reminds us, Native communities and individuals are varied, divergent, and complex—there is no monolithic "Indian voice," but there are a multiplicity of voices, and those who write about American Indian history must incorporate Native sources in their research.[44]

Women writers, specifically as historians and anthropologists, carved a niche for themselves as interpreters of the American West and its American Indian population. Many of them positioned their interpretations from an Indian perspective or claimed to represent Indian voices. From Muriel Wright's positive interpretation of western settlement as a blending of American Indian and pioneer history to the oral history approach of Eve Ball and Angie Debo to the more literary styles of Mari Sandoz, Ruth Underhill, and Alice Marriott, these varying perspectives represent the complexity of women as interpreters of the West. They, above all, shared the common desire to write about American Indian communities principally for a non-Native readership. For these women historians and anthropologists, writing was their own instrument, their own voice. Writing was their tool of communication, as a way of presenting their observations and allowing the reader to get a glimpse of their own lives in the process.

✢❧ *Conclusion* ❧✢

I n the early 1990s, anthropologist Nancy J. Parezo identified the thousands of women who were actively studying and writing about American Indian communities in the Southwest as "hidden scholars," largely unknown researchers in the field from the late nineteenth century to the mid-twentieth century. Building on this compelling notion of "hidden scholars," this study represents the first attempt to make connections between Muriel Wright, Angie Debo, and Alice Marriott as women scholars of Oklahoma's American Indian history; it is a conscious effort to reclaim these "hidden scholars," to rediscover them and contextualize them as part of the larger literature of western regionalism and identity.

The work of Parezo, Devon A. Mihesuah, Virginia Scharff, Joan Jensen, Shirley Leckie, Barbara Babcock, and others reconsiders the presence of women interpreters in the American West. In *One Foot on the Rockies*, Jensen discusses the tradition of women's creativity in such diverse fields as art, poetry, history, and anthropology in the modern American West. In a chapter entitled "With These Words: Silences/Voices," Jensen explores the academic literary tradition among western women. From the storytelling tradition of western Indian women to women anthropologists who entered the field with ambitions of preserving Indian culture, women addressed personal and professional concerns in their writings. This study takes Parezo's notion of "hidden scholars" and Jensen's examination of the "anthropological literary tradition" as its inspiration, and seeks to include both women anthropologists and women historians of Oklahoma as part of this larger tradition of women's intellectual history in the American West.[1]

Wright, Debo, and Marriott were born around the turn of the century and initiated their careers during the Depression years of the 1930s. They experienced life on different "frontiers" as children. Debo and Marriott grew up in Oklahoma Territory and each recalled not having much interaction with American Indian people. On the other hand, Wright grew up in Choctaw Nation, Indian Territory. After 1907, when Oklahoma achieved statehood by combining Oklahoma Territory and Indian Territory, all three women spent their adolescent years and early twenties experiencing the opportunities as well as the limitations the new state provided. By the 1930s, all three were actively engaged in exploring Indian reform issues in Oklahoma. The primary issue was tribal landownership and assimilationist policies. John Collier, Commissioner of Indian Affairs, introduced the Indian Reorganization Act, or the "Indian New Deal," an attempt to alter the course of 150 years of assimilationist policies by the federal government codified under the Dawes Act of 1887. Called the Indian Reorganization Act of 1934 (IRA), Collier and others ended the allotment policy under Dawes and attempted to restore tribal landownership in order to encourage the revitalization of traditional cultural practices.

Wright, Debo, and Marriott disagreed on the new policies. Both Marriott and Debo supported Collier's "Indian New Deal" because of their personal experiences and perspectives. Marriott soon took a position as a field representative for the Indian Arts and Crafts Board, and the board itself was created under Collier's program. Debo worked on the manuscript for *And Still the Waters Run* amid these national changes in Indian reform and with similar assumptions about the disastrous consequences of Dawes's policy. Wright, on the other hand, represented one of many Five Tribes people who had benefited from allotment and the program of "Americanization" or assimilation and considered a return to tribal landownership a step backward. Resistance to the Indian New Deal was so strong among Five Tribes people of Oklahoma that initially the IRA did not even include them. Two years later, when

Congress did include Oklahoma Indians under this legislation, most ignored it. In fact, of the 103,000 Oklahoma Indians eligible to organize under the IRA, 90,000 did not, and they were primarily Five Tribes people.[2]

The commonality Wright, Debo, and Marriott shared, however, was their desire to join the ranks of women anthropologists and historians who studied American Indians in the American West. Academic jobs for women in history and anthropology were scarce in the 1930s and 1940s. Women's opportunities often remained limited to women's colleges and to those professions traditionally regarded as "feminine": nursing, education, and social work. Ruth Behar describes two types of nontraditional women scholars, or those seemingly on the periphery of the academy. Many of these professionals did not hold academic positions, but influenced historical and anthropological interpretations as staff members of museums and historical societies. Wright's work within the Oklahoma Historical Society, as editor of the *Chronicles of Oklahoma* and as an active member of the historic preservation program fits the first type. Others survived without a regular paycheck, but sought part-time employment and grants to sustain their research. Marriott and Debo are examples of the second type. Debo's career, however, meandered in and out of academic employment. She taught at the college level in Texas in the late 1920s and early 1930s, but left her teaching position by the mid-1930s to return to her parents' home in Marshall, Oklahoma, to pursue her histories of American Indian people without distraction. In the 1950s, Debo returned to university employment as a librarian and researcher at Oklahoma State University. Behar acknowledges that more often than not, scholars like Debo did not attain permanent positions in academia and therefore could not train graduate students. These women, Behar writes, "had only their writing by which to stand or fall."[3] Their writings form the common thread that connects this study of Marriott, Wright, and Debo. Throughout their careers, although Debo and Marriott did not have the prestige of academic backing or support—Wright on the other hand was attached to the Oklahoma Historical Society for over fifty years—their texts defined them, providing tangible evidence of their scholarly work.

CONCLUSION

Muriel Wright, Angie Debo, and Alice Marriott took three different paths on their journeys through the American West. Wright made a career for herself at the Oklahoma Historical Society as editor of the *Chronicles of Oklahoma* and a crucial member of the historic preservation program. From her position as a public historian at the historical society, Wright wielded extensive power. She determined which sites in Oklahoma were considered historically significant, and at the same time she determined the journal's content. Debo attained the doctorate in history and secured a position at a teacher's college in Texas. Through the choices she made, Debo returned to her hometown of Marshall, Oklahoma, and spent the majority of her life as a nonacademic research historian, primarily writing about American Indian history. Marriott was an ethnologist who spent time observing American Indian communities, whether during government service with the Indian Arts and Crafts Board during the 1930s or on her own as a freelance writer. Her academic training extended no further than a second bachelor's degree and some graduate work, and some anthropologists—especially those with doctorates—may not consider her work scholarly. But with recognition from feminist scholars such as Babcock and Parezo in the 1980s, Marriott has been included in studies of women anthropologists in the American Southwest, offering a broader, more inclusive interpretation of who can be called a "historian" or an "anthropologist." This broader notion of women interpreters of the American West is a promising, recent historiographical trend.

As I have argued throughout this book, Wright, Debo, and Marriott interpreted and envisioned Oklahoma as a place of complexity, uniqueness, and paradox. At times, they focused on the region that welcomed Native communities offering a place of growth and pioneers seeking new opportunities for economic advancement and landownership. At other times, the women, as public intellectuals, instructed their readers on the restraints and conflicts the people endured as Oklahoma approached statehood. For all of the stories Wright, Debo, and Marriott told, we can accurately state that their aim was to educate a broad audience on the importance of American Indian history in the development of Oklahoma.

CONCLUSION

All three women were on the cusp of academia, and for a variety of reasons they chose to remain there. Alice Marriott offered a fresh, lively writing style that enticed people to read about American Indian narratives, especially Native women's stories. Angie Debo tackled topics that other historians would not touch for political reasons. Muriel Wright embraced her Choctaw heritage as the granddaughter of Chief Allen Wright, known for proposing the name "Oklahoma," thus ensuring Five Tribes history a place in the historical memory of the state's development. As we approach Oklahoma's centennial in 2007, we should pause, recognize, and reclaim the "hidden scholars" who lived and wrote texts about Oklahoma history, particularly American Indian history, for general audiences. Although their journeys through life were difficult, they preferred to blaze their own trails rather than take a more traveled road.

Notes

Works frequently cited have been identified
by the following abbreviations:

ADC Angie Debo Collection, Special Collections, Edmon Low Library,
    Oklahoma State University, Stillwater.

ADT Angie Debo, interviews by Glenna Matthews and Gloria Valencia-
    Webber, from 1981 to 1985, transcripts, Angie Debo Collection,
    Oklahoma State University Library, Stillwater.

AMC Alice Lee Marriott Collection, Western History Collections,
    University of Oklahoma, Norman, Oklahoma.

AMI Alice Marriott, interview by Jennifer Fox for the Daughters of the
    Desert Oral History Project, 13 March 1986, Tucson, Arizona,
    audio recording, Wenner-Gren Foundation for Anthropological
    Research, New York, New York.

EDC E. E. Dale Collection, WHC.

IMI   Ioleta Hunt McElhaney, interviewed by B. D. Timmons, 3 March
    1968, T-198-1, Doris Duke Oral History Collection, WHC.

MWC Muriel H. Wright Collection, 83–18, Indian Archives Division,
    Oklahoma Historical Society, Oklahoma City.

MWI Muriel H. Wright, interview by Frank Doyle, 8 March 1965, tape
    recording, Indian Archives Division, Oklahoma Historical Society,
    Oklahoma City.

UOPC University of Oklahoma Press Collection, WHC.

WHC Western History Collections, University of Oklahoma, Norman.

PREFACE

1. Muriel H. Wright, interview by Frank Doyle, 8 March 1965, tape recording, Indian Archives Division, Oklahoma Historical Society, Oklahoma City [hereafter cited as MWI].

2. Angie Debo, "Indian History from an Author's Point of View," 1951, folder 19, box 20, Angie Debo Collection, Special Collections, Edmon Low Library, Oklahoma State University, Stillwater [hereafter cited as ADC].

3. Angie Debo, *The Road to Disappearance: A History of the Creek Indians* (Norman: University of Oklahoma Press, 1941), ix.

4. Catherine Jane Lavender, "Storytellers: Feminist Ethnography and the American Southwest, 1900–1940" (Ph.D. diss., University of Colorado-Boulder, 1997), 1–2.

5. John Collier, "Appendix, Indian Population," in *Annual Report of the Secretary of the Interior for the Fiscal Year Ended June 30, 1933* (Washington, D.C.: Government Printing Office, 1933), 111.

6. Barbara Tedlock, "From Participant Observation to the Observation of Participation: The Emergence of Narrative Ethnography," *Journal of Anthropological Research* 47 (Spring 1991): 74–76.

7. Virginia Scharff, *Twenty Thousand Roads: Women, Movement, and the West* (Berkeley: University of California Press, 2003).

CHAPTER ONE

1. Rennard Strickland, "Oklahoma's Story: Recording the History of the Forty-Sixth State," in *Oklahoma: New Views on the Forty-Sixth State*, ed. Anne Hodges Morgan and H. Wayne Morgan (Norman: University of Oklahoma Press, 1980), 260–61.

2. Ibid., 261.

3. Carol Kammen, *On Doing Local History* (Nashville, TN.: American Association for State and Local History, 1986), 28.

4. John Walton Caughey, "The Local Historian: His Occupational Hazards and Compensations," *Pacific Historical Review* 12 (March 1943): 1–9.

5. Richard Lowitt, "Regionalism at the University of Oklahoma," *Chronicles of Oklahoma* 73 (Summer 1995): 156, 19ff.

6. Robert L. Dorman, *Revolt of the Provinces: The Regionalist Movement in America, 1920–1945* (Chapel Hill: University of North Carolina Press, 1993), 169.

7. Curtis M. Hinsley Jr., *Savages and Scientists: The Smithsonian Institution and the Development of American Anthropology, 1846–1910*

NOTES TO PAGES 5–9

(Washington, D.C.: Smithsonian Institution Press, 1981), 9–10.

8. Jerry D. Moore, "Franz Boas: Culture in Context," in *Visions of Culture: An Introduction to Anthropological Theories and Theorists* (Walnut Creek, CA: AltaMira Press, 1997), 42–52; Lavender, "Storytellers," 35–49.

9. Wilbur R. Jacobs, *On Turner's Trail: 100 Years of Writing Western History* (Lawrence: University Press of Kansas, 1994), 3–15, 61–76.

10. Douglas Hale, "The People of Oklahoma: Economics and Social Change," in Morgan and Morgan, *Oklahoma: New Views of the Forty-Sixth State*, 34; Rennard Strickland, *The Indians in Oklahoma* (Norman: University of Oklahoma Press, 1980), 160–63.

11. Hale, "People of Oklahoma," 35; Angie Debo, *And Still the Waters Run* (Princeton, N.J.: Princeton University Press, 1940), 51; F. Doran, "Population Statistics of Nineteenth-Century Indian Territory," *Chronicles of Oklahoma* 53 (Winter 1975–76): 502–12; Muriel H. Wright, *A Guide to the Indian Tribes of Oklahoma* (Norman: University of Oklahoma Press, 1951), 237.

12. Hale, "People of Oklahoma," 35; Debo, *And Still the Waters Run*, 15–17.

13. Erik M. Zissu, *Blood Matters: The Five Civilized Tribes and the Search for Unity in the Twentieth Century* (New York: Routledge, 2001), xiii.

14. Craig S. Womack, *Red on Red: Native American Literary Separatism* (Minneapolis: University of Minnesota Press, 1999), 140–48.

15. See, for example, Clara Sue Kidwell, "Indian Women as Cultural Mediators," *Ethnohistory* 39 (Spring 1992): 97–107; Margaret Connell Szasz, ed., *Between Indian and White Worlds: The Cultural Broker* (Norman: University of Oklahoma Press, 1994).

16. Devon Abbott Mihesuah, *Indigenous American Women: Decolonization, Empowerment, Activism* (Lincoln: University of Nebraska Press, 2003), 6–7.

17. Linda W. Reese, "Cherokee Freedwomen in Indian Territory, 1863–1890," *Western Historical Quarterly* 33 (Autumn 2002): 275.

18. Hale, "People of Oklahoma," 37.

19. David La Vere, *Contrary Neighbors: Southern Plains and Removed Indians in Indian Territory* (Norman: University of Oklahoma Press, 2000), 7.

20. Ibid.

21. Hale, "People of Oklahoma," 39.

22. Ibid., 40.

23. Ibid., 41.

24. Ibid.

25. Ibid., 50.

26. Albert L. Hurtado, "Romancing the West in the Twentieth Century: The Politics of History in a Contested Region," *Western Historical Quarterly* 32 (Winter 2001): 417–35.

27. John Joseph Mathews quoted in Arrell Morgan Gibson, "A History of the University of Oklahoma Press," *Journal of the West* 7 (October 1968): 554.

28. Hurtado, "Romancing the West," 428.

29. Steven Crum, "Bizzell and Brandt: Pioneers in Indian Studies, 1929–1937," *Chronicles of Oklahoma* 66 (Summer 1988): 178–91.

30. Lowitt, "Regionalism at the University of Oklahoma," 150–71.

31. John Joseph Mathews quoted in "Short List of Great, Beautiful Books Extended by One," *The Daily Oklahoman*, 20 August 1961, 68.

32. John Joseph Mathews quoted in Gibson's "History of the University of Oklahoma Press," 561.

33. Lowitt, "Regionalism at the University of Oklahoma," 157.

34. Hurtado, "Romancing the West," 433.

35. Benjamin Albert Botkin quoted in Lowitt, "Regionalism at the University of Oklahoma," 165.

36. Charles Evans, *Lights on Oklahoma History* (Oklahoma City: Harlow Publishing Corporation, 1926), v.

37. James Shannon Buchanan and Edward Everett Dale, *A History of Oklahoma* (New York: Row, Peterson and Company, 1924), v.

38. Bob L. Blackburn, "Battle Cry for History: The First Century of the Oklahoma Historical Society," *Chronicles of Oklahoma* 70 (Winter 1992–93): 363–64.

39. Strickland, "Oklahoma's Story," 207.

40. Blackburn, "Battle Cry for History," 356–59.

41. Muriel H. Wright, "Pioneer Historian and Archaeologist of the State of Oklahoma," *Chronicles of Oklahoma* 24 (Winter 1946–47): 396.

42. Backburn, "Battle Cry for History," 365.

43. Stanley Clark, "Grant Foreman," *Chronicles of Oklahoma* 31 (Autumn 1953): 228.

44. Blackburn, "Battle Cry for History," 366.

45. Michael D. Green, "Grant Foreman," in *Historians of the American Frontier*, ed. John R. Wunder (Westport, CT: Greenwood Press, 1988), 262.

46. Ibid.

47. Ibid., 263.

48. Ibid.

49. J. Stanley Clark, "Carolyn Thomas Foreman," *Chronicles of Oklahoma* 45 (Winter 1967–68): 370.

50. Green, "Grant Foreman," 265.

51. Grant Foreman, *Indian Removal: The Emigration of the Five Civilized Tribes of Indians* (Norman: University of Oklahoma Press, 1932), 386.

52. Green, "Grant Foreman," 270.

53. "Oklahoma Biographs," *Daily Oklahoman*, 21 June 1936, C-11.

CHAPTER TWO

1. Muriel H. Wright, interview by Frank Doyle, 8 March 1965, tape recording, Indian Archives Division, Oklahoma Historical Society, Oklahoma City [hereafter cited as MWI].

2. Nancy Shoemaker, introduction to *Negotiators of Change: Historical Perspectives on Native American Women*, ed. Nancy Shoemaker (New York: Routledge, 1995), 12.

3. Muriel H. Wright, typed document [n.d.], Muriel H. Wright Collection, 83–18, Indian Archives Division, Oklahoma Historical Society, Oklahoma City [hereafter cited as MWC].

4. Muriel H. Wright, "A Brief Review of the Life of Doctor Eliphalet Nott Wright, 1858–1932," *Chronicles of Oklahoma* 10 (June 1931): 180–94.

5. LeRoy H. Fischer, "Muriel H. Wright, Historian of Oklahoma," *Chronicles of Oklahoma* 52 (Spring 1974): 3.

6. Devon A. Mihesuah, "Commonalty of Difference: American Indian Women and History," in *Natives and Academics: Researching and Writing About American Indians* (Lincoln: University of Nebraska Press, 1998), 43.

7. Mihesuah, *Indigenous American Women*, xvi.

8. MWI.

9. Ibid.

10. Ibid.

11. Regarding Allen Wright and the naming of Oklahoma, see Angie Debo, *The Rise and Fall of the Choctaw Republic* (1934; repr., Norman: University of Oklahoma Press,1961), 214; W. David Baird and Danney Goble, *The Story of Oklahoma* (Norman: University of Oklahoma Press, 1994), 309.

12. MWI.

13. Muriel H. Wright, Autobiographical Notes, box 4, MWC.

14. Philip J. Deloria, *Playing Indian* (New Haven, CT: Yale University Press, 1998).

15. Ibid., 123.

16. "Miss Wright a most charming Indian-Girl," unidentified Washington, D.C., newspaper [1909], box 7, MWC.

17. Ibid.

18. Alison Bernstein, "A Mixed Record: The Political Enfranchisement of American Indian Women During the Indian New Deal," *Journal of the West* 23 (1984): 13–20.

19. Deloria, *Playing Indian*, 125.

20. W. David Baird, "Are the Five Tribes of Oklahoma 'Real' Indians?" *Western Historical Quarterly* 21 (February 1990): 16.

21. Clara Sue Kidwell, *Choctaws and Missionaries in Mississippi, 1818–1918* (Norman: University of Oklahoma Press, 1995), xvi.

22. Fischer, "Muriel H. Wright," 7–8; MWI.

23. James Smallwood, ed., *And Gladly Teach: Reminiscences of Teachers from Frontier Dugout to Modern Module* (Norman: University of Oklahoma Press, 1976), 9.

24. Wright, Autobiographical Notes; Fischer, "Muriel H. Wright," 8.

25. Joe Hubbell, "Women in Oklahoma Education," in *Women in Oklahoma: A Century of Change*, ed. Melvena K. Thurman (Oklahoma City: Oklahoma Historical Society, 1982), 150.

26. Wright, Autobiographical Notes; Ruth Arrington, "Muriel Hazel Wright," in *Notable American Women: The Modern Period*, ed. Barbara Sicheman et al. (Cambridge, MA: Belknap Press of Harvard University Press, 1980), 751–52.

27. Courtney Ann Vaughn-Roberson, "Sometimes Independent but Never Equal—Women Teachers, 1900–1950: The Oklahoma Example," *Pacific Historical Review* 53 (February 1984): 49.

28. Fischer, "Muriel H. Wright," 9–11.

29. Ibid.

30. Wright, Autobiographical Notes.

31. "Miss Muriel Wright May Be Appointed Chief of Choctaws," *Colgate Courier*, 23 January 1930, box 7, MWC; Walter Ferguson to Muriel Wright, 1 February 1930, box 1, MWC; Muriel H. Wright to Walter Ferguson, 3 February 1930, MWC.

32. Wright to Judge R. L. Williams, 22 September 1930, box 19, folder 3, MWC.

33. Fischer, "Muriel H. Wright," 12; MWI; Ben Dwight to Muriel H. Wright, 2 November 1931, box 1, MWC.

34. Wright to Joseph B. Thoburn, 20 June 1934, box 3, folder 1, MHW.

35. Wright to Judge R. L. Williams, 22 September 1930, box 19, folder 3, MHW.

36. Joseph B. Thoburn and Muriel H. Wright, *Oklahoma: A History of the State and Its People*, 4 vols. (New York: Lewis Historical Publishing Company, 1929).

37. Joseph B. Thoburn to Armacost and Royston, 13 February 1931, box 1, MWC.

38. Muriel H. Wright, editorially assisted by Joseph B. Thoburn, *The Story of Oklahoma* (Oklahoma City: Webb Publishing Company, 1929).

39. Muriel H. Wright with Lucyl Shirk, *The Story of Oklahoma: A Work Book* (Guthrie, OK: Co-operative Publishing Company, 1951); Muriel H. Wright, *Our Oklahoma: Work Book in Oklahoma History* (Guthrie, OK: Co-operative Publishing Company, 1951).

40. [unidentifiable name] to Muriel H. Wright, 26 August 1924, box 1, MWC.

41. Muriel H. Wright, *Our Oklahoma* (Guthrie, OK: Co-operative Publishing Company, 1939); Muriel H. Wright, *The Oklahoma History* (Guthrie, OK: Co-operative Publishing Company, 1955).

42. Joseph B. Thoburn, review of *Our Oklahoma*, by Muriel H. Wright, *Chronicles of Oklahoma* 17 (September 1939): 451.

43. Ibid.

44. R. L. Williams to Muriel H. Wright, 17 September 1930, box 19, folder 3, MHW.

45. Fred Smith Standley, "The Oklahoma Historical Society, 1893–1943" (M.A. thesis, University of Oklahoma, 1986), 126. For a discussion of the conflict between Thoburn and Williams, see 125–34.

46. Wright to Judge R. L. Williams, 22 September 1930, box 19, folder 3, MWC.

47. Wright to Williams, 22 September 1930.

48. Handwritten document, Wright, n.d. [mid-1970s], MWC.

49. Daniel F. Littlefield Jr., "Muriel Hazel Wright," in *Native American Women: A Biographical Dictionary*, ed. Gretchen M. Bataille (New York: Garland Publishing, 1993), 287.

50. Wright to Uncle Brookes, 24 January 1947, box 3, folder 1, MWC.

51. Muriel H. Wright, "Old Boggy Depot," *Chronicles of Oklahoma* 5 (March 1927): 4–17.

52. Ibid., 8.

53. Muriel H. Wright, Autobiographical Notes, box 4, MWC.

54. Ibid.

55. Muriel H. Wright, "Contributions of the Indian People to Oklahoma," *Chronicles of Oklahoma* 14 (June 1936): 156.

56. Ibid., 159.

57. Ibid., 161.
58. Muriel H. Wright to Hon. Joseph W. Latimer, 6 August 1932, box 1, MWC.
59. Muriel H. Wright, "The Wedding of Oklahoma and Miss Indian Territory," *Chronicles of Oklahoma* 35 (Autumn 1957): 255–60.
60. MWI.
61. LeRoy Fischer, "Muriel H. Wright, Historian of Oklahoma," *Chronicles of Oklahoma* 52 (Spring 1974): 17.
62. Wright to Williams, 22 September 1930, box 19, folder 3, MWC.
63. Muriel H. Wright, photo album, "Some Historic Sites in Southern and Southeastern Oklahoma," photographs taken on field trips made during 1930, 29 January 1930, Oklahoma Historical Society.
64. Muriel H. Wright, Biographical Notes, March 1966, box 4, MWC; Muriel H. Wright et al., *Mark of Heritage* (Oklahoma City: Oklahoma Historical Society, 1976), 185–86, 189–90, 194.
65. Muriel H. Wright, "Historic Spots on the Old Stage Line from Fort Smith to Red River," *Chronicles of Oklahoma* 11 (June 1933): 798–822.
66. LeRoy H. Fischer, "The Historic Preservation Movement in Oklahoma," *Chronicles of Oklahoma* 57 (Spring 1979): 9–10. Fischer's article provides an important overview of the historic preservation movement in Oklahoma.
67. Fischer, "Historic Preservation," 13–14.
68. Fischer, "Muriel H. Wright," 17.
69. Baird, "Are the Five Tribes of Oklahoma 'Real' Indians?" 13.
70. Muriel H. Wright to Honorable Joseph W. Latimer, 6 August 1932, box 1, MWC.
71. Ibid.
72. Wright to Honorable Elmer Thomas, U.S. Senate, 21 May 1947, Elmer Thomas Collection, Legislative Series, box 66, folder 9, Carl Albert Center, University of Oklahoma, Norman.
73. Ibid.
74. Thomas to Wright, 23 May 1947, Elmer Thomas Collection, Legislative Series, box 66, folder 9, Carl Albert Center.
75. Muriel H. Wright, *A Guide to the Indian Tribes of Oklahoma* (1951; repr. Norman: University of Oklahoma Press, 1986), 23.

CHAPTER THREE

1. Kenny Brown, "Prairie City and Its Lessons for Town Development Today," Keynote Address for Celebrating 50 Years of *Prairie City* on Angie Debo's 105th Birthday, 30 January 1995, Edmon Low Library,

Oklahoma State University, Stillwater.

2. Angie Debo, "The Site of the Battle of Round Mountain, 1861," *Chronicles of Oklahoma* 27 (Summer 1949): 187–206; Muriel H. Wright, "Colonel Cooper's Civil Report on the Battle of Round Mountain," *Chronicles of Oklahoma* 39 (Winter 1961–62): 352–97; Angie Debo, "The Location of the Battle of Round Mountain," *Chronicles of Oklahoma* 41 (Spring 1963): 70–104.

3. LeRoy Fischer, phone interview by author, 22 September 1996; Dale Chlouber, interview by author, Ripley, Oklahoma, 20 October 1996.

4. Dale Chlouber, "Revisiting the Battle of Red Fork," 1, unpublished manuscript in author's possession, 1996.

5. Debo, "Battle of Round Mountain," 190.

6. Ibid., 206.

7. Wright, "Colonel Cooper's Civil War Report," 356.

8. Chlouber, "Revisiting the Battle of Red Fork," 2.

9. Wright to Doctor Dailey, 29 January 1952, box 3, MWC.

10. Ibid.

11. Muriel H. Wright, review of *The Rise and Fall of the Choctaw Republic*, by Angie Debo, in *Chronicles of Oklahoma* 13 (March 1935): 108.

12. Ibid.

13. Wright to Doctor Dailey, 29 January 1952, box 3, MWC.

14. Debo, *Rise and Fall*, 86–90, 101–2.

15. W. David Baird, *Peter Pitchlynn: Chief of the Choctaws* (Norman: University of Oklahoma Press, 1972), 146–56; Petrina Russo Medley, "Angie Debo: In Search of Truth" (Ph.D. diss., Oklahoma State University, 2000), 24; Leckie, *Angie Debo*, 56.

16. Debo, *Rise and Fall*, 90.

17. Baird, *Peter Pitchlynn*, 153; Medley, "Angie Debo," 24.

18. Wright, review of *The Rise and Fall of the Choctaw Republic*, by Angie Debo, 115–16.

19. Ibid., 118–19.

20. LeRoy Fischer, phone interview by author, 22 September 1996.

21. Medley, "Angie Debo," 25.

22. Harry J. W. Belvin, Principal Chief, Choctaw Nation, to Angie Debo, 19 January 1971, folder 32, box 1, ADC.

23. ADT, 16 December 1981, 1.

24. W. David Baird, e-mail interview by author, 17 September 1996.

25. Courtney Vaughn and Joan K. Smith, "History and Ideology: Conflicts Between Angie Debo and Muriel Wright," *Midwest History of Education Journal* 26, no. 1 (1999): 102.

26. Muriel H. Wright, Autobiographical Notes, box 4, MWC.

27. Muriel H. Wright, "Organ Honors Memory of Indian Evangelist," *Daily Oklahoman*, 1 May 1927, box 4, MWC.

28. Shirley A. Leckie, *Angie Debo: Pioneering Historian* (Norman: University of Oklahoma Press, 2000), 93–94.

29. Quoted in Vaughn and Smith, "History and Ideology," 104.

30. Ibid.

31. Wright to Doctor Dailey, 29 January 1952, box 3, MWC.

32. Vaughn and Smith, "History and Ideology," 104.

33. Grant Foreman, review of *And Still the Waters Run*, by Angie Debo, *American Historical Review* 46 (July 1941): 936–37; Grant Foreman, review of *And Still the Waters Run*, by Angie Debo, *Mississippi Valley Historical Review* 27 (March 1941): 636–37; Dan E. Clark, review of *And Still the Waters Run*, by Angie Debo, *Journal of Southern History* 7 (August 1941): 574–75.

34. Baird and Goble, *The Story of Oklahoma*, 431; W. David Baird, e-mail interview by author, 26 November 1996.

35. Colin B. Goodykoontz, "The Forty-Third Annual Meeting of the Mississippi Valley Historical Association," *Mississippi Valley Historical Review* 37 (September 1950): 284.

36. Muriel H. Wright to Angie Debo, 3 May 1950, folder 22, box 25.2, ADC; Goodykoontz, "Forty-Third Annual Meeting," 284.

37. Angie Debo, *The Five Civilized Tribes of Oklahoma: Report on Social and Economic Conditions* (Philadelphia: Indian Rights Association, 1951).

38. Muriel H. Wright to Angie Debo, 3 May 1950, folder 22, box 25.2, ADC.

39. Ibid.

40. Muriel H. Wright, "Notes and Documents," *Chronicles of Oklahoma* 29 (Spring 1951): 243; J. B. Wright to Mr. W. O. Roberts, "Notes and Documents," *Chronicles of Oklahoma* 29 (Spring 1951): 243–47.

41. J. B. Wright to Mr. W. O. Roberts, Area Director, Muskogee Area Office, 29 June 1951, W. G. Stigler Collection, box 9, folder 39, Carl Albert Center, Norman.

42. Ibid.

43. Debo, *The Five Civilized Tribes of Oklahoma*, 24.

44. J. B. Wright to W. O. Roberts, 29 June 1951, W. G. Stigler Collection, box 9, folder 39, Carl Albert Center.

45. W. G. Stigler to J. B. Wright, 2 July 1951, W. G. Stigler Collection, box 9, folder 39, Carl Albert Center.

46. Wright to Dr. W. N. P. Dailey, 29 January 1952, box 3, MWC.

47. Angie Debo to Dr. Charles Evans, 31 January 1952, folder 18, box 31, ADC.

48. Wright to Dr. W. N. P. Dailey, 29 January 1952, box 3, MWC.

49. Muriel H. Wright to Mrs. L. E. Custer, 5 July 1947, box 4, MWC; "Notes and Documents," *Chronicles of Oklahoma* 25 (Summer 1947): 153; "Minutes of the Annual Meeting of the Oklahoma Historical Society at Pryor, May 26, 1947," *Chronicles of Oklahoma* 25 (Summer 1947): 169.

50. Arrell Morgan Gibson, foreword to *A Guide to the Indian Tribes of Oklahoma*, by Muriel H. Wright (1951; repr., Norman: University of Oklahoma Press, 1986), vii.

51. Ibid.

52. Wright, *Guide*, 27.

53. Gibson, foreword to *Guide*, viii.

54. Angie Debo, review of *A Guide to the Indian Tribes of Oklahoma*, by Muriel H. Wright, *The American Indian* 6 (Summer 1953): 45.

55. Wright to Doctor W. N. P. Dailey, Schenectady, New York, 29 January 1952, box 3, MHW.

56. Leslie Hewes, review of *A Guide to the Indian Tribes of Oklahoma*, by Muriel H. Wright, *Mississippi Valley Historical Review* 39 (June 1952): 132–33.

57. Angie Debo, interviews by Glenna Matthews and Gloria Valencia-Webber, from 1981 to 1985, transcripts, Angie Debo Collection, Oklahoma State University Library, Stillwater, Oklahoma, 16 December 1981, 2 [hereafter cited as ADT].

58. Dale Chlouber, interview by author, Stillwater, Oklahoma, 20 October 1996; LeRoy Fischer, phone interview by author, 22 September 1996; W. David Baird, e-mail interview by author, 17 September 1996; Mary Jane Warde, interview by author, Stillwater, Oklahoma, 18 October 1996.

CHAPTER FOUR

1. Angie Debo, interviews by Glenna Matthews and Gloria Valencia-Webber, from 1981 to 1985, transcripts, Angie Debo Collection, Oklahoma State University Library, Stillwater, Oklahoma, 12 December 1981, 12 [hereafter cited as date and ADT].

2. Richard White, review of "Indians, Outlaws, and Angie Debo," produced by Barbara Abrash and Martha Sandlin, *Journal of American History* 76 (December 1989): 1010.

3. Shirley A. Leckie, "Angie Debo, Pioneering Historian," public lecture at Oklahoma State University, Stillwater, Oklahoma, 29 March 1999, 3.

4. "Angie Debo: An Autobiographical Sketch, Eulogy, and Bibliography" (Stillwater: College of Arts and Sciences and Department of History, Oklahoma State University, 1988), 1–2.

5. Shirley A. Leckie, "Angie Debo, Pioneering Historian," paper delivered at the Western History Association Conference, Lincoln, Nebraska, October 1996, 7.

6. Shirley A. Leckie, *Angie Debo: Pioneering Historian* (Norman: University of Oklahoma Press, 2000), 57.

7. Ibid., 12.

8. ADT, 16 December 1981, 7.

9. "Angie Debo: An Autobiographical Sketch," 1.

10. ADT, 15 August 1983, 11, 1.

11. Ibid.

12. ADT, 20 November 1981, 1–4; Arrell Morgan Gibson, "Edward Everett Dale: The Historian," in *Frontier Historian: The Life and Work of Edward Everett Dale*, ed. Arrell Morgan Gibson (Norman: University of Oklahoma Press, 1975), 18–19.

13. ADT, 20 November 1981, 4.

14. Gibson, "Edward Everett Dale," 4.

15. Wilbur R. Jacobs, *On Turner's Trail: 100 Years of Writing Western History* (Lawrence: University Press of Kansas, 1994), 236.

16. Frederick Jackson Turner, "The Significance of the Frontier in American History," in *The Frontier in American History* (New York: Henry Holt and Company, 1920), 1.

17. Richard Lowitt, "Regionalism at the University of Oklahoma," *Chronicles of Oklahoma* 73 (Summer 1995): 156.

18. Angie Debo, "Edward Everett Dale: The Teacher," in *Frontier Historian*, 28.

19. Angie Debo, *Prairie City: The Story of an American Community* (New York: Knopf, 1944; repr., Norman: University of Oklahoma Press, 1998), xii.

20. Edward Everett Dale, "The Spirit of Soonerland," *Chronicles of Oklahoma* 1 (June 1923): 169.

21. Robert L. Dorman, *Revolt of the Provinces: The Regionalist Movement in America, 1920–1945* (Chapel Hill: University of North Carolina Press, 1993), 172–74.

22. ADT, 20 November 1981, 2–3.

23. Angie Debo to E. E. Dale, 16 January 1925, folder 12, box 17, E. E. Dale Collection, W[estern] H[istory] C[ollections] [hereafter cited as EDC].

24. Angie Debo, "Edward Everett Dale, Historian of Progress," 1930–31,

14, box 7, folder 3, Angie Debo Collection, Oklahoma State University Library, Stillwater, Oklahoma [hereafter cited as ADC].

25. Debo, "Edward Everett Dale: The Teacher,"27.

26. ADT, 20 November 1981, 4.

27. Ibid., 5.

28. Ibid., 4–8; Leckie, *Angie Debo*, 32–34, 38.

29. See Jacqueline Goggin, "Challenging Sexual Discrimination in the Historical Profession: Women Historians and the American Historical Association, 1890–1940," *American Historical Review* 97 (June 1992): 769–802.

30. ADT, 20 November 1981, 9.

31. ADT, 12 December 1981, 2.

32. Goggin, "Challenging Sexual Discrimination," 771.

33. Ibid.

34. Ibid., 3.

35. ADT, 16 February 1984, 2.

36. ADT, 16 December 1981, 4.

37. Leckie, *Angie Debo*, 38–39; Medley, "Angie Debo," 11–12.

38. Medley, "Angie Debo," 66.

39. Leckie, *Angie Debo*, 40.

40. Ibid., 41–42.

41. Ibid., 42.

42. Ibid., 51; Medley, "Angie Debo," 67–99.

43. Leckie, "Angie Debo, Pioneering Historian," 4.

44. ADT, 12 December 1981, 4.

45. E. E. Dale to Angie Debo, 7 October 1931, folder 12, box 17, EDC.

46. Joseph B. Thoburn and Muriel H. Wright, *Oklahoma: A History of the State and Its People*, 4 vols. (New York: Lewis Historical Publishing Company, 1929).

47. E. E. Dale to Angie Debo, 7 October 1931, folder 12, box 17, EDC.

48. Angie Debo to E. E. Dale, 9 October 1931, folder 12, box 17, EDC.

49. E. E. Dale to Angie Debo, 14 October 1931, folder 12, box 17, EDC.

50. Angie Debo to E. E. Dale, 19 October 1932, folder 12, box 17, EDC.

51. Ibid.

52. E. E. Dale to Angie Debo, 24 October 1932, folder 12, box 17, EDC.

53. Ibid.

54. Ibid.

55. Medley, "Angie Debo," 67.

56. Leckie, *Angie Debo*, 52.

57. Angie Debo, *The Rise and Fall of the Choctaw Republic* (Norman:

University of Oklahoma Press, 1934).

58. ADT, 12 December 1981, 5–6.

59. Rennard Strickland, "Oklahoma's Story: Recording the History of the Forty-Sixth State," in Morgan and Morgan, *Oklahoma: New Views of the Forty-Sixth State*, 261.

60. ADT, 20 November 1981, 9.

61. Annie H. Abel-Henderson, review of *The Rise and Fall of the Choctaw Republic*, by Angie Debo, *American Historical Review* 40 (July 1935): 795–96.

62. Anna Lewis, review of *The Rise and Fall of the Choctaw Republic*, by Angie Debo, *Mississippi Valley Historical Review* 21 (December 1934): 410.

63. Medley, "Angie Debo," 69–70; Leckie, *Angie Debo*, 57.

64. Leckie, *Angie Debo*, 58.

65. Angie Debo to E. E. Dale, 3 January 1934, box 12, folder 31, ADC.

66. Angie Debo to E. E. Dale, 5 January 1934, box 12, folder 31, ADC.

67. Leckie, *Angie Debo*, 66.

68. ADT, 20 November 1981, 13–14; ADT, 16 February 1984, 3; ADT, 8 June 1984, 11.

69. Angie Debo to E. E. Dale, 5 May 1938, box 12, folder 31, ADC.

70. Angie Debo to E. E. Dale, 24 March 1941, box 12, folder 31, ADC.

71. Ibid.

72. Goggin, "Challenging Sexual Discrimination," 770, 776.

73. Debo quoted in Leckie, *Angie Debo*, 71.

74. Leckie, *Angie Debo*, 72–75.

75. ADT, 17 August 1983, 1.

76. ADT, 12 December 1981, 4.

CHAPTER FIVE

1. See Patricia Nelson Limerick, *Legacy of Conquest: The Unbroken Past of the American West* (New York: W. W. Norton, 1987); Patricia Nelson Limerick, *Something in the Soil: Legacies and Reckonings in the New West* (New York: W. W. Norton, 2000).

2. Patricia Nelson Limerick, "Land, Justice, and Angie Debo: Telling the Truth To—and About—Your Neighbors," *Great Plains Quarterly* 21 (Fall 2001): 271.

3. Howard R. Lamar, "The Creation of Oklahoma: New Meanings for the Oklahoma Land Run," in *The Culture of Oklahoma*, ed. Howard F. Stein and Robert F. Hill (Norman: University of Oklahoma Press, 1993), 43, 47.

4.   ADT, 12 December 1981, 12; ADT, 9 August 1984, 34.

5.   ADT, 12 December 1981, 12–13.

6.   Debo, *And Still the Waters Run*, x–xi.

7.   Dorman, *Revolt of the Provinces*, 170.

8.   Ibid., 174.

9.   Ibid., 172.

10. Debo, *And Still the Waters Run*, 93.

11. ADT, 12 December 1981, 7.

12. Debo, *And Still the Waters Run*, x.

13. Medley, "Angie Debo," 80.

14. ADT, 12 December 1981, 9.

15. Grant Foreman, review of *And Still the Waters Run*, by Angie Debo, American Historical Review 46 (July 1941): 937.

16. Lowitt, "Regionalism at the University of Oklahoma," 19 ff.

17. Reader's Report of D'Arcy McNickle. 3 September 1936, box 65, University of Oklahoma Press Collection, WHC [hereafter cited as UOPC].

18. Lowitt, "Regionalism at the University of Oklahoma," 163–64.

19. Leckie, *Angie Debo*, 77.

20. Morris Wardell to Brandt, July 19, 1937, UOPC; Medley, "Angie Debo," 31–34; Leckie, *Angie Debo*, 77.

21. Debo, *And Still the Waters Run*, x–xi; Suzanne H. Schrems and Cynthia J. Wolff, "Politics and Libel: Angie Debo and the Publication of *And Still the Waters Run*," *Western Historical Quarterly* 22 (May 1991): 194; Lowitt, "Regionalism at the University of Oklahoma," 162–65; ADT, 12 December 1981, 8.

22. ADT, 12 December 1981, 8.

23. Joseph A. Brandt to William Bizzell, 20 July 1937, box 32, UOPC.

24. Leckie, *Angie Debo*, 80.

25. ADT, 4 May 1983, 8–9.

26. Ibid., 6.

27. Ibid., 7.

28. Angie Debo and John M. Oskison, *Oklahoma: A Guide to the Sooner State*, comp. Writers' Program, Works Progress Administration, State of Oklahoma (Norman: University of Oklahoma Press, 1941).

29. ADT, 16 December 1981, 7–8.

30. Debo, *Road to Disappearance*, ix–x.

31. Ibid., viii.

32. Mary Jane Warde, *George Washington Grayson and the Creek Nation, 1843–1920* (Norman: University of Oklahoma Press, 1999), 252.

33. LeRoy R. Hafen, review of *The Road to Disappearance*, by Angie Debo, *American Historical Review* 48 (July 1943): 827.

34. Debo, *Road to Disappearance*, 369.

35. Richard L. Power, review of *The Road to Disappearance*, by Angie Debo, *Mississippi Valley Historical Review* 29 (June 1942): 127.

36. Debo, *Road to Disappearance*, x.

37. Michael D. Green, *The Creeks: A Critical Bibliography* (Bloomington: Indiana University Press, 1979), 17.

38. ADT, 12 December 1981, 12–13.

39. Dan E. Clark, review of *And Still the Waters Run*, by Angie Debo, *Journal of Southern History* 7 (August 1941): 575.

40. Grant Foreman, review of *And Still the Waters Run*, by Angie Debo, Mississippi Valley Historical Review 27 (March 1941):636.

41. Baird and Goble, *The Story of Oklahoma*, 431; W. David Baird, e-mail interview by author, 26 November 1996.

42. ADT, 16 December 1981, 2.

43. Ibid.

44. ADT, 8 April 1983, 13.

45. ADT, 12 December 1981, 12.

46. Medley, "Angie Debo," 41.

47. ADT, 8 April 1981, 12–13.

48. Strickland, "Oklahoma's Story," 238.

49. Angie Debo, *Tulsa: From Creek Town to Oil Capital* (Norman: University of Oklahoma Press, 1943); Angie Debo, *Prairie City: The Story of an American Community* (New York: Knopf, 1944; repr., Norman: University of Oklahoma Press, 1988); Angie Debo, *Oklahoma: Foot-loose and Fancy-free* (1949; repr., Norman: University of Oklahoma Press, 1987).

50. Debo, *Prairie City*, vii.

51. Ibid., xii.

52. Ibid., vii–viii.

53. Edward Everett Dale, review of *Prairie City*, by Angie Debo, *American Historical Review* 50 (April 1945): 573.

54. Angie Debo, "Who Writes Truth," 1974, 5, folder 41, box 20, ADC.

55. ADT, 8 April 1983, 12; Debo, *Oklahoma, Foot-loose and Fancy-free*, ix.

56. Paul B. Sears, review of *Oklahoma, Foot-loose and Fancy-free*, by Angie Debo, *American Historical Review* 56 (January 1951): 364.

57. George L. Anderson, review of *Oklahoma, Foot-loose and Fancy-free*, by Angie Debo, *Mississippi Valley Historical Review* 37 (June 1950): 140.

58. Limerick, "Land, Justice, and Angie Debo," 270–71.

59. Ibid., 270.

CHAPTER SIX

1. Jennifer Fox, "The Women Who Opened Doors: Interviewing Southwestern Anthropologists," in *Hidden Scholars: Women Anthropologists and the Native American Southwest*, ed. Nancy J. Parezo (Albuquerque: University of New Mexico Press, 1993), 306.

2. Barbara A. Babcock and Nancy J. Parezo, *Daughters of the Desert: Women Anthropologists and the Native American Southwest, 1880–1980* (Albuquerque: University of New Mexico Press, 1988); Parezo, *Hidden Scholars.*

3. Alice Marriott, interview by Jennifer Fox for the Daughters of the Desert Oral History Project, 13 March 1986, Tucson, Arizona, audio recording, tape 1, side 1, Wenner-Gren Foundation for Anthropological Research, New York, New York [hereafter cited as AMI].

4. Ibid.

5. Turner S. Kobler, *Alice Marriott*, Southwest Writers Series 27 (Austin, TX: Steck-Vaughn Company, 1969), 1–2.

6. Alice Marriott, *Greener Fields: Experiences Among the American Indians* (New York: Thomas Y. Crowell Company, 1953), 2–3.

7. AMI, tape 1, side 1; Theodora Kroeber, *Alfred Kroeber: A Personal Configuration* (Berkeley: University of California Press, 1970), 164.

8. Alice Marriott to Miss E. Petty, 12 August 1937, folder 4, box 18, Alice Lee Marriott Collection, Western History Collections, University of Oklahoma, Norman, Oklahoma [hereafter cited as AMC].

9. Alice [Marriott] to Mother, 1 July [1934], folder 4, box 21, AMC.

10. Ibid.

11. Ibid. The other woman anthropologist was Ethel Alpenfels.

12. Alice [Marriott] to Casey, 15 August [1934], folder 3, box 20, AMC. The Modoc respondents Mary and Celia's last names are unknown.

13. Alice [Marriott] to Dearest, 21 August [1934], folder 2, box 21, AMC.

14. Susan Labry Meyn, *More Than Curiosities: A Grassroots History of the Indian Arts and Crafts Board and Its Precursors, 1920 to 1942* (Lanham, MD: Lexington Books, 2001), 83. See also Robert Fay Schrader, *The Indian Arts and Crafts Board: An Aspect of New Deal Indian Policy* (Albuquerque: University of New Mexico Press, 1983).

15. Meyn, *More Than Curiosities*, 86–87.

16. John Collier, *Annual Report of the Secretary of the Interior for the Fiscal Year Ending June 30, 1937* (Washington, D.C.: Government Printing Office, 1937), 250–51.

17. Alice Marriott, Specialist in Indian Arts and Crafts, to Miss Conroy, [n.d., 1942?], folder 5, box 18, AMC.

18. Alice Marriott, unpublished manuscript on the Indian Arts and Crafts Board, "Changing Times," 2, folder 23, box 78, AMC.

19. Ibid., 2–3.

20. Meyn, *More Than Curiosities*, 177; Schrader, *Indian Arts and Crafts Board*, 141.

21. Alice Marriott, "Changing Times," 2–3.

22. Ibid., 4.

23. Ibid.

24. Meyn, *More Than Curiosities*, 178.

25. Ibid., 194.

26. Alice Marriott to Miss E. Petty, Indian Arts and Crafts Board, Washington, D.C., 12 August 1937, folder 4, box 18, AMC.

27. Meyn, *More Than Curiosities*, 193–94.

28. Helen Carr, *Inventing the American Primitive: Politics, Gender and the Representation of Native American Literary Traditions, 1789–1936* (New York: New York University Press, 1996), 203.

29. "Exposition Exhibit to Further Arts and Crafts Program Here," *Anadarko Daily News*, 1 April 1937, folder 13, box 16, AMC.

30. Alice Marriott, Specialist in Indian Arts and Crafts, to Miss Conroy, [n.d., 1942?], folder 5, box 18, AMC.

31. Meyn, *More Than Curiosities*, 198.

32. Alice Marriott to Rene d'Harnoncourt, 22 December 1938, folder 6, box 15, AMC.

33. Alice Marriott to Rene d'Harnoncourt, [n.d.], folder 2, box 19, AMC.

34. Meyn, *More Than Curiosities*, 174.

35. Alice Marriott to Mrs. Mary Inkanish, 4 August 1939, folder 4, box 18, AMC.

36. Marriott, "Changing Times," 6, folder 23, box 78, AMC.

37. Marriott, *Greener Fields*, 183.

38. Ibid., 186.

39. Meyn, *More Than Curiosities*, 216.

40. Marriott, "Changing Times," 6–7, folder 23, box 78, AMC.

41. Meyn, *More Than Curiosities*, 216–17.

42. 1938–39 report, [n.d.], folder 2, box 19, AMC.

43. *Official Guidebook*, Golden Gate International Exposition World's Fair on San Francisco Bay (San Francisco: The Crocker Company, 1939), 72, folder 5, box 17, AMC.

44. Meyn, *More Than Curiosities*, 123.

45. Ibid., 184–85.

46. "Alice Marriott—Case History," 1, [n.d.], folder 23, box 78, AMC; Alice

Marriott to Miss Morrow, 16 November 1939, folder 3, box 22, AMC; Meyn, *More Than Curiosities*, 145.

47. Marriott, *Greener Fields*, 187.

48. AMI, tape 2, side 1.

CHAPTER SEVEN

1. Marriott, *Greener Fields*, 84.

2. Ibid., 79.

3. Alice Marriott, *The Ten Grandmothers* (Norman: University of Oklahoma Press, 1945).

4. James Mooney, *Calendar History of the Kiowa Indians*, Seventeenth Annual Report of the Bureau of American Ethnology, pt. 1 (Washington, D.C.: Government Printing Office, 1898).

5. AMI, tape 1, side 1.

6. Marriott, *Greener Fields*, 102.

7. AMI, tape 1, side 2.

8. Ibid.

9. AMI, tape 1, side 1.

10. Ibid.

11. Wilbur Sturtevant Nye, *Carbine and Lance: The Story of Old Fort Sill* (1937; repr., Norman: University of Oklahoma Press, 1969); Wilbur Sturtevant Nye, *Bad Medicine and Good: Tales of the Kiowas* (Norman: University of Oklahoma Press, 1962).

12. Claribel F. Dick, *The Song Goes On: The Story of Ioleta Hunt McElhaney* (Philadelphia: Judson Press, 1959), 27.

13. Nye, *Bad Medicine and Good*, xix.

14. Dick, *Song Goes On*, 22–23. See also Clyde Ellis, *To Change Them Forever: Indian Education at the Rainy Mountain Boarding School, 1893–1920* (Norman: University of Oklahoma Press, 1996).

15. Dick, *Song Goes On*, 29.

16. Ibid., 53.

17. Marriott, *Greener Fields*, 65.

18. Marriott wrote a children's book, *Kiowa Annie*, which offers a positive treatment of the captivity narrative based on Millie Durgan.

19. Marriott, *Greener Fields*, 114.

20. Ibid.

21. AMI, tape 1, side 1.

22. Ibid.

23. Throughout Marriott's correspondence, she refers to Ioleta Hunt McElhaney as "Isleta" and appears to use Ioleta and

Isleta interchangeably.

24. AMI, tape 1, side 1.

25. Ioleta Hunt McElhaney, interviewed by B. D. Timmons, 3 March 1968, T-198-1, Doris Duke Oral History Collection, WHC [hereafter cited as IMI].

26. Ibid.

27. Ibid.

28. Dick, *Song Goes On*, 95.

29. IMI.

30. Ibid.

31. Marriott, *Greener Fields*, 102–3.

32. Dick, *Song Goes On*, 104.

33. Marriott, *Ten Grandmothers*, xi.

34. AMI, tape 1, side 1.

35. Marriott, *Ten Grandmothers*, xi.

36. Ibid., xi.

37. In correspondence with Clyde Ellis and Eric Lassiter, they contend that most Kiowas refer to the bundles as "the bundles" or the "boy bundles." In the Kiowa language, the word for grandmother is *tawlee*; for boy it is *tahlee*. Perhaps Marriott or her interpreter, Ioleta Hunt McElhaney, made this mistake in translation. Once the term was printed as the "grandmother bundles," it became the standard description.

38. Marriott, *Ten Grandmothers*, viii.

39. James Silverhorn, interviewed by Julia A. Jordan, 6 June 1969, T-18, transcript, Doris Duke Oral History Collection, WHC.

40. Ibid.

41. Alice Marriott, *Kiowa Years: A Study in Culture Impact* (New York: Macmillan Company, 1968), 156–57.

42. Guy Quoetone, interviewed by Julia A. Jordan, 30 March 1971, T-638, transcript, Doris Duke Oral History Collection, WHC.

43. Louise Lamphere, "Gladys Reichard Among the Navajo," in Parezo, *Hidden Scholars*, 159–60.

44. AMI, tape 1, side 1.

45. Alice [Marriott] to Darling, 4 July [1935], folder 5, box 21, AMC.

46. AMI, tape 1, side 1.

47. Marriott, *Greener Fields*, 103.

48. Ibid., 103.

49. Ibid., 103–4.

50. Marriott, *Ten Grandmothers*, 142.

51. Ibid., 74.

52. Ibid., 75.

53. Ibid., 76.

54. Ibid., 220.

55. Ibid., 221.

56. Gretchen M. Bataille and Kathleen Mullen Sands, *American Indian Women: Telling Their Lives* (Lincoln: University of Nebraska Press, 1984), 45.

57. Alice [Marriott] to Darling, 20 July [n.d.], folder 5, box 21, AMC.

58. Marriott, *Greener Fields*, 112.

59. Ibid.

60. Luke E. Lassiter, *The Power of Kiowa Song: A Collaborative Ethnography* (Tucson: University of Arizona Press, 1998), 9.

61. Alice [Marriott] to Dearest, 10 July [n.d.], folder 5, box 21, AMC.

62. Alice [Marriott] to Dear darlings, 8 February 1937, folder 4, box 20, AMC.

63. Marriott, Ten Grandmothers, 239.

64. Ibid., 244.

65. Ibid., 240.

66. Ibid., 246.

67. Ibid., 247.

68. Ibid.

69. Alice [Marriott] to Darling, 5 July [n.d.], folder 5, box 21, AMC.

70. Ibid.

71. Alice [Marriott] to Darling, 9 July 1936, folder 4, box 20, AMC.

72. Alice [Marriott] to Darlings, 13 July [1936], folder 4, box 20, AMC.

73. Ibid.

74. In letters between Alice Marriott and George Hunt, they refer to each other as "Dear Father" and "Dear Daughter." For examples, see Geo. Hunt to Alice Marriott, 11 October 1939, folder 3, box 22, AMC; Alice Marriott to George Hunt, 15 November 1939, folder 3, box 22, AMC.

75. Alice [Marriott] to Darlings, 5 July [1936], folder 1, box 20, AMC.

76. Ibid.

77. Alice [Marriott] to Darlings, 13 July [1936], folder 4, box 20, AMC.

78. Alice [Marriott] to Darlings, 5 July [1936], folder 1, box 20, AMC.

79. Marriott, *Greener Fields*, 124.

80. Ibid., 125.

81. Ibid., 124–29.

82. Alice [Marriott] to Darlings, 13 July [1936], folder 4, box 20, AMC.

83. Ibid.

84. Ibid.

85. Ibid.; Leslie Spier, *Yuman Tribes of the Gila River* (Chicago: University of Illinois Press, 1933); Ruth M. Underhill, *The Autobiography of a Papago Woman*, Memoirs of the American Anthropological Association no. 46 (Menasha, WI: American Anthropological Association, 1936).

86. Marriott, *Ten Grandmothers*, xi.

87. Lassiter, *Power of Kiowa Song*, 13.

88. Forrest [Clements] to Alice [Marriott], 28 January 1943, folder 3, box 22, AMC.

89. Louis [McElhaney] to Alice [Marriott], 7 March 1945, folder 3, box 22, AMC.

90. Ernest Wallace, review of *The Ten Grandmothers*, by Alice Marriott, *Southwestern Sciences Quarterly* 26 (June 1945): 99–100.

91. Ibid.

92. Angie Debo to Alice Marriott, 16 December 1946, folder 9, box 32, AMC.

93. Clark Wissler, review of *The Ten Grandmothers*, by Alice Marriott, *American Anthropologist* 47 (July–September 1945): 439.

94. Ibid., 440.

95. Marriott, *Greener Fields*, 261.

96. Ibid.

97. Ibid., 262.

98. Ibid.

99. Ibid.

100. Lassiter, *Power of Kiowa Song*, 78.

101. Ibid., 78–79.

102. Marriott, *Greener Fields*, 255.

103. AMI, tape 1, side 1.

104. Typed document, "Dedication of the Kiowa Cultural Center," 24 June 1983, 3–4, folder 11, box 78, AMC.

105. Ibid.

CHAPTER EIGHT

1. Nancy J. Parezo, "Matilda Coxe Evans Stevenson," in *Women Anthropologists: A Biographical Dictionary*, ed. Ute Gacs et al. (Westport, CT: Greenwood Press, 1988), 338.

2. Mary Hershberger, "Mobilizing Women, Anticipating Abolition: The Struggle Against Indian Removal in the 1830s," *Journal of American History* 86 (June 1999): 15–40.

3. Shirley A. Leckie, "Women Writers Who Explored the Legacy of Conquest Out on Their Own Frontier," paper delivered at the

American Historical Association, Pacific Coast Branch Conference, Maui, Hawaii, 7 August 1999, 6; Valerie Sherer Mathes, *Helen Hunt Jackson and Her Indian Reform Legacy* (Norman: University of Oklahoma Press, 1997).

4. Siobhan Senier, *Voices of American Indian Assimilation and Resistance: Helen Hunt Jackson, Sarah Winnemucca, and Victoria Howard* (Norman: University of Oklahoma Press, 2001), 50.

5. Ibid., xiii.

6. Frederick E. Hoxie, *A Final Promise: The Campaign to Assimilate the Indians, 1880–1920* (Lincoln: University of Nebraska Press, 1984), 25–28; Joan T. Mark, *A Stranger in Her Native Land: Alice Fletcher and the American Indians* (Lincoln: University of Nebraska Press, 1988).

7. Carr, *Inventing the American Primitive*, 169.

8. Brigitte Georgi-Findlay, *The Frontiers of Women's Writing: Women's Narratives and the Rhetoric of Westward Expansion* (Tucson: University of Arizona Press, 1996), 13.

9. Ibid., x.

10. Ibid., 290.

11. Leah Dilworth, *Imagining Indians in the Southwest: Persistent Visions of a Primitive Past* (Washington, D.C.: Smithsonian Institution Press, 1996), 4.

12. Parezo, "Anthropology: The Welcoming Science," in *Hidden Scholars*.

13. Babcock and Parezo, *Daughters of the Desert*, 7.

14. Wilbur R. Jacobs, *On Turner's Trail: 100 Years of Writing Western History* (Lawrence: University Press of Kansas, 1994), 72; Allan G. Bogue, *Frederick Jackson Turner: Strange Roads Going Down* (Norman: University of Oklahoma Press, 1998), 237. For the history of women in the historical profession, see Peter Novick, *That Noble Dream: The "Objectivity Question" and the American Historical Profession* (1988; repr., Cambridge, UK: Cambridge University Press, 1993), 366–67, 491–510; Goggin, "Challenging Sexual Discrimination," 769–802.

15. Babcock and Parezo, *Daughters of the Desert*, 4.

16. Joan M. Jensen, *One Foot on the Rockies: Women and Creativity in the Modern American West* (Albuquerque: University of New Mexico Press, 1995), 117.

17. Beatrice Medicine, "Ella Cara Deloria," in Gacs et al., *Women Anthropologists*, 45–46.

18. Ibid.; Raymond J. Demallie, "Ella Cara Deloria," in *Notable American Women*, ed. Barbara Sicherman et al. (Cambridge, MA: Belknap Press of Harvard University Press, 1980), 183–85; Janet L.

Finn, "Ella Cara Deloria and Mourning Dove: Writing for Cultures, Writing Against the Grain," in *Women Writing Culture*, ed. Ruth Behar and Deborah A. Gordon (Berkeley: University of California Press, 1995), 131–47.

19. Medicine, "Ella Cara Deloria," 47.

20. Ella Deloria to Franz Boas, 11 July 1932, quoted in Finn, "Ella Cara Deloria and Mourning Dove," 140.

21. Ella Deloria to H. E. Beebe, 1952, quoted in Finn, "Ella Cara Deloria and Mourning Dove," 132.

22. Ella Deloria, *Speaking of Indians* (New York: Friendship Press, 1944); Medicine, "Ella Cara Deloria," 48.

23. Medicine, "Ella Cara Deloria," 48.

24. Finn, "Ella Cara Deloria and Mourning Dove," 132.

25. Ella Deloria, *Dakota Texts* (New York: G. E. Stechert and Co., 1932); Ella Deloria and Franz Boas, *Dakota Grammar*, Memoirs of the National Academy of Sciences 23, Second Memoir (Washington, D.C.: Government Printing Office, 1941).

26. Ella Deloria, *Waterlily* (Lincoln: University of Nebraska Press, 1988).

27. Jennifer Scanlon and Shaaron Cosner, "Rachel Caroline Eaton," in *American Women Historians, 1700–1990s* (Westport, CT: Greenwood Press, 1996), 65–66.

28. Muriel H. Wright, "Rachel Caroline Eaton, 1869–1938," *Chronicles of Oklahoma* 16 (December 1938): 509.

29. Scanlon and Cosner, "Grace Raymond Hebard," in *American Women Historians*, 107.

30. Susan Horan, "Guide to Grace Raymond Hebard Papers," 2, Grace Raymond Hebard Collection, American Heritage Center, University of Wyoming, Laramie, Wyoming; Scanlon and Cosner, "Grace Raymond Hebard," 107–8; Virginia Scharff, "Marking Wyoming: Grace Raymond Hebard and the West as Woman's Place," in *Twenty Thousand Roads* (Berkeley: University of California Press, 2003), 94–114.

31. Virginia Scharff, "What If Molly Had a Ph.D.? Women Professors and the Civilizing of Wyoming," paper presented at the American Heritage Center Symposium, "Schoolmarms and Scholars: Women Educators of the American West," 19 September 1998, American Heritage Center, Laramie, Wyoming.

32. Scharff, "Marking Wyoming," 109.

33. Dwight L. Smith, "Louise Phelps Kellogg," in *Historians of the American Frontier: A Bio-Bibliographical Sourcebook*, ed. John R. Wunder (New York: Greenwood Press, 1988), 352.

34. Louise Phelps Kellogg, "The American Colonial Charter: A Study of English Administration in Relation Thereto, Chiefly After 1688," *Annual Report, American Historical Association* 1 (1903): 187–341; Smith, "Louise Phelps Kellogg," 352.

35. William E. Unrau, "Mari Sandoz," in Wunder, *Historians of the American Frontier*, 575–85.

36. Mari Sandoz, *Old Jules* (Boston: Little, Brown, 1935); Melody Graulich, "Violence Against Women: Power Dynamics in Literature of the Western Family," in *The Women's West*, ed. Susan Armitage and Elizabeth Jameson (Norman: University of Oklahoma Press, 1987), 113.

37. Mari Sandoz, *Crazy Horse: The Strange Man of the Oglalas* (New York: Alfred A. Knopf, 1942).

38. Mari Sandoz, *Cheyenne Autumn* (New York: McGraw Hill, 1953).

39. Unrau, "Mari Sandoz," 576, 581–82.

40. Kimberly Moore Buchanan, "Eve Ball," in Wunder, *Historians of the American Frontier*, 46–55.

41. Lynda A. Sanchez, "Eve Ball," *New Mexico Magazine* 59 (April 1981): 26.

42. Eve Ball, *Indeh, An Apache Odyssey* (Provo, UT: Brigham Young University Press, 1980), xix.

43. Quoted in Sanchez, "Eve Ball," 27.

44. See Mihesuah, *Indigenous American Women*, Devon A. Mihesuah, ed., *Natives and Academics: Researching and Writing About American Indians* (Lincoln: University of Nebraska Press, 1998); Womack, *Red on Red*.

CONCLUSION

1. Mihesuah, *Indigenous American Women*; Scharff, *Twenty Thousand Roads*; Jensen, *One Foot on the Rockies;* Parezo, *Hidden Scholars;* Babcock and Parezo, *Daughters of the Desert*.

2. Baird, "Are the Five Tribes of Oklahoma 'Real' Indians?" 13.

3. Ruth Behar, "Introduction: Out of Exile," in *Women Writing Culture*, ed. Ruth Behar and Deborah Gordon (Berkeley: University of California Press, 1995), 17.

✖✖ Selected Bibliography ✖✖

ARCHIVAL MATERIALS

Laramie, Wyoming. American Heritage Center, University of Wyoming.
   Grace Raymond Hebard Collection
Norman, Oklahoma. Carl Albert Congressional Research and Studies
Center, University of Oklahoma.
   W. G. Stigler Collection
   Elmer Thomas Collection, Legislative Series
Norman, Oklahoma. Western History Collections, University of Oklahoma.
   E. E. Dale Collection
   Alice Lee Marriott Collection
   Alice Lee Marriott and Carol K. Rachlin Collection
   University of Oklahoma Press Collection
Oklahoma City, Oklahoma. Archives and Manuscripts Division, Oklahoma
Historical Society.
   Muriel H. Wright Papers
Stillwater, Oklahoma. Special Collections and University Archives,
Oklahoma State University.
   Angie Debo Collection

ORAL HISTORIES AND INTERVIEWS

Baird, W. David. Interview via e-mail to author, 17 September 1996; 26
   November 1996, Stillwater, Oklahoma.
Chlouber, Dale. Interview by author, 20 October 1996, Ripley, Oklahoma.
Debo, Angie. Interviews conducted by Glenna Matthews and Gloria
   Valencia-Webber, 1981–85. Transcripts. Angie Debo Collection,

BIBLIOGRAPHY

Special Collections and University Archives, Oklahoma State University, Stillwater, Oklahoma.

Fischer, LeRoy. Telephone interview by author, 22 September 1996, Stillwater, Oklahoma.

McElhaney, Ioleta Hunt. Interview conducted by B. D. Timmons, 3 March 1968, T-198-1, Doris Duke Oral History Collection, University of Oklahoma, Norman.

Marriott, Alice. Interview conducted by Jennifer Fox for the Daughters of the Desert Oral History Project, 13 March, 1986, Tucson, Arizona. Audio Recording. Wenner-Gren Foundation for Anthropological Research, New York, New York.

Quoetone, Guy. Interview conducted by Julia A. Jordan, 30 March 1971, T-638, Doris Duke Oral History Collection, University of Oklahoma, Norman.

Schaefer, Gerry. Interview by author, 16 October 1996, Marshall, Oklahoma.

Silverhorn, James. Interview conducted by Julia A. Jordan, 6 June 1969, T-18, Doris Duke Oral History Collection, University of Oklahoma, Norman.

Warde, Mary Jane. Interview by author, 18 October 1996, Stillwater, Oklahoma.

Wright, Muriel H. Interview conducted by Frank Doyle, 8 March 1965. Audio Recording. Oklahoma Historical Society, Oklahoma City, Oklahoma.

GOVERNMENT DOCUMENTS

Collier, John. "Appendix: Indian Population," in *Annual Report of the Secretary of the Interior for the Fiscal Year Ending June 30, 1933.* Washington, D.C.: Government Printing Office, 1933.

———. *Annual Report of the Secretary of the Interior for the Fiscal Year Ending June 30, 1937.* Washington, D.C.: Government Printing Office, 1937.

NEWSPAPERS

Colgate Courier
Daily Oklahoman
Muskogee Daily Phoenix

PUBLISHED PRIMARY SOURCES

Debo, Angie. "Edward Everett Dale: The Teacher." In *Frontier Historian: The Life and Work of Edward Everett Dale*, ed. Arrell Morgan Gibson, 21–37. Norman: University of Oklahoma Press, 1975.

BIBLIOGRAPHY

―――. *The Five Civilized Tribes of Oklahoma: Report on Social and Economic Conditions.* Philadelphia: Indian Rights Association, 1951.

―――. "The Location of the Battle of Round Mountain." *Chronicles of Oklahoma* 41 (1963): 70–104.

―――. *Oklahoma, Foot-loose and Fancy-free.* Norman: University of Oklahoma Press, 1949.

―――. "Oklahoma History Goes to Press." *Bulletin of the Oklahoma State Library* 1 (1948): 67–80.

―――. *Prairie City: The Story of an American Community.* New York: A. A. Knopf, 1944.

―――. "Realizing Oklahoma's Literary Potential." *Oklahoma Librarian* 16 (1966): 67–75.

―――. Review of *A Guide to the Indian Tribes of Oklahoma*, by Muriel H. Wright. *American Indian* 6 (Summer 1953): 45–46.

―――. *The Rise and Fall of the Choctaw Republic.* Norman: University of Oklahoma Press, 1934.

―――. *The Road to Disappearance: A History of the Creek Indians.* Norman: University of Oklahoma Press, 1941.

―――. "The Site of the Battle of Round Mountain, 1861." *Chronicles of Oklahoma* 27 (1949): 187–206.

―――. *And Still the Waters Run: The Betrayal of the Five Civilized Tribes.* Princeton, NJ: Princeton University Press, 1940.

―――. "Termination and the Oklahoma Indians." *American Indian* 7 (1955): 17–23.

―――. *Tulsa: From Creek Town to Oil Capital.* Norman: University of Oklahoma Press, 1943.

―――. "What Oklahoma Indians Need." *American Indian* 7 (1956): 13–21.

―――. "Writing Local History." *Writer* 55 (1942): 19–22.

Debo, Angie, and John M. Oskison. *Oklahoma: A Guide to the Sooner State*, comp. Writers' Program, Work Progress Administration, State of Oklahoma. Norman: University of Oklahoma Press, 1941.

Marriott, Alice. *Greener Fields: Experiences Among the American Indians.* New York: Thomas Y. Crowell Co., 1953.

―――. *Kiowa Years: A Study in Culture Impact.* New York: Macmillan Co., 1968.

―――. *Maria: The Potter of San Ildefonso.* Norman: University of Oklahoma Press, 1948.

―――. *The Ten Grandmothers.* Norman: University of Oklahoma Press, 1945.

―――. *The Valley Below.* Norman: University of Oklahoma Press, 1949.

Marriott, Alice, and Carol K. Rachlin. *Dance Around the Sun: The Life of*

BIBLIOGRAPHY

Mary Little Bear Inkanish: Famed Cheyenne Craftswoman Who Bridged Two Cultures, Old and New, Indian and White. New York: Thomas Y. Crowell Co., 1977.

Thoburn, Joseph B., and Muriel H. Wright. *Oklahoma: A History of the State and Its People*. 4 vols. New York: Historical Publishing Co., 1929.

Wright, Muriel H. "The American Indian Exposition in Oklahoma." *Chronicles of Oklahoma* 24 (Summer 1946): 158–65.

———. "Brief Outline of the Choctaw and Chickasaw Nations in the Indian Territory, 1820 to 1860." *Chronicles of Oklahoma* 7 (December 1929): 388–418.

———. "A Brief Review of the Life of Doctor Eliphalet Nott Wright (1858–1932)." *Chronicles of Oklahoma* 10 (June 1932): 267–86.

———. "Colonel Cooper's Civil War Report on the Battle of Round Mountain." *Chronicles of Oklahoma* 39 (Winter 1961–62): 352–97.

———. "Contributions of the Indian People to Oklahoma." *Chronicles of Oklahoma* 14 (June 1936): 156–61.

———. "Fifty Oklahoma Historical Markers Completed, 1949." *Chronicles of Oklahoma* 27 (Winter 1949–50): 488–92.

———. *A Guide to the Indian Tribes of Oklahoma*. Norman: University of Oklahoma Press, 1951.

———. "Historic Spots on the Old Stage Line from Fort Smith to Red River." *Chronicles of Oklahoma* 11 (June 1933): 798–822.

———. *Oklahoma Historic Sites Survey*. Oklahoma City: Oklahoma Historical Society, 1958.

———. "Oklahoma Historical Markers Completed, 1950." *Chronicles of Oklahoma* 28 (Winter 1950–51): 488–92.

———. *The Oklahoma History*. Guthrie, OK: Co-operative Publishing Co., 1955.

———. "Old Boggy Depot." *Chronicles of Oklahoma* 5 (March 1927): 4–17.

———. *Our Oklahoma*. Guthrie, OK: Co-operative Publishing Co., 1939.

———. *Our Oklahoma: Work Book in Oklahoma History*. Guthrie, OK: Co-operative Publishing Co., 1951.

———. "Pioneer Historian and Archaeologist of the State of Oklahoma." *Chronicles of Oklahoma* 24 (Winter 1946–47): 396.

———. "Rachel Caroline Eaton, 1869–1938." *Chronicles of Oklahoma* 16 (December 1938): 509–10.

———. "The Removal of the Choctaws to the Indian Territory, 1830–1833." *Chronicles of Oklahoma* 6 (June 1928): 103–28.

———. Review of *The Removal of the Choctaw Indians*, by Arthur H. DeRosier Jr. *Chronicles of Oklahoma* 49 (Spring 1971): 126–27.

BIBLIOGRAPHY

———. Review of *The Rise and Fall of the Choctaw Republic*, by Angie Debo. *Chronicles of Oklahoma* 13 (March 1935): 108–20.

———. "The Wedding of Oklahoma and Miss Indian Territory." *Chronicles of Oklahoma* 35 (Autumn 1957): 255–60.

Wright, Muriel H., and LeRoy H. Fischer. *Civil War Sites in Oklahoma*. Oklahoma City: Oklahoma Historical Society, 1967.

Wright, Muriel H., and George H. Shirk. *Mark of Heritage: Oklahoma Historical Markers*. Oklahoma City: Oklahoma Historical Society, 1958.

Wright, Muriel H., editorially assisted by Joseph B. Thoburn. *The Story of Oklahoma*. Oklahoma City: Webb Publishing Co., 1929.

Wright, Muriel H., with Lucyl Shirk. *The Story of Oklahoma: A Work Book*. Guthrie, OK: Co-operative Publishing Co., 1951.

PUBLISHED SECONDARY SOURCES

Abel-Henderson, Annie H. Review of *The Rise and Fall of the Choctaw Republic*, by Angie Debo. *American Historical Review* 40 (July 1935): 795–96.

Albers, Patricia. "From Illusion to Illumination: Anthropological Studies of American Indian Women." In *Gender and Anthropology: Critical Reviews for Research and Teaching*, ed. Sandra Morgen, 132–70. Washington, D.C.: American Anthropological Association, 1989.

Albers, Patricia, and Beatrice Medecine. *The Hidden Half: Studies of Plains Indian Women*. Washington, D.C.: University Press of America, 1983.

Allen, Paula Gunn. *The Sacred Hoop: Recovering the Feminine in American Indian Tradition*. Boston: Beacon Press, 1986.

Anderson, George L. Review of *Oklahoma: Foot-loose and Fancy-free*, by Angie Debo. *Mississippi Valley Historical Review* 37 (June 1950): 140–41.

Anderson, Karen. *Changing Woman: A History of Racial Ethnic Women in Modern America*. New York: Oxford University Press, 1996.

Angie Debo: An Autobiographical Sketch, Eulogy and Bibliography. Stillwater: College of Arts and Sciences and Department of History, Oklahoma State University, 1988.

Armitage, Susan, and Elizabeth Jameson, eds. *The Women's West*. Norman: University of Oklahoma Press, 1987.

Arrington, Ruth. "Muriel Hazel Wright." In *Notable American Women: The Modern Period*, ed. Barbara Sicheman and Carol Hurd Green, 751–52. Cambridge, MA: Belknap Press of Harvard University Press, 1980.

Babcock, Barbara A., and Nancy J. Parezo. *Daughters of the Desert: Women Anthropologists and the Native American Southwest, 1880–1980*. Albuquerque: University of New Mexico Press, 1988.

BIBLIOGRAPHY

Baird, W. David. "Are the Five Tribes of Oklahoma 'Real' Indians?" *Western Historical Quarterly* 21 (February 1990): 4–18.

———. *Peter Pitchlynn: Chief of the Choctaws.* Norman: University of Oklahoma Press, 1972.

Baird, W. David, and Danney Goble. *The Story of Oklahoma.* Norman: University of Oklahoma Press, 1994.

Ball, Eve. *Indeh, An Apache Odyssey.* Provo, Utah: Brigham Young University Press, 1980.

Bataille, Gretchen M., and Kathleen Mullen Sands. *American Indian Women: Telling Their Lives.* Lincoln: University of Nebraska Press, 1984.

Behar, Ruth, and Deborah A. Gordon, eds. *Women Writing Culture.* Berkeley: University of California Press, 1995.

Bell, Diane, Pat Caplan, and Wazir Jahan Karim, eds. *Gendered Fields: Women, Men and Ethnography.* New York: Routledge, 1993.

Berkhofer, Robert F. Jr. *The White Man's Burden: Images of the American Indian from Columbus to the Present.* New York: Knopf, 1978.

Bernstein, Alison. "A Mixed Record: The Political Enfranchisement of American Indian Women During the Indian New Deal." *Journal of the West* 23 (1984): 13–20.

Bieder, Robert E. *Science Encounters the Indian, 1820–1880: The Early Years of American Ethnology.* Norman: University of Oklahoma Press, 1986.

Blackburn, Bob L. "Battle Cry for History: The First Century of the Oklahoma Historical Society." *Chronicles of Oklahoma* 70 (Winter 1992–93).

———. "Oklahoma Historians Hall of Fame: Angie Debo." *Chronicles of Oklahoma* 72 (Winter 1994–95): 456–59.

———. "Oklahoma Historians Hall of Fame: Muriel Wright." *Chronicles of Oklahoma* 71 (Winter 1993–94): 450–54.

Bogue, Allan G. *Frederick Jackson Turner: Strange Roads Going Down.* Norman: University of Oklahoma Press, 1998.

Brew, J. O., ed. *One Hundred Years of Anthropology.* Cambridge, MA: Harvard University Press, 1968.

Brumberg, Joan Jacobs, and Nancy Tomes. "Women in the Professions: A Research Agenda for American Historians." *Reviews in American History* 10 (June 1982): 275–96.

Buchanan, James Shannon, and Edward Everett Dale. *A History of Oklahoma.* New York: Row, Peterson and Co., 1924.

Carr, Helen. *Inventing the American Primitive: Politics, Gender and the Representation of Native American Literary Traditions, 1789–1936.* New York: New York University Press, 1996.

Caughey, John Walton. "The Local Historian: His Occupational Hazards and Compensations." *Pacific Historical Review* 12 (March 1943): 1–9.

Chase, Richard. "Ruth Benedict: The Woman as Anthropologist." *Columbia University Forum* 2 (1959): 19–22.

Clark, Dan E. Review of *And Still the Waters Run,* by Angie Debo. *Journal of Southern History* 7 (August 1941): 574–75.

Clark, J. Stanley. "Carolyn Thomas Foreman." *Chronicles of Oklahoma* 45 (Winter 1967–68): 370.

———. "Grant Foreman." *Chronicles of Oklahoma* 31 (Autumn 1953): 228.

Clifford, James. *The Predicament of Culture: Twentieth-Century Ethnography, Literature, and Art.* Cambridge, MA: Harvard University Press, 1988.

Clifford, James, and George Marcus, eds. *Writing Culture: The Poetics and Politics of Ethnography.* Berkeley: University of California Press, 1986.

Clifton, James, ed. *Being and Becoming Indian: Biographical Studies of North American Frontiers.* Chicago: Dorsey Press, 1989.

Comer, Krista. *Landscapes of the New West: Gender and Geography in Contemporary Women's Writing.* Chapel Hill: University of North Carolina Press, 1999.

Cott, Nancy. *The Grounding of Modern Feminism.* New Haven, CT: Yale University Press, 1987.

Crum, Steven. "Bizzell and Brandt: Pioneers in Indian Studies, 1929–1937." *Chronicles of Oklahoma* 66 (Summer 1988): 178–91.

Dale, Edward Everett. Review of *Prairie City,* by Angie Debo. *American Historical Review* 50 (April 1945): 573.

———. "The Spirit of Soonerland." *Chronicles of Oklahoma* 1 (June 1923): 167–78.

Deloria, Ella. *Dakota Texts.* New York: G. E. Stechert and Co., 1932.

———. *Speaking of Indians.* New York: Friendship Press, 1944.

———. *Waterlily.* Lincoln: University of Nebraska Press, 1988.

Deloria, Ella, and Franz Boas. *Dakota Grammar.* Memoirs of the National Academy of Sciences 23, Second Memoir. Washington, D.C.: Government Printing Office, 1941.

Deloria, Philip J. *Playing Indian.* New Haven, CT: Yale University Press, 1998.

Dick, Claribel F. *The Song Goes On: The Story of Ioleta Hunt McElhaney.* Philadelphia: Judson Press, 1959.

Dilworth, Leah. *Imagining Indians in the Southwest: Persistent Visions of a Primitive Past.* Washington, D.C.: Smithsonian Institution Press, 1996.

Dippie, Brian W. *The Vanishing American: White Attitudes and U.S. Indian Policy.* Middletown, CT: Wesleyan University Press, 1982.

Dodson, Shirleen L. "Smithsonian Women: Seizing the Opportunities." In

BIBLIOGRAPHY

Women's Changing Roles in Museums, ed. Ellen C. Hickes, 35–37.
Washington, D.C.: Smithsonian Institution, 1986.

Doran, F. "Population Statistics of Nineteenth-Century Indian Territory."
Chronicles of Oklahoma 53 (Winter 1975–76): 502–12.

Dorman, Robert L. *Revolt of the Provinces: The Regionalist Movement
in America, 1920–1945.* Chapel Hill: University of North Carolina
Press, 1993.

Edmunds, R. David. "Native Americans, New Voices: American Indian
History, 1895–1995." *American Historical Review* 100 (June 1995): 717–40.

Ellis, Clyde. *To Change Them Forever: Indian Education at the Rainy
Mountain Boarding School, 1893–1920.* Norman: University of
Oklahoma Press, 1996.

Etulain, Richard W. *Re-imagining the Modern American West: A Century of
Fiction, History, and Art.* Tucson: University of Arizona Press, 1996.

Evans, Charles. *Lights on Oklahoma History.* Oklahoma City: Harlow
Publishing Corporation, 1926.

Faragher, John Mack. *Rereading Frederick Jackson Turner: "The
Significance of the Frontier in American History" and Other Essays.*
New York: Henry Holt and Co., 1994.

Fischer, LeRoy H. "The Historic Preservation Movement in Oklahoma."
Chronicles of Oklahoma 57 (Spring 1979): 3–25.

———. "Muriel H. Wright, Historian of Oklahoma." *Chronicles of
Oklahoma* 52 (Spring 1974): 3–29.

Fitzpatrick, Ellen. *Endless Crusade: Women Social Scientists and
Progressive Reform.* New York: Oxford University Press, 1991.

Fixico, Donald L., ed. *Rethinking American Indian History.* Albuquerque:
University of New Mexico Press, 1997.

Foreman, Grant. *Indian Removal: The Emigration of the Five Civilized
Tribes of Indians.* Norman: University of Oklahoma Press, 1932.

———. Review of *And Still the Waters Run,* by Angie Debo. *American
Historical Review* 46 (July 1941): 936–37.

———. Review of *And Still the Waters Run,* by Angie Debo. *Mississippi
Valley Historical Review* 27 (March 1941): 636–37.

Freed, Stanley A., and Ruth S. Freed. "Clark Wissler and the Development
of Anthropology in the United States." *American Anthropologist* 85
(1983): 800–825.

Furnish, Patricia L. "Women and Labor on the Panhandle-Plains,
1920–1940." *Panhandle-Plains Historical Review* 68 (1995): 14–36.

Gacs, Ute, Aisha Khan, Jerrie McIntyre, and Ruth Weinberg, eds. *Women
Anthropologists: A Biographical Dictionary.* Westport, CT:

Greenwood Press, 1988.

Garfield, Viola E., and Pamela T. Amoss. "Erna Gunther." *American Anthropologist* 86 (1984): 394–99.

Geertz, Clifford. *Works and Lives: The Anthropologist as Author.* Stanford, CA.: Stanford University Press, 1988.

Georgi-Findlay, Brigitte. *The Frontiers of Women's Writing: Women's Narratives and the Rhetoric of Westward Expansion.* Tucson: University of Arizona Press, 1996.

Gibson, Arrell Morgan, ed. *Frontier Historian: The Life and Work of Edward Everett Dale.* Norman: University of Oklahoma Press, 1975.

———. "A History of the University of Oklahoma Press." *Journal of the West* 7 (October 1968).

Goggin, Jacqueline. "Challenging Sexual Discrimination in the Historical Profession: Women Historians and the American Historical Association, 1890–1940." *American Historical Review* 97 (June 1992): 769–802.

Goodykoontz, Colin B. "The Forty-Third Annual Meeting of the Mississippi Valley Historical Association." *Mississippi Valley Historical Review* 37 (September 1950): 265–88.

Gordon, Deborah. "Writing Culture, Writing Feminism: The Poetics and Politics of Experimental Ethnography." *Inscriptions* 3, no. 4 (1988): 7–24.

Gravitt, Winnie Lewis. "Anna Lewis: A Great Woman of Oklahoma." *Chronicles of Oklahoma* 40 (1962–63): 326–29.

Green, Michael D. *The Creeks: A Critical Bibliography.* Bloomington: Indiana University Press, 1979.

Green, Rayna. "Native American Women." *Signs* 6 (Winter 1980): 248–67.

———. "The Pocahontas Perplex: The Image of Indian Women in American Culture." *Massachusetts Review* 16 (Autumn 1975): 698–714.

———. *Women in American Indian Society.* New York: Chelsea House Publishers, 1992.

Gridley, Marion E. *American Indian Women.* New York: Hawthorn, 1974.

Hafen, LeRoy R. Review of *The Road to Disappearance*, by Angie Debo. *American Historical Review* 48 (July 1943): 826–27.

Hebard, Grace Raymond. *The Bozeman Trail.* Cleveland: Arthur H. Clark Co., 1922.

———. *Sacajawea.* Glendale, CA: Arthur H. Clark Co., 1933.

———. *Washakie: Chief of the Shoshones.* With a foreword by Richard Clemmer. Cleveland: A. H. Clark Co., 1930. Reprint, Bison Books, 1995.

Herring, Rebecca. "Their Work Was Never Done: Women Missionaries on the Kiowa-Comanche Reservation." *Chronicles of Oklahoma* 64 (Spring 1986): 69–83.

Hershberger, Mary. "Mobilizing Women, Anticipating Abolition: The Struggle Against Indian Removal in the 1830s." *Journal of American History* 86 (June 1999): 15–40.

Hewes, Leslie. Review of *A Guide to the Indian Tribes of Oklahoma*, by Muriel H. Wright. *Mississippi Valley Historical Review* 39 (June 1952): 132–33.

Hinsley, Curtis M. *Savages and Scientists: The Smithsonian Institution and the Development of American Anthropology, 1846–1910.* Washington, D.C.: Smithsonian Institution Press, 1981.

Howe, Barbara J. "Women in Historic Preservation: The Legacy of Ann Pamela Cunningham." *Public Historian* 12 (Winter 1990): 31–61.

Hoxie, Frederick. *A Final Promise: The Campaign to Assimilate the Indians, 1880–1920.* Lincoln: University of Nebraska Press, 1984.

Hurtado, Albert. "Romancing the West in the Twentieth Century: The Politics of History in a Contested Region." *Western Historical Quarterly* 32 (Winter 2001): 417–35.

Hyatt, Marshall. *Franz Boas, Social Activist: The Dynamics of Ethnicity.* New York: Greenwood Press, 1990.

Jacobs, Margaret D. *Engendered Encounters: Feminism and Pueblo Cultures, 1879–1934.* Lincoln: University of Nebraska Press, 1999.

Jacobs, Wilbur R. *On Turner's Trail: 100 Years of Writing Western History.* Lawrence: University Press of Kansas, 1994.

Jaimes, Marie Annette. "Towards a New Image of American Indian Women: The Renewing Power of the Feminine." *Journal of American Indian Education* 22 (October 1982): 18–32.

Jameson, Elizabeth, and Susan Armitage, eds. *Writing the Range: Race, Class, and Culture in the Women's West.* Norman: University of Oklahoma Press, 1997.

Jensen, Joan M. *One Foot on the Rockies: Women and Creativity in the Modern American West.* Albuquerque: University of New Mexico Press, 1995.

Jensen, Joan M., and Darlis Miller. "The Gentle Tamers Revisited: New Approaches to the History of Women in the American West." *Pacific Historical Review* 49 (May 1980): 173–212.

Johansen, Dorothy O., and Charles M. Gates. *Empire of the Columbia: A History of the Pacific Northwest.* New York: Harper, 1957.

Kammen, Carol. *On Doing Local History.* Nashville, TN: American Association for State and Local History, 1986.

Kellogg, Louise Phelps. "The American Colonial Charter: A Study of

English Administration in Relation Thereto, Chiefly After 1688."
Annual Report, American Historical Association 1 (1903): 187–341.

Kelly, Lawrence C. "Anthropology and Anthropologists in the Indian New
Deal." *Journal of the History of the Behavioral Sciences* 16 (1980): 6–24.

Kidwell, Clara Sue. *Choctaws and Missionaries in Mississippi, 1818–1918.*
Norman: University of Oklahoma Press, 1995.

———. "Indian Women as Cultural Mediators." *Ethnohistory* 39 (Spring
1992): 97–107.

Kobler, Turner S. *Alice Marriott.* Southwest Writers Series 27. Austin, TX:
Steck-Vaughn Co., 1969.

Kolodny, Annette. *The Lay of the Land: Metaphor as Experience and
History in American Life and Letters.* Chapel Hill: University of
North Carolina Press, 1975.

Kroeber, Theodora. *Alfred Kroeber: A Personal Configuration.* Berkeley:
University of California Press, 1970.

Lassiter, Luke E. *The Power of Kiowa Song: A Collaborative Ethnography.*
Tucson: University of Arizona Press, 1998.

Lassiter, Luke E., Clyde Ellis, and Ralph Kotay. *The Jesus Road: Kiowas,
Christianity, and Indian Hymns.* Lincoln: University of Nebraska
Press, 2002.

Lavender, Catherine Jane. "Storytellers, Feminist Ethnography and the
American Southwest, 1900–1940." Ph.D. diss., University of
Colorado–Boulder, 1997.

La Vere, David. *Contrary Neighbors: Southern Plains and Removed Indians
in Indian Territory.* Norman: University of Oklahoma Press, 2000.

Layton, Robert. *An Introduction to Theory in Anthropology.* New York:
Cambridge University Press, 1997.

Leach, William. *Land of Desire: Merchants, Power and the Rise of a New
American Culture.* New York: Pantheon Books, 1993.

Lears, T. J. Jackson. *No Place of Grace: Antimodernism and the
Transformation of American Culture, 1880–1920.* New York:
Pantheon, 1981.

Leckie, Shirley A. *Angie Debo: Pioneering Historian.* Norman: University of
Oklahoma Press, 2000.

———. *Elizabeth Bacon Custer and the Making of a Myth.* Norman:
University of Oklahoma Press, 1993.

Lewis, Anna. Review of *The Rise and Fall of the Choctaw Republic,* by Angie
Debo. *Mississippi Valley Historical Review* 21 (December 1934): 410.

Lewis, David Rich. "Still Native: The Significance of Native Americans in
the History of the Twentieth-Century American West." *Western*

BIBLIOGRAPHY

Historical Quarterly 24 (May 1993): 203–27.

Limerick, Patricia Nelson. "Land, Justice, and Angie Debo: Telling the Truth to—and About—Your Neighbors." *Great Plains Quarterly* 21 (Fall 2001): 261–73.

———. *The Legacy of Conquest: The Unbroken Past of the American West.* New York: W. W. Norton, 1987.

———. *Something in the Soil: Legacies and Reckonings in the New West.* New York: W. W. Norton, 2000.

Limerick, Patricia Nelson, Clyde A. Milner II, and Charles E. Rankin, eds. *Trails: Toward a New Western History.* Lawrence: University Press of Kansas, 1991.

Littlefield, Daniel F. Jr. "Muriel Hazel Wright." In *Native American Women: A Biographical Dictionary*, ed. Gretchen M. Bataille, 287. New York: Garland Publishing, 1993.

Loughlin, Patricia. "The Battle of the Historians of Round Mountain: An Examination of Muriel Wright and Angie Debo." *Heritage of the Great Plains* 31 (Spring/Summer 1998): 277–84.

Lowitt, Richard. "'Dear Miss Debo': The Correspondence of E. E. Dale and Angie Debo." *Chronicles of Oklahoma* 77 (Winter 1999): 372–405.

———. "Regionalism at the University of Oklahoma." *Chronicles of Oklahoma* 73 (Summer 1995): 150–71.

Lurie, Nancy O. "Women in Early Anthropology." In *Pioneers of American Anthropology: The Early Uses of Biography*, ed. June Helm, 29–81. Seattle: University of Washington Press, 1966.

Lyon, William H. "Gladys Reichard at the Frontier of Navajo Culture." *American Indian Quarterly* 13 (1989): 137–63.

McIntosh, Kenneth. "Geronimo's Friend: Angie Debo and the New History." *Chronicles of Oklahoma* 66 (Summer 1988): 164–77.

Mark, Joan. *Four Anthropologists: An American Science in Its Early Years.* New York: Science History Publications, 1980.

———. *A Stranger in Her Native Land: Alice Fletcher and the American Indians.* Lincoln: University of Nebraska Press, 1988.

Mathes, Valerie Sherer. *Helen Hunt Jackson and Her Indian Reform Legacy.* Norman: University of Oklahoma Press, 1997.

Mead, Margaret. "Changing Styles of Anthropological Work." *Annual Review of Anthropology* 2 (1973): 1–26.

Mead, Margaret, and Ruth L. Bunzel, eds. *The Golden Age of American Anthropology.* New York: George Braziller, 1960.

Medicine, Beatrice. "Learning to be an Anthropologist and Remaining 'Native.'" In *Applied Anthropology in America*, ed. Elizabeth Eddy and

BIBLIOGRAPHY

William Partridge, 182–96. New York: Columbia University Press, 1978.

Medley, Petrina Russo. "Angie Debo: In Search of Truth." Ph.D. diss., Oklahoma State University, 2000.

Meyn, Susan Labry. *More Than Curiosities: A Grassroots History of the Indian Arts and Crafts Board and Its Precursors, 1920 to 1942*. Lanham, MD: Lexington Books, 2001.

Mihesuah, Devon Abbott. "American Indians, Anthropologists, Pothunters, and Repatriation: Ethical, Religious and Political Differences." *American Indian Quarterly* 20 (Spring 1996): 229–37.

———. *Cultivating the Rosebuds: The Education of Women at the Cherokee Female Seminary, 1851–1909*. Urbana: University of Illinois Press, 1993.

———. *Indigenous American Women: Decolonizing, Empowerment, Activism*. Lincoln: University of Nebraska Press, 2003.

———, ed. *Natives and Academics: Researching and Writing about American Indians*. Lincoln: University of Nebraska Press, 1998.

Mooney, James. *Calendar History of the Kiowa Indians*. Seventeenth Annual Report of the Bureau of American Ethnology, pt. 1. Washington, D.C.: Government Printing Office, 1898.

Moore, Jerry D. *Visions of Culture: An Introduction to Anthropological Theories and Theorists*. Walnut Creek, CA: AltaMira Press, 1997.

Morgan, Anne Hodges, and H. Wayne Morgan. *Oklahoma: New Views of the Forty-Sixth State*. Norman: University of Oklahoma Press, 1982.

Norwood, Vera. *Made from This Earth: American Women and Nature*. Chapel Hill: University of North Carolina Press, 1993.

———. "Women's Place: Continuity and Change in Response to Western Landscapes." In *Western Women: Their Land, Their Lives*, ed. Lillian Schlissel, Vicki L. Ruiz, and Janice Monk, 155–81. Albuquerque: University of New Mexico Press, 1988.

Norwood, Vera, and Janice Monk, eds. *The Desert Is No Lady: Southwestern Landscapes in Women's Writing and Art*. New Haven, CT: Yale University Press, 1987.

Novick, Peter. *That Noble Dream: The "Objectivity Question" and the American Historical Profession*. 1988. Reprint, Cambridge, UK: Cambridge University Press, 1993.

Nye, Wilbur Sturtevant. *Bad Medicine and Good: Tales of the Kiowas*. Norman: University of Oklahoma Press, 1962.

———. *Carbine and Lance: The Story of Old Fort Sill*. 1937. Reprint, Norman: University of Oklahoma Press, 1969.

Parezo, Nancy J. "Cushing as Part of the Team: The Collecting Activities of the Smithsonian Institution." *American Ethnologist* 12 (1985): 763–74.

———. "The Formation of Ethnographic Collections: The Smithsonian Institution in the American Southwest." In *Advances in Archaeological Method and Theory*, vol. 10, ed. Michael Schiffer, 1–47. Orlando, FL: Academic Press, 1987.

———. ed. *Hidden Scholars: Women Anthropologists and the Native American Southwest*. Albuquerque: University of New Mexico Press, 1993.

Power, Richard L. Review of *The Road to Disappearance*, by Angie Debo. *Mississippi Valley Historical Review* 29 (June 1942): 127.

Prucha, Francis Paul. *The Great Father: The United States Government and the American Indians*. Vol. 2. Lincoln: University of Nebraska Press, 1984.

Reese, Linda W. "Cherokee Freedwomen in Indian Territory, 1863–1890." *Western Historical Quarterly* 33 (Autumn 2002): 273–96.

———. *Women of Oklahoma, 1890–1920*. Norman: University of Oklahoma Press, 1997.

Reichard, Gladys. *Dezba, Woman of the Desert*. New York: J. J. Augustin, 1939.

Rice, Julian. *Deer Women and Elk Men: The Lakota Narratives of Ella Deloria*. Albuquerque: University of New Mexico Press, 1992.

Rosaldo, Michelle Zimbalist, and Louise Lamphere, eds. *Woman, Culture, and Society*. Stanford, CA: Stanford University Press, 1974.

Rosenberg, Rosalind. *Beyond Separate Spheres: Intellectual Roots of Modern Feminism*. New Haven, CT: Yale University Press, 1982.

Rossiter, Margaret W. *Women Scientists in America: Struggles and Strategies to 1940*. Baltimore: Johns Hopkins University Press, 1982.

Sanchez, Lynda A. "Eve Ball." *New Mexico Magazine* 59 (April 1981): 26–33.

Sandoz, Mari. *Cheyenne Autumn*. New York: McGraw-Hill, 1953.

———. *Crazy Horse: The Strange Man of the Oglalas*. New York: Alfred A. Knopf, 1942.

———. *Old Jules*. Boston: Little, Brown, 1935.

Scanlon, Jennifer, and Shaaron Cosner. *American Women Historians, 1700–1990s*. Westport, CT: Greenwood Press, 1996.

Scharff, Virginia. *Twenty Thousand Roads: Women, Movement, and the West*. Berkeley: University of California Press, 2003.

Schmidt, Delores B., and Earl R. Schmidt. "The Invisible Woman: The Historian as Professional Magician." In *Liberating Women's History: Theoretical and Critical Essays*, ed. Bernice A. Carroll, 42–54. Urbana: University of Illinois Press, 1976.

Schrader, Robert Fay. *The Indian Arts and Crafts Board: An Aspect of New Deal Indian Policy*. Albuquerque: University of New Mexico

Press, 1983.

Schrems, Suzanne H., and Cynthia J. Wolff. "Politics and Libel: Angie Debo and the Publication of *And Still the Waters Run*." *Western Historical Quarterly* 22 (May 1991): 184–203.

Sears, Paul B. Review of *Oklahoma: Foot-loose and Fancy-free*, by Angie Debo. *American Historical Review* 56 (January 1951): 364–65.

Senier, Siobhan. *Voices of American Indian Assimilation and Resistance: Helen Hunt Jackson, Sarah Winnemucca, and Victoria Howard*. Norman: University of Oklahoma Press, 2001.

Seymour, Flora Warren. *Bird Girl: Sacagawea*. New York: Bobbs-Merrill Co., 1945.

———. "Delusion of the Sentimentalists." *The Forum* 71 (March 1924): 274.

———. *Pocahontas: Brave Girl*. New York: Bobbs-Merrill Co., 1946.

———. *The Story of the Sioux Indians*. Girard, KS: Haldeman-Julius Co., 1924.

———. *Women of Trail and Wigwam*. New York: The Woman's Press, 1930.

Shapiro, Judith. "Anthropology and the Study of Gender." In *A Feminist Perspective in the Academy*, ed. E. Langland and W. Gove, 110–29. Chicago: University of Chicago Press, 1981.

Shoemaker, Nancy, ed. *Negotiators of Change: Historical Perspectives on Native American Women*. New York: Routledge, 1995.

Sicherman, Barbara, et al. *Native American Women*. Vol. 2. Cambridge, MA: Belknap Press of Harvard University Press.

Sklar, Kathryn Kish. "American Female Historians in Context, 1770–1930." *Feminist Studies* (Fall 1975): 171–84.

Smallwood, James, ed. *And Gladly Teach: Reminiscences of Teachers from Frontier Dugout to Modern Module*. Norman: University of Oklahoma Press, 1976.

Smith-Rosenberg, Carroll. *Disorderly Conduct: Visions of Gender in Victorian America*. New York: Alfred A. Knopf, 1985.

Solomon, Barbara Miller. *In the Company of Educated Women: A History of Women and Higher Education*. New Haven, CT: Yale University Press, 1985.

Spier, Leslie. *Yuman Tribes of the Gila River*. Chicago: University of Illinois Press, 1933.

Stacey, Judith. "Can There Be a Feminist Ethnography?" *Women's Studies International Forum* 11 (1988): 21–27.

Standley, Fred Smith. "The Oklahoma Historical Society, 1893–1943." M.A. thesis, University of Oklahoma, 1986.

Stein, Howard F., and Robert F. Hill, eds. *The Culture of Oklahoma*. Norman: University of Oklahoma Press, 1993.

BIBLIOGRAPHY

Strickland, Rennard. *The Indians in Oklahoma.* Norman: University of
　　Oklahoma Press, 1980.

Szasz, Margaret Connell, ed. *Between Indian and White Worlds: The
　　Cultural Broker.* Norman: University of Oklahoma Press, 1994.

Tedlock, Barbara. "From Participant Observation to the Observation of
　　Participation: The Emergence of Narrative Ethnography." *Journal of
　　Anthropological Research* 47 (Spring 1991): 69–94.

Thoburn, Joseph B. Review of *Our Oklahoma,* by Muriel H. Wright.
　　Chronicles of Oklahoma 17 (September 1939): 450–51.

Thurman, Melvena K., ed. *Women in Oklahoma: A Century of Change.*
　　Oklahoma City: Oklahoma Historical Society, 1982.

Trenton, Patricia, ed. *Independent Spirits: Women Painters of the American
　　West, 1890–1945.* Berkeley: University of California Press, 1995.

Trinh, T. Minh-ha. *Woman, Native, Other: Writing Postcoloniality and
　　Feminism.* Bloomington: Indiana University Press, 1989.

Turner, Frederick Jackson. *The Frontier in American History.* New York:
　　Henry Holt and Co., 1920.

Underhill, Ruth M. *The Autobiography of a Papago Woman.* Memoirs of
　　the American Anthropological Association no. 46. Menasha, WI:
　　American Anthropological Association, 1936.

Vaughn, Courtney, and Joan K. Smith. "History and Ideology: Conflicts
　　Between Angie Debo and Muriel Wright." *Midwest History and
　　Education Journal* 26, no. 1 (1999).

Vaughn-Roberson, Courtney Ann. "Sometimes Independent But Never
　　Equal—Women Teachers, 1900–1950: The Oklahoma Example."
　　Pacific Historical Review 53 (February 1984): 39–58.

Wallace, Ernest. Review of *The Ten Grandmothers,* by Alice Marriott.
　　Southwestern Sciences Quarterly 26 (June 1945): 99–100.

Warde, Mary Jane. *George Washington Grayson and the Creek Nation,
　　1843–1920.* Norman: University of Oklahoma Press, 1999.

Watson, Mary Jo. "Oklahoma Indian Women and Their Art." Ph.D. diss.,
　　University of Oklahoma, 1993.

White, Richard. *"It's Your Misfortune and None of My Own": A New History
　　of the American West.* Norman: University of Oklahoma Press, 1993.

———. Review of "Indians, Outlaws, and Angie Debo," produced by
　　Barbara Abrash and Martha Sandlin. *Journal of American History* 76
　　(December 1989): 1010–11.

Wickett, Murray R. *Contested Territory: Whites, Native Americans, and
　　African Americans in Oklahoma, 1865–1907.* Baton Rouge: Louisiana
　　State University, 2000.

BIBLIOGRAPHY

Williams, Walter L. "Twentieth-Century Indian Leaders: Brokers and Providers." *Journal of the West* 23 (July 1984): 3–6.

Wissler, Clark. Review of *The Ten Grandmothers*, by Alice Marriott. *American Anthropologist* 47 (July–September 1945): 439.

Womack, Craig S. *Red on Red: Native American Literary Separatism*. Minneapolis: University of Minnesota Press, 1999.

Wrobel, David M., and Michael C. Steiner, eds. *Many Wests: Place, Culture, and Regional Identity*. Lawrence: University Press of Kansas, 1997.

Wunder, John R., ed. *Historians of the American Frontier: A Bio-Bibliographical Sourcebook*. New York: Greenwood Press, 1988.

UNPUBLISHED PAPERS

Brown, Kenny. "Prairie City and Its Lessons for Town Development Today." Keynote Address for Celebrating 50 Years of Prairie City on Angie Debo's 105th Birthday, 30 January 1995, Edmon Low Library, Oklahoma State University.

Chlouber, Dale. "Revisiting the Battle of Red Fork." Unpublished paper in author's possession, 1996.

Jensen, Joan M. "Native American Women Photographers: Artists and Chroniclers." Paper delivered at the Western History Association Conference, Sacramento, California, October 1998.

Leckie, Shirley A. "Angie Debo, Pioneering Historian." Public lecture delivered at Oklahoma State University, Stillwater, Oklahoma, 29 March 1999.

———. "Angie Debo, Pioneering Historian." Paper delivered at the Western History Association Conference, Lincoln, Nebraska, October 1996.

———. "Women Writers Who Explored the Legacy of Conquest Out on Their Own Frontier." Paper delivered at the American Historical Association, Pacific Coast Branch Conference, Maui, Hawaii, August 1999.

Scharff, Virginia. "What if Molly Had a Ph.D.? Women Professors and the Civilizing of Wyoming." Paper presented at the American Heritage Center Symposium, "Schoolmarms and Scholars: Women Educators of the American West," American Heritage Center, Laramie, Wyoming, 19 September 1998.

✣ℬ Index ✣ℬ

Page numbers in italic type refer to illustrations.

INDEX

INDEX

INDEX

INDEX

INDEX

INDEX

INDEX

INDEX